WHITE MAN ~~~
THEY WERE LIKE BROTHERS . . .
UNTIL THE LOVE OF A WOMAN
CAME BETWEEN THEM

Jim Bridger waited another hour until the deep purple sunset had faded. The trees were shadows against the horizon and the lodges gleamed like lanterns lit by their warm fires. . . . Hoisting himself out of the compound, he straddled the log barricade. The time had come to settle matters with Ear-of-the-Fox.

A screaming fury rushed out of the night. Without warning, Ear-of-the-Fox swept down, a death cry on his lips, a powerful horse pounding the earth beneath him. . . .

Bridger spun around. A tomahawk dug into his shoulder, just below the neck. Dazed by the blow, he grabbed his knife in one lightning motion. In that instant, he looked straight into the face of his attacker.

Ear-of-the-Fox had stripped himself of everything but his breechcloth. His skin shone with sacred unguents. His teeth were bared in a horrible grimace. In his right hand was the raised tomahawk tinged with Bridger's blood.

"You will die, white man!" the warrior gasped. "You stand between me and the Spirit World!"

"Not for long, you bastard!" Bridger growled back. He put a hand to his neck to wipe away the blood that trickled from the gash in his flesh. His eyes never left the young warrior.

"You will no longer ride the whore, Little Fawn," the Shoshone taunted. "When I am done with you, I will make her clean your scalp and stretch it for me."

Bridger looked into the blood-tinged eyes of the mad warrior and knew he must kill him. It seemed inconceivable that Ear-of-the-Fox was the same man who had once saved his life. . . .

JIM BRIDGER
MOUNTAIN MAN

CANADA

BLACKFOOT

FLATHEAD

CONTINENTAL DIVIDE

MARIAS R.

NEZ PERCE

JEFFERSON

Three Forks

MADISON R.

GALLATIN R.

Colter's Hell

CROW

SALMON R.

YELLOWSTONE LAKE

POPO AGIE R.

N

Pierre's Hole

SNAKE R.

South Pass

WIND RIVER RANGE

IDAHO

GREEN R.

UTAH

CACHE VALLEY

SHOSHONE

GREAT SALT LAKE

Jim Bridger

1830 ◆ 1833

49°

Fort Union

MISSOURI RIVER

YELLOWSTONE RIVER

N. DAKOTA

MONTANA

BIGHORN RIVER

BIGHORN MTS.

S. DAKOTA

N. PLATTE R.

NEBRASKA

ST. LOUIS

WYOMING

COLORADO

JIM BRIDGER
MOUNTAIN MAN

Laura Parker

A Dell/Standish Book

Published by

Miles Standish Press, Inc.
37 West Avenue
Wayne, Pennsylvania 19087

Dell ® TM 681510, Dell Publishing Co., Inc.

ISBN: 0-440-04229-1
Printed in the United States of America
First printing—November 1981

For Denise

Prologue

Yellowstone River—Spring 1830

The winds howled down the narrow canyon, driving arrow-sharp needles of ice into the unprotected face of the lone rider. Beyond the horizon the setting sun cast the last of its eerie, brittle light over the land before heavy-bellied storm clouds overtook it.

Jim Bridger checked his horse just short of the ridge. The cries were clearer now despite the echoing wind. Caution, bred of eight years in the Upper Missouri wilderness, made him dismount before moving closer. With cold, cramped fingers he lifted the Hawken rifle from his saddle and slid silently to the ground. With a whisper of reassurance, he ran a gentling hand over the flank of his horse to stop its nervous pawing at the frozen earth. He smelled the subtle odor of death, hoping this time he would be cured of the gut-wrenching weakness that squeezed cold sweat from his body and turned the spit sour on his tongue. For three years he had scouted for the fur company owned by Jedediah Smith, Big Bill Sublette, and David Jackson. He never grew accustomed to the scene that too often greeted him at the end of the trail of a missing trapper.

He knew what he would find even before he lowered himself to his belly and slithered forward to the lip of the canyon. Below, a village of migrant Blackfoot Indians occupied a sandbar that jutted out into the river from the shallows. Their buffalo-skin lodges stood in stiff resistance to the frigid winds. Slowly Bridger's gaze traveled the length of the camp, checking for sentries and numbering the warriors at near fifty. Then his eyes came to rest on a sight from the bowels of hell.

Stretched out and staked spread-eagle was the missing man. Even at this distance and with nightfall moments away, Bridger could tell that the man had been skinned, stripped of his hide as cleanly as a flayed beaver. The bloody bared flesh gleamed an oily black in the campfire light.

Bridger swallowed his own bile. "Damn them dog-eating, soul-rotted savages!" he cursed softly.

The pitiful moans that occasionally reached his ears told Bridger that the man still lived. But not for long. The braves would break from the circle around the main campfire when "counting coup" (touching the enemy) was done and return to their victim for the final horror. But one man alone could not hope to defeat an armed camp. Even if he did manage to kill a few of them, he could not save the trapper. A sane man would back away, mount up, and hope to put a few miles between himself and the warriors before he settled down to an uneasy night's sleep.

He reckoned the distance from his vantage point to the center of the camp to be one hundred and fifty yards, precious little advantage once the village was alerted to his presence. He edged forward, feeling with moccasined feet for a toehold in the rocky surface of the cliff below. He lowered himself gently over the side with one hand, his Hawken rifle gripped tightly in the other. Pebbles gave and skipped beneath his feet, but the new layer of snow muffled their descent. Bridger crouched down. The top of the canyon wall loomed six feet above him now. He would get one chance. The recoil of his rifle could send him soaring over the side. If he slipped on the snow, he would tumble into the Blackfoot camp like an offering from one of their manitous. He would have perhaps five minutes to climb back up and ride out before a war party mounted up and gave chase. Less time if there were outriders on the cliffside with him.

His thoughts shifted abruptly back to the camp below. A howling shriek issued from the tortured man as two of the braves dragged him upright after cutting him loose. With sticks and rifle butts they urged him forward toward the center of the circle of lodges where a pole had been sunk. The man stumbled and fell. Wild cries burst from his throat as the women of the tribe pushed forward to rake him with talonlike nails.

Bridger gritted his teeth and waited, praying that the cries would cease. But they did not. Finally the braves stepped forward again and pulled the man to his feet. It was the moment Bridger had waited for. Without a single thought for his own hide, he lifted the rifle to his shoulder and took aim. The trapper jerked in response to his fire. Bridger did not linger a moment. He jumped to his feet and, grabbing the trunk of a bush growing just above his head, heaved himself back over the edge of the canyon.

The dream came again that night.

Bridger awoke suddenly, his finger tightening on the trigger of the rifle in his lap as he staggered to his clad only in elkskin, he became vulnerable to the icy feet. The buffalo robes slid off him. Sweat-soaked and drafts of daybreak. Bracing cold brought him to reality quickly and once more he sank down, gathering the bedroll about him.

He thought himself a fool. He really expected to wake to the feel of his bones being crushed between the great jaws of a grizzly tearing at his flesh. Bridger shuddered and burrowed deeper into the musky robes.

It had been a long time. He thought the dream had gone for good. He should have realized the dream was never far from him. It drove him on when other men, sensible to the odds, turned back. It taunted him to prove to himself that his reluctance was not a lack of courage. The familiar nightmare had returned the night before in unspoken challenge. The trapper would have died before dawn. The stake had been set to roast him alive. But Jim Bridger had never left a man to his fate—not after the first time.

"Seven years is a long spell," he murmured under his breath. As a boy of nineteen he had been the baby of Ashley's Brigade. Still haunted by that memory, this weathered veteran of twenty-six years could now aim and fire a shot into the chest of a fellow trapper in an act of mercy, as kind as the cradling of a crying child.

Bridger snorted and spat, dusting the frozen dew from his beard as he rose to his feet. Blackfoot had trailed him well into the night, forcing him to ride north while his brigade traveled south toward the Wind River Mountains.

The sunrise swam irresolutely into the chill blue sky of Montana as he swung into the saddle, as hungry and cold as a man could be. But fire would bring the curious. And he was more than two days' ride from a friendly face.

Chapter 1

In an isolated spot on the bank of the Popo Agie River, Bridger paused to shuck his leather shirt and trousers. The heavy muscles of a blacksmith's apprentice still lingered in his broad shoulders. Little else remained of the rangy eighteen-year-old indentured servant who had run away from St. Louis in 1822 to hunt beaver in the Three Forks region of the Missouri River. The blue-gray eyes were as clear as a mountain stream. His stern features—a hooked nose and high cheekbones—were weathered to a leathery brown, aging his appearance well beyond his twenty-six years.

Bridger scratched the growth of whiskers on his chin while debating for the fifth time in as many years whether to slice away the beard. His hand strayed down to scratch the thick mat of hair on his chest, and a smile played on his lips. It seemed a shame to tamper with what nature so obviously intended to be his lot.

"That Cap'n Bridger got the hair o' the grizzly on him!" He had often heard that sentiment murmured behind his back after a successful tangle with the Crow or Blackfoot, or when one of the brigade men had enough Taos Lightning in him to loosen his tongue.

Reckon they must be part right, he answered the thought. His sun-bleached hair hung to his shoulders and golden fur covered his arms, chest and legs.

Consigning the razor to perdition, he waded into the icy stream and began the task of scrubbing off a whole season's grime and stink. The lye soap borrowed from a fellow trapper helped. Half an hour later he waded out to spread himself on the tall grasses of the riverbank to dry. Gnats tickled his nose and the odor of the ripening grass teased his nostrils as he drifted off to sleep.

The first splash brought him fully awake. Automatically he reached for the Green River skinning knife beside his clothes, though his instinct for survival told him that no human enemy would announce himself so boldly.

The sound of female laughter sent his brows upward. As the splashing increased so did the laughter. He could stand it no longer. He stretched himself out in the grass and parted the reeds on the riverside. The sight that met his eyes more than made up for the irritation of having his sleep interrupted.

On the opposite bank were half a dozen Indian girls in varying states of undress. They, too, had sought the solitude of the river in which to bathe. Bridger cautiously fingered a few more blades of grass out of his way, his face split into a wide grin. Apparently this was his lucky day. He had planned to go down to the Indian villages this very evening, but this was better than the brief glimpses he would be allowed of the enticing young women who expected payment for their favors in advance.

Eagerly his eyes roamed the lithe figures. Shoshone squaws, he decided. There was no mistaking those lovely pouting faces and long limbs. One girl was pregnant, her rounded abdomen the color and curvature of an acorn. As the squaws splashed and played in the shallows, Bridger feasted on the sight of their firm, chocolate-tipped breasts and temptingly rounded buttocks. In his mind's eye he joined them on the sweet grass of the far bank, lustily rolling with one, then another until he was spent and limp.

"Come night, Jim. Just you wait till night," he counseled himself. The squaws were willing—just how willing he knew from experience—but there were rules. An Indian girl could be had for a few pennies' worth of glass beads or a fancy-looking glass. It was her right, her due. To a trapper, a handful of "foofaraw"— trinkets, baubles, necklaces—in the wilderness could buy more happiness than a claim to all the lands and titles in Europe. Funny thing about that. He had never had the chance to try a woman of his own kind— a white woman. But if what he heard tell was true, he did not mind the lack. It was said a white woman did not like the mating act, found it repugnant, and submitted to her man through sufferance. That wasn't the way with an Indian girl. Did they like it? They went so far as to beckon their favored man into the cottonwoods themselves. No, he did not mind what he missed by being so far from what some folks called civilization.

"Over here, Jake!" a voice cried, breaking in on Bridger's thoughts. "Told ya I heared women. Hoo-ee! They's naked, too!"

Three buckskinned figures broke from the woods a few yards from where Bridger lay. Fanning out, they ran toward the shallow river, whooping like savages, waving a bottle of whiskey in one hand and glass bead necklaces in the other.

"Come on, little darlin's. Who's gonna be the first

in the cottonwoods with ol' Milt?" the tallest of the three yelled.

With shrieks of fear and pleasure, the naked band of squaws dashed from the water and scrambled for the shelter of the cottonwood grove like a disturbed bevy of quail. But the long-legged mountain men were experts at tracking their prey, and gamely followed, splashing up the opposite bank within yards of the fleeing females.

Bridger watched with amusement the antics of Big Bill Sublette's brother, Milt, and the other trappers. The last man to gain the far bank slipped in the mud and fell, breaking his bottle of whiskey. Another man caught up with one of the girls and brought her to the ground with a flying leap. They struggled for a brief moment. The Indian girl reached out to gouge at the man's eyes, until the trapper caught her attention by swinging a pair of copper bracelets before her nose. Hesitantly she reached for them, then snatched them from him. Bridger heard her giggle and knew the man had won.

Not one to get much pleasure from spying on another man's fun, he squatted down to collect his clothing when a scream, unlike the others, brought him back to his feet. Running with a speed that made the most of her long, slim legs, a young Indian girl raced from the cottonwoods and headed straight for the bank just opposite him. He was surprised to see that she was younger than the others—without the full curves of womanhood yet. He had paid little attention to her during his moments of solitary spying. But there was something pleasingly graceful about the kick of her pale brown legs and the swing of the blue-black hair reaching her naked hips. As she plunged into the water, another figure emerged from the trees.

"Hey! Wait up, you bloodthirsty little savage!"

The man had lost his beads and whiskey, and ran toward the river with one hand clamped to his bleeding cheek.

Sizing up the odds and knowing Milt's temper when he was riled, Bridger strode over to the river in time to fish the girl out as she reached his side. "Easy, little gal. Ain't no—" His words of assurance were cut off by a well placed kick from a slender foot. Releasing the girl, Bridger made a protective grab for his groin, deflecting a second blow.

"Damnit! You crazed squaw, can't you tell when a man's helping?" Startled and angered, he made the near-fatal mistake of reaching for her a second time. More swiftly than he could credit, she ducked under his arm and, grasping the handle of his knife that lay in the grass, swung around on him making a slashing gesture at his middle.

"That's it! You keep her busy, Gabe!" Milt yelled to Bridger, calling the trapper by his nickname. Milt waded across the river and gained the bank. Throwing his arms open, he closed in on the girl. "Come on, honey. Give Milt a nice ol' kiss and then we'll go a-huntin' them beads we lost back in the trees," he coaxed, a big grin on his nail-raked face.

An expression of sheer terror entered the girl's eyes, but Bridger knew enough of Indian upbringing to realize she meant deadly harm to the first man who touched her. "Back off, Sublette," he ordered in a low voice. "You scared the gal half out of her wits." Bridger's glance flickered from his friend to the girl, and he raised his hand in the universal sign of friendship. Then he made the sign for Shoshone with his fingers, thinking that he should have done it in the first place and saved himself an aching groin. The girl did not relax, but kept her fingers tightly wrapped about the knife. He repeated the peculiar wriggling hand gesture that had led many of the Plains tribes to refer to the Shoshones as "The Snakes."

"Appears to me she don't like yer idea o' bein' friends," Milt teased, and thrust a hand out to grab her. "Let me have a . . . Ho!" Quickly, he drew his hand back. A thin bloody streak appeared where the blade had passed lightly over it.

"Damn slut! What'd you go and do that for?" he yelped.

"Let her be, Milt. She's just a babe," Bridger said quietly, and bent down slowly to retrieve his leather shirt.

The girl followed his movements, but Bridger was careful not to give her a reason to use her weapon a second time. He lifted the shirt over his head and saw the flicker of relief in her gaze. Quicker than a coiled rattler he whipped out his arm and caught the knife in the folds of his shirt. She did not have time to react before he twisted her wrist back and snatched his knife.

"Much obliged," Milt called as he grabbed her from behind. She swore at him in Shoshone, tearing at his hands. When Milt swung her off her feet with a roar of laughter, she bent her head and immediately sank her teeth into his wrist.

"Yow!" Milt squawked and dropped her at his feet. "Just for that I ain't gonna give you them pretty things I brought," he grumbled and kicked at her half-heartedly.

"Aw, Milt," Bridger drawled in his best joshing tone. "Don't be a sore loser. Just look what she's done to my only shirt." He held up the buckskin garment displaying a broad slash across the front.

The snort of derision surprised both men and they turned to stare at the naked girl sitting in the grass. Milt's lazy gaze wandered over the delicately boned girl, then rose to meet Bridger's amused glance.

"Reckon she is just a child," he muttered sheepishly. "Only, how's a man supposed to think when his eyes is full of riper . . ." He paused, his weathered face a dull red above his dark beard. "Must be the whiskey," he muttered. "Yeah, first day of rendezvous and all. Musta been the whiskey Bill sold me."

"Bill's in camp?" Bridger's slow speech belied the pleasure the news brought him.

"Hell, yeah. Don't think there'd be a rendezvous if brother Bill didn't get through with the whiskey and supplies." Milt shot him a keen glance. "Why ain't you down to camp with the rest o' Jed's brigade?" His gaze went to the Indian girl and back. "Don't tell me she's . . . ?" He let the question hang.

"If I was to think you was serious, I'd have to stuff your tongue down your throat," Bridger returned lightly and reached for his britches.

"What do we do with her?" Milton hunched a shoulder in the squaw's direction as she scrambled upright.

"Better send her home." Bridger turned to her, choosing his words carefully. The Shoshone tongue was one of the many he had become familiar with over the years. "Where are your people?"

The girl's dark eyes rested on him for a full minute before she spoke. "I am Shoshone. I am called Little Fawn, eldest daughter of the great chief Washakie."

"Washakie's daughter?" Bridger echoed in surprise. "Why do you come to the river with the other girls? The daughter of my great friend Washakie does not need to peddle herself for foofaraw."

The disapproval in the white man's voice made Little Fawn's amber skin blush, but her voice was full of contempt. "I want no foofaraw. That is for the Ute and Crow sows. I come only to bathe."

Her eyes traveled up and down Bridger's body, acknowledging his nakedness for the first time. A man's body was not unknown to her, as she had tended many a wounded warrior in the short span of her thirteen years. But this six-foot bearded white man with golden fur covering his limbs was unlike the Indians she knew who had hairless brown limbs. Her curious gaze lingered for an instant below his waist, then she turned abruptly and dashed into the underbrush.

"Looks to be you frightened her, Gabe. Guess she ain't had a man after all." Milton shook the water from his soaked buckskins. "She cost me plenty, to no account."

"Come on, Milt. It ain't like you to fret," Bridger said as he examined his ruined shirt. "Buy you a whiskey when we get into camp."

"That a fact?" Milton's bushy brows quirked in interest. "What're we waitin' for?" He grinned. " 'Cept you best get them britches on 'afore you scare off the rest of them squaws."

Little Fawn sprinted through the narrow stand of sweet cottonwoods, but paused at the edge of the forest to think of a way out. Her village lay in the valley formed by the fork of the Bighorn Mountains to the north and the Wind River Range to the south, their rounded peaks dark smudges against the soft summer sky. They were camped on the Popo Agie, which formed the southeastern border of the triangular valley. Tepees stretched out through the middle distance of the valley floor. Only one lodge stood out in her mind. Washakie's tepee was near the center of their village. It would be impossible to reach it without attracting the attention of the whole camp of braves, squaws, children and dogs.

"Damn the Gray Eyes," she muttered and

stamped her bare foot on the soft forest floor. She knew only a few words of English, most of it learned by listening when her father sat in counsel to smoke with the white trappers. It was, of course, unacceptable language for a young girl, whether American or Shoshone. She was not afraid of the drunk trapper or his friend, yet she could not go back for her clothing. That would be admitting that she had made a mistake or had been frightened off. No, she would have to find a way to return to her father's lodge without suffering a loss of pride.

The faint whinny of a horse attracted her attention. A short distance away she saw a small party of Indian braves leading a group of ponies past the cottonwoods to graze in the tall summer grasses of the open prairie. She backed behind a waist-high shrub and waited.

Bringing up the rear, his bow slung negligently over his right shoulder, was Ear-of-the-Fox, her father's adopted son and her best friend.

Quickly Little Fawn put her fingers to her lips and produced a credible imitation of the oriole's song. When he halted with head canted, she repeated the clear flutelike whistles. A moment later he waved off his friends and turned in her direction.

Ear-of-the-Fox displayed no unusual interest in Little Fawn's nudity, but he noted with satisfaction that her tiny breasts had begun to swell. It would not be many more summers before he could claim her as his own. But a deep frown formed on his serious young face when she did not at once dissolve into giggles or launch into one of her wild tales of having been attacked by bears. It was like her to hide her clothes and pretend some fantastic tale. The silence was unlike her.

"Why do you call me?" he asked coldly. "Do you not see that I have men's work to do? I am no longer a child. I will earn the right to ride with a war party this fall."

Little Fawn wrinkled her nose in disrespect. "Who is so foolish as to let a mere boy ride with great warriors?" It was understood between them that Little Fawn considered herself his equal and, until recently, the understanding did not disturb Ear-of-the-Fox. It was a private matter between friends, and she had never embarrassed him in public. But the sight of her standing defiantly before him without a stitch of clothing made Ear-of-the-Fox uncomfortable. "Where are your skins? You should be in the village helping your mother, Blue Feather, dress the new hides."

Little Fawn bit her lip. Ear-of-the-Fox seldom spoke sharply to her, but things were changing. "I left them on the riverbank. Trappers came upon us as we bathed." Young though she was, she fully appreciated the look of anger that leaped into her friend's eyes.

"They—they took your clothes?" The words trembled out, so great was the brave's fury.

Secretly pleased by his obvious jealousy, she turned away, shrugging her slender shoulders. "I am not afraid of the white men." She whirled back, the next thought making her forget the game she had begun. "Do you know the white man has skin the color of a prairie dog's underbelly?"

The news did not meet with the expected results. Ear-of-the-Fox's right hand shot out, leaving its scarlet imprint on her cheek. Enraged, Little Fawn flew at him, a tiny thunderbolt of flailing limbs and sharp teeth. They tumbled to the ground, rolling in the damp carpet of fetid leaves and grass. Ear-of-the-Fox knew he could easily overpower her. He found an unexpected pleasure in this attack, allowing her several stinging blows in return for the chance to run his hands over the soft skin of her back and buttocks.

The pleasure was short-lived. Little Fawn's knee made contact for the second time that day, and Ear-of-the-Fox rolled away from her with a groan.

"That will teach you who you may strike," she cried, and rose to pick the clinging leaves from her shoulders and legs.

Fifteen is a difficult age, especially for a young man smitten with a young woman. Ear-of-the-Fox felt that his pride had been assaulted by Little Fawn and his physical pain made matters worse. But his sense of dignity would not allow him to acknowledge either his embarrassment or his discomfort. He bounded quickly to his feet, and bent to collect his bow and arrow case. "I have work to do. You stay and hide your shame in the woods. It is fitting," he announced, and started toward the clearing.

"Wait!" Little Fawn ran to his side and placed a hand on his arm. "I am not dishonored." At his skeptical look she added saucily, "I ran away—but not before I counted coup on both of the white men."

"Ah, that is wild woman talk."

Little Fawn lifted her chin. "I can prove it. When next you are in the white men's camp, look for two men, one with a knife slash across the back of his hand and another with a buckskin shirt slit from shoulder to waist. Both of these things I have done."

Impressed with the certainty of her tone, Ear-of-the-Fox felt anger rising within him once more. Little Fawn was to be his woman; he would share her with no man. He gave her a long look. "If it is as you say, I will kill these men for touching you."

Little Fawn smiled quickly, but was tempered by uncertainty as she stared into his contorted face. "I do not need you to avenge me. I have taken my victory. I need you to get a robe for me so that I may go home."

Ear-of-the-Fox stood his ground. The rage in his

blood demanded that he take some action. He could not be certain which man to blame unless he walked the length of the trappers' camps many days searching for a torn shirt. Little Fawn's smile grew and his resolve wavered. He had promised Washakie that he would not make war on the white man. But would her father hold him to that promise if he learned of his daughter's shame? "You say they did not harm you. Is this truth?"

Little Fawn answered, "Go and look for yourself. You will find the men I described."

"What you reckon is the worst case o' cabin fever you ever seen, Gabe?"

Bridger grumbled and lifted his head from his chest. His lids felt lined with sand as they slid back over a pair of startlingly red eyes. The rendezvous, the trappers' yearly trade fair, was nearly two weeks old. Endless nights of drinking, gorging, and retching had begun to pall as an entertainment, and a few men had gathered to recount their exploits of past years.

Bridger belched and shifted his weight only to discover that his "pillow" was a rather plump Indian girl who did not like being elbowed in the stomach. She wriggled under him, yowling like a cat. Groggy but determined, he sat up and shoved her away. She was bare to the waist in her summer costume of buckskin skirt and a dozen necklaces. Aware of the white man's eyes on her and hoping to add another necklace to her collection, she sat up, pushed the dark hair from her eyes, and smiled, revealing a wide gap where two front teeth should have been.

Bridger recoiled in disgust. "Bejesus! Where'd you come from?"

Laughter erupted from the trappers. "Don't you remember, Gabe? You bet a few o' us shyer fellers you'd bed every squaw in the Crow village 'afore rendezvous is done," one replied.

Bridger's lips turned in a sickly smile. "Did I win?"

"Hell! Who cares?"

Bridger glared across the fire to find Tom Fitzpatrick, his best friend, grinning at him. Fitzpatrick's boyish face had been scraped clean of the auburn beard that usually hid a mass of freckles. Instead of the usual fringed buckskins, he wore a crudely made suit of vile green and red plaid that he had bought, no doubt, with part of his cache of beaver pelts. "Go on, Gabe. Tell these pork-eaters about the time you spent your first winter at Fort Henry," Fitzpatrick encouraged.

Gabe? Bridger shook his head, then immediately regretted it. Whiskey was a luxury not often indulged in and the potent mixture called Taos Lightning was worst of all. Made of raw spirits cut with an equal amount of water and flavored with tobacco and cayenne pepper, the concoction almost crippled his faculties. But he was pretty certain his name was Jim Bridger. After a moment's reflection he remembered where the name had come from. Gabe—Gabriel. Jed Smith had dubbed him that at last year's rendezvous.

"Bless it all, Bridger, if your face ain't longer than a summer's day. Looks like Gabriel come to tell Daniel of the Day of Judgment," Jed had pronounced when he had come upon Bridger staring woefully at a ruined cache of pelts. By nightfall all the camp had heard the nickname. Those with the right to address Bridger intimately chopped it off to "Gabe." Bridger snorted. Just like that Bible-toting Jed to burden him with a highfalutin name like that.

"Cap'n Bridger, sir? I'd like to hear that story," encouraged one of the younger pork-eaters, a new camp tender recruited to Bridger's brigade.

Bridger stretched out full on his buffalo robe and rested his head on his arms. He enjoyed telling of his adventures, and in a land where tall tales were a fact of life, his were the most respected. "Was my first winter out with the Missouri Fur Company. Major Henry was in charge. Musta been two dozen men wintering at Fort Henry, all squashed into a space that'd pain a pair of dogs."

He shut his eyes, remembering back a world ago. "The Missouri froze up long before midwinter. Ice musta been four feet thick in places. Snow drifts reached up to the top of the stockade by January. Men and horses and dogs shut up tighter'n a grave. Weren't nothing to break the silence but the howling of them damned wolves. Lined up on the fort wall, they did, a-beggin' and a-pleadin' to share our heat. Wasn't long before many a man was snarling at his best friend like one of the maddened wolves. Ain't every man can keep from breaking when faced with that kind of living death."

His low, methodical voice drew his audience into the scene he painted, setting more than one old-timer to reflecting on his own vivid memories. "We lost two men that year. Funny thing. It was spring when it happened. The first thaw sorta broke the dam o' feelings. We had a legend with us, fellers. The damnedest, ugliest, meanest riverman this country's ever seen. Ol' Mike Fink spent that winter at Fort Henry. And it was his last on this God's earth. He'd been a-grumblin' all winter. Boasted he'd been everywhere and done everything this world had to offer. But he'd never been up against the soul-wrenching, mind-busting winter of the Upper Missouri. About midwinter he picked a fight with the two men he'd been most friendly with. Killed one in outright murder. Shot his head clean off. Other feller grabbed up a pistol and put a ball in Fink's heart. Buried the two side by side. Seemed fitting somehow. Bad winter, '32."

The hush lingered when he was done until Fitzpatrick roared out, "Always could tell the best goddamn stories around, Gabe." He took a long pull on his tin cup in salute. "Hell, I got chilblains just thinking about it!"

Bridger rose at dawn. Muted pastels streaked the morning sky. He threw back the flap of his tepee and set about stirring the embers of the campfire. In spite of the carousal of the last few weeks, a serious matter rested uneasily on his shoulders. Upon riding in the first day of rendezvous, he had heard rumors that the long-time partnership of Jed Smith and Bill Sublette was breaking up. He did not believe this talk, but a brief conversation with Jed only the night before confirmed it. Now was the time for him to make his own decision.

Bridger sighed. It had been a long time since he had given a thought to his future. Ever since he had left St. Louis to take up the life of a trapper, he figured his future was set. A man lived a lifetime just making it from rendezvous to rendezvous. He had been around since the very first one back in '25. The future? That meant planning out what there was left of his time on earth. The Indians said only the mountains endured forever. He wasn't a mountain. His future was uncertain. The dream that plagued him had made another visit during the night, reminding him that he had not yet outlived the shame of having once left a wounded, defenseless man to die in the wilderness. That dream was his private damnation. Unless he lived down that cursed dream, he did not have any future worth troubling over. Still, things would change with Bill and Jed leaving after all these years.

While he considered this problem he mixed beans with water, set the kettle to brew coffee over the fire, sat back on his heels and waited. Sure enough, the smell of coffee roused Fitzpatrick, who staggered to the tepee entrance within minutes, the jacket of his city suit missing.

"Sure'n and if 'tisn't that most heav'nly of brews that set my nostrils a-quiver," he rhapsodized in the broad Irish brogue he saved for whimsical moments. He rubbed the sleep from his face with both hands and joined Bridger.

Bridger nodded and reached for two of the battered tin cups lying about on the ground. He filled them, then gave one to Fitzpatrick. "Never figured on nothing like this, Fitz," he began. "Thought we'd all be together till the last of us went under. Don't seem right, Jed and Bill giving over the business when they're doing so well. Hell! Trapping ain't never been better, what with the brigades grown to a size them skulking Blackfoot think twice about attacking." He shook his head. "Don't seem right."

Fitz cocked his head thoughtfully. He had known Bridger as long as he had been in the wilderness. Knew him better, probably, than any man alive. Yet there was a part of him no one could plumb. He had seen Bridger plow into the midst of the worst fighting, then turn the next moment and shake his head over the wanton destruction of the area by the multitude of new trappers and traders infesting the Upper Missouri. A strange mixture of ferocity and gentleness was Jim Bridger.

"Why did you come West, Gabe?"

The question surprised Bridger but he answered it. "Same as the next, I reckon. Came West to make a living, make a place for myself."

Fitz nodded. "Fair enough. Most men are looking

for something and that something for most of us is a chance to get rich." He grinned, a thousand Irish imps dancing in his light blue eyes. "Reckon it's our turn, Gabe. Jed and Bill is handing it to us for the taking."

Bridger stared at the fire. "You suggesting we buy out Smith, Jackson and Sublette? Know what they're asking? Twenty thousand U.S. American dollars, that's what. Where the hell are we to get that kind of money?"

The news did not daunt the Irishman. "We'll offer them the same deal they did Ashley four years back: an IOU for sixteen thousand dollars in beaver pelts to be paid back over a period of years." Fitz leaned nearer and said in a conspiratorial tone, "If them ol' codgers could do it, you and me sure as hell can."

Bridger hunched his shoulders and chewed thoughtfully on a strip of jerky he had pulled from his pocket. "Ain't no need for you to paint rosy pictures for me. I ain't no fool and running a fur company takes more doing than trapping and skinning beaver. Jed and Bill got the schooling to go with their experience in the field." He lifted his head but did not look directly at the man next to him. "I can't even write my name. All that figuring and selling and record-keeping—it ain't in me."

Fitz sighed. Men of learning, even those who knew only their letters and a spot of figuring, were in the minority out here and few cared that it was so. But Bridger was a proud man and Fitz knew the admission had cost him. Fitz was older by four years, but there were parts of Bridger that seemed as old as the hills themselves. He had seen Bridger read in the debris floating on the surface of a stream signs that meant a party of Blackfoot had camped upriver, as well as other equally astonishing deductions from less information. Marks made on paper might be incomprehensible to Bridger, but his mind was quick and his reasoning nearly infallible. Fitz wanted the fur company, wanted it bad, and Bridger was the man he wanted as a partner.

" 'Tis a wee bit of scrawling you're bothering your fine head about? Faith! I'm making you the offer on the condition that you leave the easy part to me." Fitz reached out and walloped his friend on the back. "You thickheaded, plew-stripping grizzly bear, did you think *I* want Captain of Brigades? Now that is a lovely thought—you behind a desk in St. Louis mulling over a ledger while I drag a brigade of green *engagés* into Blackfoot country." More seriously he said, "If you take the field I'll be responsible for supplies and the like. Leave the caravans to me and I'll rest easy with you in charge out here."

Bridger's gray gaze turned with full force on his friend. "Ain't you forgetting something? That lone tepee over on the far side of camp. Ain't you thought to ask whose it is? That's McKenzie's man, Fontenelle. The American Fur Company has come to rendezvous. That ain't good, Fitz. I figure Bill and Jed aim to sell out before the real trouble starts. Word is McKenzie's got marching orders to run all competition out of the Rockies. Fontenelle made Jed an offer this morning. Could be we're buying a worthless company."

"Could be," Fitz agreed mildly.

"On the other hand, I don't see giving them fancypants Easterners a clear shot at our livelihood," Bridger went on. "It was you and me and folks like Jed and Bill what first came out here when no white man had ever set foot in this territory. Appears to me we owe it to ourselves to stick around a while and give them big city fellers a run for their lives."

"You mean just to sorta spoil the game for them," Fitz ventured with a sweet smile.

"Couldn't have said it better myself," Bridger answered. "Likely we'll be skinning McKenzie men before the season's out."

Chapter 2

William Henry Vanderburgh paced the ground of his tent as he waited for the arrival of Lucien Fontenelle. For weeks Vanderburgh had hastened over the dangerous terrain from Fort Union to Cache Valley only to learn that rendezvous had taken place elsewhere. Impatiently he waited for news from the Wind River Valley where the hundreds of trappers had gathered.

Tall and fair-haired, Vanderburgh knew he cut a commanding figure in his clean, neatly tailored buckskins and boots. A West Point graduate and son of a wealthy Indiana judge, he expected to accomplish much in the fur business for which he had given up a military career. Had he not been picked to lead the American Fur Company's brigades in the field? John Jacob Astor's monopoly of the American fur trade would be complete with the addition of the Upper Missouri traffic, and Vanderburgh had the opportunity of handing the trade to Mr. Astor's man, Kenneth McKenzie, on a silver platter. Such a coup should assure him a permanent niche in the world and more money than he required.

The thought of success temporarily soothed his impatience, but when the Frenchman finally arrived, Vanderburgh's anger had rekindled with the length of the delay. His eyes ran contemptuously over the elegantly dressed man who, in his spotless black riding coat and leather trousers, looked too well rested to have hurried himself.

"Well, what did you find out?" Vanderburgh demanded. "Did Smith and Sublette accept McKenzie's offer?"

Lucien Fontenelle gritted his teeth, cautioning himself against displaying resentment of the American's rudeness. Slender and of medium height, he appeared to be as genteel as his aristocratic Creole background would proclaim him. But beneath the courtly exterior pulsed a dark moody streak.

"What the devil's the matter with you?" Vanderburgh struck the tabletop with his fist. "Just answer my question and get out."

"But of course, *mon ami*." Fontenelle's tone was amicable, but his eyelids began to flutter in betrayal of temper. "We are too late. Smith, Jackson, and Sublette have sold out to the Rocky Mountain Fur Company."

Vanderburgh lifted his head sharply. "What nonsense is this? There's no such company. If you're pulling one of your idiotic stunts, I'll have you sent back to Fort Union!"

"Tsk, tsk. Such a temper, m'sieur. Can nothing happen that you do not direct?"

"What the hell is that supposed to mean?" Vanderburgh replied.

Fontenelle shrugged. "What I say, m'sieur. A new company has formed headed by Messieurs Bridger and Fitzpatrick. In addition they have sold shares to M'sieur Sublette's younger brother Milton, the Dutchman, Fraeb, and Jean-Baptiste Gervais."

Vanderburgh swore under his breath, his fists working by his sides for a moment. "What was the price?"

Again Fontenelle shrugged, enjoying prolonging the other man's discomfort. "Rumor is rumor, m'sieur. It says the company signed an IOU for sixteen thousand dollars to be paid off in pelts."

"Shit!"

"As you say, m'sieur." Fontenelle's face remained blank, but secretly Vanderburgh's defeat pleased him. The Frenchman had trapped the Mississippi and Arkansas Rivers for a number of years, and for men like Bridger and Fitzpatrick, who trapped in country still openly hostile, he had nothing but admiration. Often in the last weeks he had wondered if he had made a mistake in accepting McKenzie's generous offer. Still, his work for the American Fur Company was business and he always accomplished his assignments.

"It does not change anything, it only makes our job more difficult," Vanderburgh declared with an effort to rally his spirit. "Better read this." He picked up a paper from the table and thrust it at Fontenelle. "It comes from New York direct. Seems the Astor Trust anticipated such an eventuality."

Fontenelle took the paper, skimming it at will until a passage caught his attention.

> You are under no restraint with regards to prices, but to get the trade even if the returns you make should not pay the first costs of the goods. You are well aware that this is the object of the company and their positive instruction. . . .

Vanderburgh drummed his fingers on the tabletop while the Frenchman read. Their orders were specific but limited. Anything short of pitched battle would serve. Under orders from back East he was to outbid and undercut the current western market prices until no man in the Rockies could show a profit. His men were to bribe away the independent trappers, gain the support of the Plains Indians by whatever methods proved most effective, and spoil where possible the chances of a successful hunt by the "Opposition," as the American Fur Company termed its newest adversaries. Finally, his most pressing business was to learn the secret grounds of the mountain men. After that, the Company would simply outman the Opposition and drive them out or round them up to work for them.

"Our first order of business in the fields is to learn the terrain," Vanderburgh said when Fontenelle lifted his eyes. "Anything short of murder is acceptable."

"*Écraser toute opposition.* How delightfully phrased." Fontenelle sent the letter skimming across the room. "So, there is to be no method too ruthless, no trick too low. It suits us, *non*? The cutthroat tactics of the 'King of the Missouri' shall be carried out by a son of the French aristocracy and the West Point soldier, while our officious leader, McKenzie, lords it on the Upper Missouri. *Mais oui.* We are a fine pair. *Félicitations, m'sieur.* I salute you in your finest hour." With a flick of his hand Fontenelle turned smartly on his heel.

Piqued by the man's highhanded manner, Vanderburgh bawled after him, "Just be certain your men are ready to leave when the Rocky Mountain Company pulls out for their fall hunt. This isn't the Mississippi, Fontenelle. You'll have to prove yourself all over again to McKenzie."

Fontenelle merely lifted his shoulders slightly, his back to the American.

"Another thing," Vanderburgh continued. "You and Drips will hunt together. Follow any of the brigades but the one commanded by Jim Bridger." A smile broke the harsh line of his features. "Met the backwoods ruffian a few years back. He's the key to our success, I'll wager. And he's my game."

"Where's Cap'n Bridger?" Fitz demanded of the young engagé who brought him his horse.

The man, named Loretto, flung an arm toward the Shoshone village. "Capitán Bridger goes to smoke the peace pipe with Chief Washakie. He says he will catch up."

Fitz cursed and spit at the ground near his own foot. "Ain't we got enough to do without him gallivant-ing off to parley? Of all the—" Fitz caught himself up, realizing that the young Mexican was staring at him, mouth agape, and swore again. To the new recruits, Bridger ranked just below the Holy Trinity in respect and awe. "Get your mess mounted up, Loretto, and tell that Blackfoot wife of yours she's to keep close to you. If you consider yourself married, and if you ain't up to sharing her, she best be kept outta sight."

The Mexican's dark eyes grew hard. "Any man who touch my woman, he gets his throat cut." With a quick movement he whipped the skinning knife from his leggings and drew it across his own throat.

Fitz merely shrugged when the man walked away. "Loco Mexican," he muttered to himself. "Near about as crazy as Gabe and his belief in Indian medicine." Fitz had no doubt that a blessing on this year's brigade was Bridger's real motive for approaching Washakie.

Washakie was glad to welcome his tall, steely-eyed guest. "The Shoshone welcome our friend, the white medicine man Peejatowahooten," he intoned formally when Bridger stood before him at the en-trance of his lodge. "We will smoke together and ask

the Great spirit for guidance so that you may find
many rivers filled with beaver."

Bridger nodded solemnly, and with his hand
raised, two fingers extended upward, he made the sign
for friend. Washakie was young, only a few years older
than Bridger himself, yet he had eight daughters. The
feeling of common purpose ran in both men's veins,
drawing them to one another. It was a friendship
prized by Bridger. Unlike many of the older chiefs,
Washakie saw the future of his people bound up in the
fortunes of the white man. For his own part, Bridger
saw the life and customs of the Shoshone perfectly
suited to the land that he now claimed as his own.

The lodge flap was held open by one of
Washakie's four wives, and both men passed inside.
Bridger glanced around, envious of the comforts of the
primitive setting. The pounded earth floor had been
swept clean and two willow-stick backrests were placed
beside the fire smoldering in the center of the lodge.
The dew cloth had been lifted back to facilitate air cir-
culation. In one corner sat Washakie's first wife, Blue
Feather.

Bridger's eyes went back to the tall, gaunt but
well-muscled man who was his host. His painted buckskin shirt was decorated with the treasured porcupine
quills, and the fringed seams worked with beads. Long,
unbound black hair, shining with a fresh application
of bear grease, framed his handsome face of wide
cheekbones and Roman nose. Washakie seemed at
peace with his world and it with him, Bridger thought.

The soapstone pipe was ceremoniously filled and
lit. Bridger savored the rich tobacco, better than the
blend he traded beaver for, and watched his exhaled
breath rise as prayer to intermingle with the higher
powers. The Indians believed that through the act of
smoking a man could reach to the level of the spirit

world. Bridger understood this feeling of oneness. Brief enough were the moments of harmony in a man's life; they should be appreciated.

In due time the pipe was put away and a meal served consisting of meat stew from the simmering pot, a salad of roots, leaves and buds, and fried pemmican into which pulverized dried wild cherries had been added. This last delicacy drew Bridger's attention to Blue Feather, and he gave her a bobbing nod while holding out his bowl to show his approval. To Washakie he said in the formal Shoshone tongue, "Fortunate, indeed, is a man whose wife's cooking gladdens the heart and fills the belly."

Washakie's face was grave as he replied, "The man who finds himself such a wife will curse the day of his birth if he cannot learn the taming of her spirit. The pemmican is the work of my eldest daughter and already I despair of her learning the humility owed a man by his woman. Still, you honor us with your words." To Blue Feather he said, "Go and bring your daughter to me. It is a great honor our guest bestows upon her. Let her come in meek manner to hear of it." Blue Feather nodded silently and ducked through the open flap.

In the clearing beyond the village, Little Fawn was hard at work on one of the buffalo skins Washakie's hunting party had brought back days earlier. Having washed the blood from the hide, she rolled it up and prepared it for dressing. This morning it had been staked out on the ground and her job was to work free the remaining flesh, sinew, and integument with a scraping tool. Afterwards, an adz-shaped tool would be used on the skin to reduce the hide to uniform thickness. Finally she would apply a mixture of buffalo brains, liver, and fat to the hide several times to assure a smooth texture. Dirty work of this kind was dreaded

by most Indian women, but Little Fawn looked upon it
with pleasure. She had a special reason for taking an
interest in this skin. Women of the tribe were not often
allowed to keep anything of value beyond the trinkets
given to them by warriors or trappers. Only the daughter of a chief occasionally received skins of her own.
And this one, she reflected happily, would be special.
She would not scrape the thick coarse hair from it as
one did when preparing a tepee cover. It would be
made into a warm, fur-lined robe as a gift for her future husband. Upon it she would record in paint the
images received in her sacred "vision."

Little Fawn stood up and rubbed a handful of dry
dirt between her palms to clean them. Soon she would
be going on her quest. The Mysterious Spirits inhabit-
ing the sky and earth imparted their wisdom and protection to those who sought it by trial and sacrifice.
When the white men were gone from the plain to hunt
pelts in the mountain streams, she would leave her village. Traveling alone and without food or water, she
would seek an isolated spot in the mountains to pray
for a revelation that would bind her life and future to
the spirit who offered her protection.

Not many Indian women cared to subject themselves to the torture required by abstinence from food
and drink, or the vulnerability to wolves and bears, as
well as the special danger to an unprotected woman.

But, thought Little Fawn, I am different. In her
veins ran the blood of the great Shoshone chiefs and,
even more, the savior of her people, Sacajawea, the
most honored of all her women ancestors. She would
face whatever danger lay in her path to earn the favor
of the Mysterious Spirit.

She looked up at her mother's call and turned
toward her father's lodge after a last satisfied glance at
her work. So fixed were her thoughts upon her secret

desires that upon reaching the lodge she failed to notice that her father was not alone. She greeted him with an impulsive embrace just inside the doorway where he stood.

"Father, you have sent for me?" she asked with a quick smile for her adored parent.

"We have a guest," Washakie said and placed a restraining hand on his daughter's shoulder. "Your skill with the pemmican earns you the honor to stand before a great friend of the Shoshone nation." To Bridger he said, "Peejatowahooten, my daughter, Little Fawn, accepts your praise with a humble heart."

Little Fawn's black eyes swung to the guest the instant her father had pronounced his Indian name, which meant Mysterious Medicine Chief. It was a name well known and respected among her tribe. Peejatowahooten was the white man of powerful magic who had taught her father the medicine of the fire stick. It was said he could charm the beaver from their lodges, so numerous were the pelts he brought to rendezvous. But her eyes slid from Bridger almost as soon as they encountered him. She recognized him immediately from the incident beside the river. Yet her curiosity was greater for the wonderful image of Peejatowahooten.

"My child, why do you not greet our guest? Or have you at last met with a man who can silence your loose tongue?" Washakie teased gently.

Little Fawn's eyes traced the empty interior of the lodge. Then they hurried back to Bridger, widening in incredulity. "This is Peejatowahooten?"

Washakie heard the scorn in her words, and his face darkened in anger. "You shame your mother with your lack of manners. Go," he commanded.

"Wait." Bridger's light eyes met the girl's dark

ones in challenge. When hers flickered to the unskillful
mending of the knife tear in his shirt he knew what
prompted her skepticism. What great medicine man
would allow a mere squaw child to come so near to
ending his life with his own knife? "It is not the child's
fault that she expects a great spirit and is given only a
man to look upon." He grinned at her flushing cheeks.
"We are not strangers, are we, Little Fawn?"

Little Fawn stood between the two tall men, one
dark and proud, and the other pale and self-assured.
The tales she had heard of Peejatowahooten had led
her to expect a being of exceptional stature and wonder. She had seen this man without his skins and knew
him to be like any other. But, she reasoned, if her father found the Gray Eyes worthy of respect, so must
she. "We have met, Peejatowahooten, at the riverbank," she replied with a quick downsweep of her
lashes.

"Your daughter is as brave as she is beautiful,"
Bridger said, hedging his bet with the little spitfire. He
had never met a woman yet who couldn't be turned
around with a fancy word.

Little Fawn's head jerked up at the words, a new
light in her eyes. He was as tall as she remembered, his
red-gold beard fuller now that it was dry, but she noted
a difference in him. He might look like all the other
trappers who chased squaws on the riverbank for the
past two weeks, but she sensed that, like an Indian, he
was not without honor. Perhaps she had misjudged
him. "You have split your skins."

"Fighting Indians," Bridger replied promptly and
his mouth twitched, suppressing a laugh. She had not
forgotten, by damn.

"My wife will mend it for you," Washakie offered,
stung once more by his child's rudeness. "Or, perhaps,

Little Fawn could repay your kind words with the mending."

Bridger saw the look of rebellion that sprang into the girl's face and quickly volunteered, "Chief Washakie is a most gracious host to offer the service and I am honored, but my men wait for me." He drew from his pocket a bracelet of silver hawkbells. He did not recall buying them nor what they had cost. He held them out. "For the child, a trinket to remember Peejatowahooten by."

Her cheeks flushed in anger as Little Fawn beheld the gift. As the lovely bells tinkled in the breeze and the silver gleamed enticingly, she told herself her friendship could not be bought for foofaraw, no matter the quality.

Unaware of his daughter's defiance, Washakie accepted the gift. "Little Fawn will be most pleased to have you accept as a gift in return three pouches of her berry pemmican to take to your fall hunting grounds." He turned to Blue Feather who hovered in the background and sent her for the present. "Will my friend not sit by the fire until Blue Feather returns? I would speak with you—friend to friend."

Bridger sat down. The silver bracelet he placed before Washakie, but when the chief looked up he discovered that his daughter had disappeared. "A willful child. I wish her husband a long life, many sons, and a stout lodgepole," he murmured.

Bridger chewed the corner of his moustache in amusement. Little Fawn would not long remain with the man who took a lodgepole to her in discipline.

Washakie was slow to speak. His thoughts gave him difficulty and he chose his words carefully. "You have lived in the land of my people for many seasons. You learn from the Shoshone how best to build your lodges, how to find the beaver, where to look for the many streams that run in the mountains. Many of my people are not certain that the white man can be trusted. They see him come and squander the abundance that the land offers. They shake their heads and think, 'The white man, he is like a willful child to destroy what he cannot consume.' I, too, think on these things. I ponder what is best for my people. I see the spoiled man-child that is the trapper and I see you, Peejatowahooten. In you the way of the Shoshone makes strong the medicine of your guardian spirit. You learn from the Shoshone. It is good. The Shoshone must learn from you, too. The old ones, they are set on their paths. It is for the young that the way of the new life must make itself known."

Bridger listened intently to the speech. Most of his dealings in the Shoshone or any other Indian tongue were about the land or trading. Grand thoughts were difficult to follow. But, little by little, he realized that an important responsibility was being placed upon him, and he did not like it.

"Your words are good, Washakie, but I am a plain man." He shook his head slowly. "If you would know of the white man's world you must ask those who live there. I have been away from my home so long that folks would consider me more Indian than white."

"That is bad?" Washakie asked in surprise.

Bridger gave him a considering glance. "The things prized in the wilderness do not have much value in a city like St. Louis. Of course the reverse also holds true."

"A wise man is a fool in the next village," Washakie agreed. "Even if what you say is true, it does not matter. The Shoshone will not go to live in your city. We are people of the land. We live here. You live here with us. Teach us your ways that we may prosper as you do."

Bridger stroked his chin. What was it Washakie wanted? Were the Shoshone, after all these years, ready to take up trapping beaver? Had news of the riches to be had at Fort Union melted the disdain they had long held for the trade? Damn it all, he thought irritably, it ain't as if we ain't got troubles enough. Me and my damned appetite for good grub. That's what had gotten him into this mess. It'd serve him right if the pemmican in his stomach turned and made him sick.

Finally Bridger said, "Chief Washakie, you are a great warrior and wise man. Your thoughts are as swift and pure as the white water. I will do what I can for your people, for they are the mountain man's friend. I'd be less than honest if I said I am what you would call prosperous. What I own I carry on my back. But I will try. What does Washakie ask of me?"

The words seemed to please the young chief, for he smiled and slapped Bridger's knee several times. "You are a good man, Peejatowahooten. I ask you to take Ear-of-the-Fox with you into the wilderness. He is the son of Broken Wing, killed last year when our people made war on the Blackfoot. I hold him as my own son and would have him learn from you the white man's way. Like you and me, he has fire in his blood and waits to earn the right to call himself warrior. It is fitting that he should be the first of our tribe to earn his feathers on the white man's path."

Bridger knew his sigh was audible. He could not help it. Washakie had not asked for the precious steel traps that made his way of trapping beaver far more accurate than the Indian way with spear and arrow. He had not asked for pelts in payment for hospitality. And, thank the saints, he had not offered that wildcat Little Fawn as a mate. Bridger sighed again. Now that he thought of it, marriage with any woman was the last thing on his mind. There were too many willing squaws to be had for little or nothing. Why should he consider shackling himself with one begging, bawling woman?

"I would be proud to take the brave but I do not have the time to set him up proper," Bridger answered.

Washakie turned to his wife once more. "Ear-of-the-Fox knows of my desire and holds himself in readiness to go with Peejatowahooten. Send for him at once."

Bridger rose to his feet in one motion. He felt cramped by the announcement that he must shoulder the responsibility for a young brave's life, and yet he was neatly trapped. At least it would not be as bad as having a greenhorn American boy on his hands. The Shoshone taught their children well how to provide for themselves. It might be worth it just to watch the boy read trails and track buffalo.

The face of the young brave who thrust aside the lodge flap wore a deep scowl. The smooth features bore no weathering marks, but formed clean planes of cheek and brow. The narrow lips were pulled tightly over clenched teeth. In his oily black hair he wore a single ornament, a red foxtail tied into a plait. He had a young, slim build but his legs were sturdy and strong. If not for the thunderous expression in his black eyes, Bridger would have welcomed this addition to his brigade. But the piercing dark look, aimed steadily at him, promised that he would never gain the friendship or even approval of his new ward.

Why the hell is he staring at my shirt? Bridger

wondered silently. Ain't nobody in this village ever seen a ripped buckskin? Aloud he said, "You ready, boy? I ain't got all day. You and me, we're going to hunt some beaver."

Chapter 3

Fitz reined in his horse when he came abreast of the brigade's bourgeois. "I'd have thought twice about offering you the job of brigade leader if I'd remembered the 'little booshway' had to bring up the rear."

Bridger glanced over at his friend, whose position as company clerk was to maintain discipline at the back of the line. Fitz's hair, beard and buckskins were all the same dull brown, covered in a thick layer of prairie dirt.

"Sorry about that, Fitz. But don't know as if I'd trust just any man back there." Bridger jerked his head in the direction of the half-mile-long snaking formation of men and mules that made up the brigade. "Milt's scouting ahead with the hunters. Could be he's willing to ride with the rear guard awhile."

Fitz shrugged. "Wouldn't mind half so much if it weren't for that damned caravan of squaws and wee ones. It's a wearisome business keeping them moving tight with the rest."

Bridger's gaze wandered back over the column he led. Right behind him came the pack of mules led by camp tenders and then the small army of trappers. To the rear of them came an auxiliary band of friendly Utes and Crows with their horse-drawn travois bearing their women and children. They, too, were heading for home in the mountains.

"Gonna have to push them a bit," he said slowly. "Stragglers got no place in this brigade. We'll be in Blackfoot country soon. Ain't got time to wait on nobody. If they can't keep up, throw them out. Them Blackfoot'll welcome the chance to pick them off."

"Ah, Gabe," Fitz chided. "You're a-worrying over much. Those folks aren't likely to stray too far behind."

Bridger grunted noncommittally and pulled his wide-brimmed hat lower on his brow. It was not the Indians in camp that irked him. Neither was it the daily reports of Blackfoot skulking in the gullies just at the edge of his trail. Deep in his gut gnawed an unfamiliar concern. Never before had he been responsible for anyone but himself. He liked the freedom to roam at will the uncharted land that was as familiar to him as the lines mapping his own face. So what if trapping was a lethal occupation? Every man present knew it. If the Gros Ventres or Piegans did not get a man, there were a thousand other hazards waiting. Like the time the river bank had given way beneath Bridger's own feet, and he had been plunged head first into an ice-choked river that could freeze a man's joints in a matter of seconds. He had been lucky, finding a gnarled root of a felled tree to cling to till he could catch his breath and climb out. There was dysentery from bad meat, the chance that a neglected wound might putrefy, snake bites, and God knows what else.

"Don't want and don't need a pack of bellyaching trappers and half-breed youngsters to make my fall season," he grumbled to himself.

Fitz took a long pull on his water skin, watching Bridger with one eye. He did not need to speculate on the man's mood nor the reason for it. But he was not about to let it get to him. His motive in having Bridger by his side in this new venture was a selfish one. Gabe commanded the respect of the old-timers. He spoke their language in a way Fitz himself could not. Bridger packed the pungent-smelling castoreum with him even at rendezvous when some of the more fastidious men put away their beaver bait.

Of course, he's guarding his secret formula, more than likely, Fitz thought enviously. Bridger was a better trapper. Call it mountain medicine, as the Indians did, or just plain uncanny good luck, as the Irish would. Whatever it was, Bridger had it and the Rocky Mountain Fur Company might as well be the one to capitalize on it.

"Hate to spoil your good mood, laddie, but you may as well hear it from me," Fitz began smoothly. "We got company."

"Can't be Blackfoot," Bridger drawled in seeming unconcern.

"Faith no! Not with a cloud of dust the size of a twister trailing them. Milt thinks it's some of McKenzie's men."

"Fontenelle?"

"Doesn't appear so. Some ramrod-backed, yellow-haired man is in the lead."

Bridger rubbed his chin thoughtfully. "Reckon I should take a look?"

Fitz grinned. "Reckon maybe you had better, 'less you plan to conduct them on a tour of our trapping grounds."

Bridger grunted. "Shaking them won't be no problem. Only I'm itching to take the measure of the man foolhardy enough to venture out into the wilderness on another man's errand."

"Take care, Gabe," Fitz warned when Bridger had turned his horse. "If rumor be true, McKenzie's men aren't above bushwhacking a fellow."

Bridger was grinning as he rode out past the rear of his brigade. Here was something that called for action. He wasn't much good at flowery speeches and the kind of diplomacy called for in town, but on the prairie he was in his element.

He found the American Company's brigade not far from the campsite his own people had abandoned the day before. In grim satisfaction he recorded the fact that they were not only trailing him, but they were using his footprints as roadsigns. Must be unsure of themselves to stick so close, he thought.

He reached down and retrieved the white kerchief he reserved for such occasions. After tying it to the barrel of his rifle, he walked his mount into open ground and waited for the American Company brigade to reach him.

Vanderburgh recognized the figure ahead instantly, though he had met Bridger only once before. Not many men sat in the saddle like their horses were an extension of themselves, and the golden bristle of beard and flat-crowned hat were unmistakable. His face was grim as he rode forward to meet the trapper. He fully realized that he had been found out and was not certain of what to expect from a man known to pack a Blackfoot scalp or two upon occasion.

"Don't be an idiot," Vanderburgh mumbled to himself. "The man would not show himself if he had murder in mind."

Bridger eyed the man coming toward him with equal interest. The tall, slim figure sat his horse well, but the very strictness of his posture and the gentleness of the sun-blushed complexion proved he was not a mountain man. Nor was he likely to reach Bridger within half an hour.

Vanderburgh? The recognition did not help his mood. Bridger groaned to himself and sat back in his saddle. He had met the man six years before. The trappers and the Arikaras were at war. Colonel Leavenworth stepped in, turning the fight into a fiasco, and earning the army the everlasting contempt and enmity of the mountain men. And who should McKenzie send after him but Leavenworth's second-in-command, Vanderburgh.

Maybe he should have sent Fitz after all, Bridger reflected. He remembered the pompous braggart well. He would probably be asked to tea. Hell!

Vanderburgh reined in his horse. He sat perfectly still to let the trapper have his say first. But Bridger had known too many Indians to be discomfited by the silence, and after a moment, took to cleaning his teeth with a straw he kept tucked away.

Aware that the continued silence was working against him, Vanderburgh decided to speak. "Mister Jim Bridger, I presume? Welcome to the American Fur Company's camp. We will soon be stopping for a spell. Will you join me for a cup of tea?" Not waiting for a reply, Vanderburgh turned and kicked his horse into a gallop.

Bridger followed after a suitable interval, quite proud of himself for not laughing in his host's face. Tea. Hell!

A little later, as he lounged against the trunk of a tree, Bridger's eyes ranged over Vanderburgh's company of men. He recognized a few of them, men who had gone back to trap the Mississippi after a season on the Missouri. The others were straight from the forts of the lower Mississippi, their bodies clothed in heavy woolens and their feet shod in boots that would soon become impractical when they reached the mountains.

Let them find out for themselves, he thought with an inward smile, just like they were about to find out about traveling in the wilderness without a night's lodging waiting for them. The place where they stood at this moment had been used the day before by his own men.

Vanderburgh made a great ritual of consuming his jerky and biscuits. If Bridger wanted a game of nerves he was well able to play. "Cup of tea, Mister Bridger?" he offered congenially.

Bridger stared at the pale brew in the cup put before him and shook his head. "Looks like it'd rot my gut. Got to be careful out here, mister. Most anything suspicious'll put a man under quicker'n a Crow quiver," he replied in a thick, slurred accent.

"Really?" Vanderburgh's brows rose skeptically. "I take it, then, that you're here for a reason other than to share my hospitality."

Bridger straightened up slowly. "Wondered when you'd get to the point. This here is the Missouri, mister, and we don't hold with the tactics McKenzie's brought out from back East. You figgering to trap beaver, you go ahead and try."

He moved from the tree and walked over to stand before Vanderburgh, who was seated in front of his portable table. Leaning forward, Bridger placed one hand on either side of the man's plate. "You just go ahead and try," he repeated softly. "But sure as there's sky above us, you'd better keep your men outta my tail hairs. Ain't gonna warn you twice." He reached out to flick Vanderburgh's pale blond forelock. "That there piece o' hair'd look mighty fine attached to a Blackfoot lance. You hear tell what they can do to a man they catch alive? Was one poor wretch they caught tending his traps alone. Stretched him out like a hide to dry.

Cut out his tongue so he couldn't make no noise and stuffed his mouth with his own balls. When night came they built a fire. Built it right on his belly, they did. Burned him clean through to the ground. Hate to see the like happen to you." He paused to stare at his opponent. "Some men ain't lucky. You ain't got the looks of a lucky man, mister. Go back home."

Vanderburgh continued to stare after him long after Bridger had mounted up and disappeared out onto the prairie. It was not that he had never heard stories of Blackfoot atrocities, nor was he afraid of Bridger's subtle threat. But there had been something in those steely-gray eyes that would have made any man hesitate, he told himself.

"He's tried to frighten me. Must be we've got him worried," he said to his steward, who had stood by in silence the entire time. "Yes, that must be it. We've badly scared Mr. Bridger and he thought to warn us off with a grisly bedtime story. Have the men mounted in ten minutes, Fletcher. We've got a brigade to track."

If Bridger wanted a fight he would get it. But not with knives and rifles. That would be too easy. Vanderburgh would hit Bridger and his Rocky Mountain Fur Company where it could do most harm and earn himself the most glory. The secret beaver streams, that's what he needed to learn. And like it or not, Bridger was going to lead him to them.

Vanderburgh mounted up, feeling refreshed and anxious. He was glad it was in the open. He had not liked spying on a man like a thief. His orders were straightforward. His enemy was alerted. Whatever happened now would be aboveboard.

Vanderburgh's spirits were still running high when they camped that night in the exact spot that Bridger's brigade had abandoned at dawn. But the next day the tracks they followed dwindled before noon.

" 'Pears like they split up, sir," Vanderburgh's scout reported when they paused at midmorning. "See that there trail? It splits like a forked twig not half a mile ahead. Me and two of the boys followed one fork about another mile and then it split right in two again."

More annoyed than worried, Vanderburgh ordered his scouts back into the field. "A baby could have followed the path Bridger's brigade left by now. You call yourselves scouts; earn the pay I'm offering."

By sundown they were unable to pick up a single clue. "Seems like they vanished," voiced an old trapper to several of his companions around their mess fire. "Don't rightly know if it be truth but some say that Cap'n Bridger's done told stories of going to hell and comin' back at will. Reckon they done slipped down a tunnel to hell for a spell?"

Vanderburgh ignored the talk. But by the third day of forced marches, which led them deeper into hostile territory and nearer their prey, the grumble of disgruntled voices could not be overlooked.

"Mr. Vanderburgh, sir. A few of us trappers figure to cache up in them hills ahead," the spokesman for the dissenters said when granted a few moments of their partisan's time. He pointed toward the Bighorn Mountains to the east. "They's plenty o' beaver in them streams up yonder. We'd do right nicely up there."

"We're not here to hunt beaver," Vanderburgh reminded the group. "We're here to scout out new preserves. If the Rocky Mountain Company did not find the Bighorn worth trapping, they must have found a better place, and it's our job to track it down." Vanderburgh mounted his horse and rode off before the men could protest further.

Yet by noon, Vanderburgh himself was beginning to feel the uncertainty of his situation. He paced the grassy carpet beneath the shelter of poplars where they had paused to rest. They had been moving hard and fast. Hardly a man among them was used to the thin, ear-buzzing altitude of this country where every mile seemed like three. Soon there would be snow. Already the peaks surrounding the prairie were dusted with flakes.

"Should I turn back?" he murmured aloud. "What will I say to McKenzie?"

The first shots in the distance did not cause Vanderburgh immediate concern. He had sent out a detachment to hunt for fresh meat. But a moment later the entire camp was roused by cries of "Injuns! Grab your guns! It's the Piegans!"

Vanderburgh pulled his pistol from his belt and ran toward open ground. On the narrow valley floor below, twelve of his men were riding pell-mell before a mounted party of fifty Blackfoot warriors, all whooping and waving rifles.

The first man to be shot from the saddle slowed the advance of the Indians as each warrior pulled in rein to touch the fallen man with lance or rifle butt, giving the other men a chance to reach the shelter of the company camp.

"We never seen 'em comin'!" yelled the first man to make it to the little rise where his party had been resting. "God Almighty! Them redskins got Freeman!"

Vanderburgh emptied his pistol in useless fire. The warriors had halted yards beyond the range of a pistol, and had begun returning the camp's fire with their own rifles. For some minutes the exchange continued. Suddenly the Indians ceased firing, circled once just out of range, and disappeared back over the shallow rise that had hidden their advance.

Stunned by the intensity and suddenness of the unexpected attack, Vanderburgh and his men sank into

silence. McKenzie had promised them free passage into
Blackfoot country, saying that he had a man in the
field explaining an elaborate treaty he hoped to have
signed by the mightiest warriors of the Plains.

"Mr. Vanderburgh, sir, we got lots more trouble."
The company scout nodded in the direction the Indians
had taken. "They's a whole village of them savages
over yonder. Freeman and me near about fell into it
'afore we saw 'em. Reckon it's our fault we ain't spied
their camp 'afore this. Only they musta been waitin' for
us. They was mounted and took out after us lickety-
split. Guess we done wrong, comin' in like we done.
D'you notice they ain't fired a shot till we was in view
o' camp? Used us as bait, in a manner o' speakin'.
Damn clever for savages."

"Damned stupid of you to let them," Vanderburgh spat back. "Thanks to you we're all in danger. In
the Army such blundering would not go unpunished."

The scout eyed his brigade leader up and down.
"If this here was the Army, we'd a been tucked up safe
in Fort Leavenworth, glad them Injuns is a-huntin'
good-for-nothin' trappers instead o' soldiers."

"Insolent whoreson!" Vanderburgh's hand shot
out and delivered a backhanded slap. The scout reeled,
reached for his knife in his leggings, and came back
toward the partisan ready to fight. Vanderburgh expected the move and had drawn his pistol. "Don't try
it. You will ride back to the Piegans' camp and tell
them that we are from Fort Union and bring gifts for
their chiefs. And if you are not back by dusk, then we
will try something else."

The scout's sneer faltered. He had accounted the
man a bully and coward, but his actions were those of
a man in full command of himself. "Don't like you,"
the scout volunteered. "Ain't sayin' I'd not like to slit
your gullet neither. But maybe it is my fault them

two-legged timber wolves found the rest o' us. So's I'm goin'. And I'll be back," he added, sheathing his knife. "There's a trick or two in me yet. You just wait and see."

Vanderburgh turned his back on the man, more angry with himself for allowing his temper to surface than at the man's insolence. If the Indians had been waiting as the man surmised, then they had known of the company's activities and did not need to be led in. And if the Piegans knew that the American Fur Company was in the neighborhood, in all likelihood they would know of the whereabouts of the Rocky Mountain brigade.

Vanderburgh chuckled. He had lost a man and regretted it, but the chance meeting with the Blackfoot might yield fruitful results yet.

He set a guard with three loaded rifles at his side, and called in his outriders. By dusk the camp had settled into an edgy restlessness. They did not know what to expect but were prepared for the worst. A little closer to nightfall, the lookout's cry of "Rider! Coming in!" drew taut the bow of anticipation.

"It's the scout!" the lookout yelled. "And he's got a party of warriors with him. They're sporting a white flag!"

Vanderburgh gave orders to wave the riders in and retired to his tent to replace his dusty wool coat with an American Company tunic complete with epaulets and saber. He had been told of the Indian love of ceremony and thought it wise to humor his touchy, if ignorant, guests. He would show them how it was done, in fine military style.

"They're in camp, Mr. Vanderburgh," Fletcher announced with some awe. "Seven big bucks leading our scout on a leather thong."

Vanderburgh affixed his last button before replying. "Very well, Fletcher. But first we'll let them cool their heels. That should show them we are not anxious for our safety." So saying, he sat down and dipped his quill into the inkwell. "Twenty minutes should be about right. Make them comfortable, Fletcher. A small cup of whiskey should service our cause, I imagine."

The steward gave his employer a funny look but did not answer. He would do his duty and hope he would not be repaid with a naked skull.

When Vanderburgh finally emerged from his tent, the last of the autumn sunset had slid behind the distant edge of the Snowy Range to the west. In the light of the camp's fire he saw several of his men stationed in a loose circle about the Indians. The Blackfoot were sipping from tin cups in silence, their buffalo robes tucked about them to keep out the cold.

Vanderburgh approached them in long, easy strides, quite pleased with his strategy. It did not take much to please these barbarians, he thought. With a few trinkets and the promise of continuing good will at Fort Union, he might be able to persuade his guests to take their grievances out on the Rocky Mountain Company.

"I bring you greetings from my employer, Kenneth McKenzie, owner of Fort Union," Vanderburgh said in loud, distinct tones when he reached the Piegans. He signed the word "peace" although he believed that it was just as well that the Blackfoot learned English quickly, for they would soon need the skill. Vanderburgh then looked at the scout he had sent out. The man sat cross-legged on the ground, the leather rope about his neck staked to the ground as if he were a pack mule.

The scout rose slowly to his feet, his eyes wide and fixed on his captors. "You got to get me outta this, Mr. Vanderburgh. I done like you said. They's here.

But this child ain't happy at all. You gotta do somethin' about this," and he jerked on the collar about his neck.

Surprise flickered in Vanderburgh's face. The scout's voice was low yet edged with hysteria. "Keep your wits, man. You're in camp again. What could possibly happen here?" His gaze swung back to the warriors. "Since these . . . gentlemen do not seem to realize they've been addressed, perhaps you'd be good enough to speak to them in their own tongue."

The scout knew precious little of the Blackfoot language, but he made known the presence of his boss. The announcement brought the warriors to their feet.

Vanderburgh could see their faces now, and only supreme self-control kept the look of repugnance from his features. Below a squared-off forelock, their faces were smeared with war paint. Blue powder covered their cheeks, vermilion rimmed their eyes and slashed down their arms and chests, and swinging from every rifle butt was at least one scalp. One of the warriors stepped forward, the only one wearing buckskins. Vanderburgh noted with horror that the seams of his shirt were interwoven with human hair. The Indian's hand came forward in the American gesture of the handshake, and he smiled slightly when Vanderburgh hesitated in putting his hand in the heavily calloused redman's. The man spoke rapidly, his face impassive.

"What does he say?" Vanderburgh demanded when the warrior finished.

"He says he's called Two Buffalo, Chief of the Bear Warriors. He asks why we're here," the scout supplied. "Says this here land is his people's. Don't belong to the white man."

Vanderburgh sighed. So that was it. Similar announcements were the usual forerunners of demands for gifts. "Tell the men to break out the trinkets and hand them a pouch of shot and powder each, the ones that were drenched in the river crossing last week." He smiled slightly and nodded to his guests. "Tell Chief Two Buffalo that these are gifts from the Great White Chief McKenzie, and that they will receive other gifts if they take their skins and pelts to Fort Union to trade."

The warriors waited patiently while the usual gifts were laid out, and then they lifted the pouches containing ammunition from the pile without touching the rest. Two Buffalo turned to the tethered scout and spoke rapidly.

The scout looked from the Indians to his boss. He opened his mouth and shut it twice before he found his voice. "Mr. Vanderburgh, sir, they're demandin' fifty rifles, fifty horses, and all our pelts before we turn back."

"Impossible!" Vanderburgh shook his head, a heavy frown on his face. "Tell Two Buffalo we do not trade with his people in the wilderness. They must go to Fort Union."

The scout hesitated, his face growing pinched. "That ain't all they want, sir. They's askin' for *me*!"

Vanderburgh turned fully to his man. "Why? What have you done? Come, man, this is no time for lies."

The scout reached automatically for his knife but remembered he had been disarmed. "Ain't no man could call me a liar if I had my Green River. But these thievin' varmints took it. I ain't afraid to tell what I done. I killed one o' them savages when we was makin' our getaway this mornin'. What'd you expect? They's after my hide."

"If you'd told me that, I'd have sent another man," Vanderburgh said tightly. "Tell one of the camp tenders to bring me two mules," he said in an aside to

Fletcher. "It'll be docked from your pay, scout. You should have told me in the first place."

"Damned Blue Belly," the scout grumbled. "Ain't I supposed to kill Injuns? Ain't that my job?"

"Your job is to follow orders. Be glad I haven't let them have you," Vanderburgh murmured.

The rest of the camp had gathered about to witness the deal. Just as well, Vanderburgh thought. Let them see my actions and know I demand obedience.

Two Buffalo looked at the mules brought to him in surprise, then turned quickly and struck the scout with his crop. The lash raised a bloody welt on the man's face. He staggered, choking as the rawhide rope tightened about his throat, and dropped to his knees.

Vanderburgh drew his pistol. "Tell Two Buffalo to leave," he ordered the injured scout. "He should be grateful that I don't have my men open fire on him. Tell him if he does not leave at once I will take back the mules *and* the gunpowder."

But the warrior did not wait for a translation. He spoke back, his own voice raised in anger.

This time another man, a trapper, stepped forward to explain. "Two Buffalo says you will give him all the pelts you have trapped in Blackfoot land, together with fifty rifles and eighty horses."

Vanderburgh permitted himself a small smile. The man's audacity in the face of such odds was astounding. "I see. Tell Two Buffalo that our pelts are not from Blackfoot land. We trapped the beaver in the land of the Crow and Shoshone. Tell him we are following a brigade of bad men who break the Blackfoot laws by trapping in their land. Ask him if he has seen these men we seek."

But Two Buffalo was not interested in Vanderburgh's problems. The trapper heard him out and shrugged. "Two Buffalo says you must go back. He says you will give him the pelts, for it is your word against the beaver's where you got the skins and the beaver cannot tell. He says if you do not give him the pelts and rifles and horses his people will burn you out."

"I'd think on it a piece 'afore I makes a decision," another of the trappers advised from the shadows at the edge of the campfire. "We're on a rise. We ain't got much water. We're mostly in the open. Them Injuns could wait us out if they was of a mind to. Nothin' we can do. And a fire . . ."

"You ever seen a prairie fire, Mr. Vanderburgh?" chimed in another. "Moves faster'n a stampede of buffalo. Winds'd whip it up this rise in no time. Them savages'd be there, waitin' to pick us off as we fled."

Two Buffalo said no more, but Vanderburgh had the sudden irksome suspicion that the Indian knew of the dissension in his camp. If he tried to force the issue he knew he would lose. He had seen the force of the warriors in the village nearby. He knew if they killed seven Blackfoot warriors in camp they could be massacred. What were a few pelts compared with preserving peace?

"Tell Two Buffalo that we will hand over our pelts, taken in Crow and Shoshone territory, to prove our goodwill," Vanderburgh said dryly. "And tell him we will return to Fort Union. Ask him to keep a sharp eye out for those trappers I warned him about. As a friend of the Blackfoot, we do not want those men to go unpunished."

"What about me, sir?"

Vanderburgh turned to the scout. "Offer Two Buffalo two horses for your release."

Two Buffalo shook his head over the offer. "The Blackfoot take one scalp for every pelt stolen from them. Should we accept less for the life of one of our people?"

Vanderburgh drew a deep breath in surprise. So the chief knew English all the time. He was in a tough spot, but McKenzie had hired him for his ability to wriggle out of such places. "The Blackfoot killed one of my men. My man killed one of yours. A scalp for a scalp. We do not ask for the warriors who killed Freeman. An Indian is dead in his place. You cannot have two lives for one."

Two Buffalo listened to the words and recognition of a kindred spirit flashed in his dark eyes. Lifting his rifle into the air he gave a war cry that echoed balefully under the canopy of trees before he mounted up and galloped out of camp with his men.

"Reckon they forgot about the pelts?" the scout asked when he had been untied.

"What do you think?" Vanderburgh ground out between his teeth. He had not liked the taste of being bested. "Keep out of my sight, scout. You've cost me more than a cache of pelts. You've cost me Jim Bridger."

Chapter 4

After finally shaking Vanderburgh off his trail, Bridger called a meeting of his trappers, both partisans and independents. He and Fitz passed out just enough of their cache of whiskey to whip up their spirits but not loosen the war edge of competitiveness.

"Tomorrow marks our last full day on the Plains," Bridger said to the ring of bearded faces around his campfire. "After that we're heading up the mountains to the Three Forks area. No need to tell you what that means. We're out for beaver. Every man here knows the beaver is getting hard to find in the old hunting grounds. And they all know where there's plenty of them. That's why we're here. But to get them pelts, we're gonna have to use our heads. Gonna have to keep your eyes peeled and your rifles tucked close. Don't need me to tell you that Blackfoot know we're here. Scout's been picking up their sign for nearly a week.

"Yep, we got to be on the alert. Every man keeps his rifle loaded, his powder dry, and shot pouch filled. I ain't telling you twice. Any man who won't take orders from me had best clear out before morning. Won't hold it against you but I ain't gonna be responsible for getting other men killed 'cause one man won't obey orders. Any questions?"

"Ye aim to march straight into Blackfoot territory just like a preacher come to meetin'?" one trapper asked.

"What's the matter, Dupree, you losing interest in the hunt?" a big-bellied man retorted to a general round of snickers.

A silver blade flashed into being like lightning across a summer-heated night sky. A shout of warning broke up the circle of men, and they scattered. Bridger was prepared and in a deliberate manner reached down and lifted his Hawken to his knees.

"Any man what's looking for his funeral will find me willing to oblige. But come morning, sixty pelts will be docked from the man who does the killing. We need every man we got. And the man who deprives me of a hand is expected to make it up."

"What if this child ain't one o' your brigade, Cap'n?" shouted the man with the knife. "What if he's an independent?"

"If he's that almighty independent he won't want to stay with me." The words were evenly spoken but the threat was clear. "Now, listen up," he continued when the Green River had found its scabbard again. "I ain't saying a man ain't got a right to settle his grievances. If we go killing off each other we'll be saving them Blackfoot a mighty lot of trouble. Only me—I'd prefer spending my lead on them howling savages than on the man next to me. Knife fights and fist fights is legal but the man who lets off a shot within the camp better have aimed it at his own head if he ain't killed an Indian."

"Fair enough!" roared one man while the general sounds of agreement of the others backed him up.

"One thing more," Fitz shouted. "We're forming a hunting party for morning. Milt here and his boys spotted a sizable herd of buffalo just over that rise, the other side of the creek. We'll be needing men experienced in riding and shooting and killing and skinning to go after them."

"Reckon there's one or two who knows a mite about it," cried a voice in the crowd. The laughter that followed saw fifty men volunteer.

The thin gray of dawn seeped across the sky when the shout of, "*Lêve! Lêve!*" broke the stillness.

At the sound of the wake-up call, Bridger rolled over onto his back, unwrapping the frost-crusted robe that had been his cover. The days were still warmed by the "chinook" winds of the Eastern Rockies, but that would soon change. The sky looked more chilled with each day, the blue thinning to ivory near the horizon. Any day now a "norther" would appear, running black, hunchbacked clouds before it like a herd of buffalo. Winds would whip all before it, plummeting the mercury fifty degrees at a single sweep across the plains.

Bridger shivered involuntarily and rose. Today they would hunt buffalo, and by nightfall he planned to be crammed with at least ten pounds of the sweet, fat meat.

The party of hunters was twenty strong. Those left behind were given the task of breaking camp and moving to a new shelter by sundown.

Bridger swung into the saddle, his Hawken loaded and ready. He looked forward to the exercise. The days spent plodding along in front of the column had stiffened his limbs and set his feet itching for adventure.

"Peejatowahooten!"

The shout made Bridger grind his teeth. There was another reason he was anxious to be away from camp for the day. In the two weeks since leaving the Wind River Valley, Ear-of-the-Fox had addressed no more than ten words to him. But whenever he looked up, the brave was there, watching with those inscrutable black eyes. The boy hated his guts and he didn't even know why. Bridger raised his head to watch the boy's approach.

Ear-of-the-Fox, too, had had his fill of camp life. From what little of it he had witnessed, the life of a white man was far from glorious. In camp there seemed to be no distinction between warrior and slave. Neither was there any distinction between the work of men and women. Most of the men had no women. They gathered their own firewood, did the cooking, even mended their own clothes.

In a rare moment, his dislike for the white man called Bridger had taken a back seat to his curiosity and he had asked a question. "Why are you reduced to squaw work? Have white men no women?"

He recalled now with contempt the big golden-haired man's reply. "Our womenfolk are not of much use in a land like this," the trapper had said. "They are delicate and could not endure the cold of the winters or the heat of the summers."

Ear-of-the-Fox had thought of this often in the past few days and decided if this were so, the Shoshone had little to fear from the white man. Most of them would not live far from their own kind and those who came to the mountains would be killed or swallowed up in his people's way of life. How much better were the women of his own tribe. Not only were they pleasant to look upon and mount but they were sturdy, able to carry great burdens long distances, and deliver fine strong sons. Little Fawn would give him many sons.

The thought swiped the pleasure from his smile. The white man had once looked upon her. Little Fawn had cut his shirt in defending herself. He did not care to be Bridger's friend. The white man was the enemy to be watched.

Ear-of-the-Fox greeted the mounted man with sign language. "I go," he said stiffly in English.

Bridger regarded the young brave, with his quiver of arrows and bow, before extending his hand, palm upward, and swinging it to the right, the sign for "no."

Ear-of-the-Fox fell back a step, his face cold. "Why?"

Bridger felt the hairs rise on his neck. He didn't trust the boy—didn't want him at his back in the midst of the confusion that was a buffalo hunt. It was a sensing of an enemy that had no explanation. "You ain't got a horse, son. We're riding."

"Now what you reckon that is all about?" "Black-jack" Henry had come up beside Fitz who was watching Bridger's conversation from a distance.

"It would seem the Shoshone brave would like to hunt buffalo and Gabe's denying him," Fitz replied. He was grinning, wondering how his partner would get out of taking the boy.

The men's voices got louder as the English was abandoned for Shoshone. "Ear-of-the-Fox says it is his right to hunt with the brigade. He says he must become a warrior this season, and to do so he must hunt."

Blackjack looked hopeful. "Reckon there's gonna be a fight?"

"You can't go. That's the end of it!" Bridger turned his horse, his jaw working in anger.

Ear-of-the-Fox went pale first, then furiously red. With an exclamation of rage he leaped at Bridger and tried to tear the reins from his hands.

The action sent Fitz dashing across the space between them. "Gabe, lad! Don't be telling me you're depriving the wee one a chance to hunt the most terrible wrath on hoof?" The words were breathless but they seemed to hold Bridger from whatever his next action might have been.

Bridger's eyes never left the brave's face. He had easily wrestled back control of his horse and they stood facing each other, one on foot and the other still astride his mount.

"The boy ain't got a horse," Bridger said after a moment, his voice flat. "We'll be traveling fast and hard." His silver gaze cut across to Fitz. "Maybe you'd like to carry him piggyback."

Fitz's eyes zigzagged from his friend to the Indian. He wondered if the boy knew how close he'd come to death. "Is that the trouble, Gabe, lad?"

Bridger nodded silently.

"Aye, then, there comes to mind that extra horse of mine." Fitz gave the two angry parties his best smile. "What if I was to loan it to the lad?"

Bridger leaned his arms on his saddle. "He won't take it. He has to earn a horse—or steal one." A slow thinning of his lips that could have been a smile stretched his mouth. "You care to let him steal your horse?"

Fitz threw up his hands and turned on his heels. He had done what he could. Gabe be damned.

Fitz had crossed more than half the distance back to his saddled horse when a strong hand fell on his shoulder, spinning him around.

"I'd be obliged if I could borrow that nag of yours a spell." Bridger stood before him, his Hawken in one hand and supplies slung over his shoulder.

"What? You gave him your horse?" Fitz asked in astonishment.

"In a manner of speaking." Bridger looked back over his shoulder to where Ear-of-the-Fox sat on horseback. "Told him his people broke that mount for me last year only he's still a mite shy of them buffalo. Ear-of-the-Fox said he could correct the fault if I'd let him. How could I refuse?"

Fitz's brows rose and disappeared under the bush of bright red hair over his forehead. " 'Tis a fair bit of talking you done in ten seconds."

Bridger shrugged. "Me and Ear-of-the-Fox are men of few words."

The feel of a new animal beneath him gave Bridger momentary pause to regret his generous impulse. Then the feeling was shed like an old skin. The air sang clean and clear past his ears as he led a cantering party across the plateau toward the watering hole that would attract their game. It was the mating or "running" season when huge herds of two hundred to two thousand buffalo banded together from the smaller groups that usually roamed the grasslands. With luck the trappers would kill enough animals to feed the entire camp for several weeks while the rest of the meat was dried and cured or put up as pemmican.

The thought of pemmican brought the delicate face of a young Shoshone girl to Bridger's mind, and he felt a queer tug in his gut. Little Fawn was uncommonly pretty. Shoshone girls always were a sight for sore eyes. Maybe she would have filled out a bit by the next rendezvous. As the heat of passion warmed him momentarily, Bridger thought he would like that just fine. Maybe next time she would not run away.

They rode on for another hour, two men in the lead and the others fanned out to the flanks and rear. They were hunters who did not want to become hunted. Finally they crested a ridge, Bridger in the lead, and immediately he raised a hand to halt his party. There below them in the distance, grazing on the grama grass, were the buffalo they sought.

"Hot damn! Must be near on a thousand of 'em!" Milt urged his horse into a canter and started down the rocky slope. The others were right behind him.

Poor of eyesight and not particularly smart, the buffalo did not know they were being stalked as long as the hunters stayed upwind. They rode in on the herd warily, slowing as they neared within three hundred yards.

Bridger gave Fitz a tight grin, and cast one considering glance at his ward, Ear-of-the-Fox, who had abandoned a saddle for a blanket and moved away from the main body of men. He then eyed the animals carefully, selecting from the nearby grazers a fat cow whose calf dogged her every step. The sandy calf probably weighed in at a couple of hundred pounds, but his mother was close to a ton. A perfect target.

"There's my girl," Bridger cooed softly as he lifted his rifle. "Give me your shoulder, honey, so old Jim can plant his ball—"

It happened so quickly he did not have time to lower his rifle before kicking his horse forward. A buffalo, which one he never knew, had caught the scent of man and faster than wildfire the alert had spread through the herd as they cut downwind at full gallop.

A roar of the chase went up beside him as several trappers shot forward. Then there was nothing but the rush of wind and dust and the insistent pounding of hooves as they raced after the animals.

Bridger felt the pounding echo in his chest, the wild exhilarating feel of the pursuit. He never tired of it. The gallop might last five full miles but the horses were well-rested, having traveled at a sedate pace for two weeks, and would last until the herd turned. Along with the rest of the party Bridger yelled, crying out in joy for the excitement of the hunt. Sweat ran in rivulets from his brow and pasted his buckskins to his back and thighs. The thin air of the high plains rushed in and out of his lungs until they ached. Still he raced on with his companions, oblivious to all else but the dark humps of straining muscle and sinew racing before them.

When at last the herd ran into a narrow canyon, Bridger knew the moment had come, and without breaking his horse's stride lifted his Hawken again in readiness. Before him everything was covered in the red-brown dust kicked up by the herd's passage. His ears hummed with the bleating, snorting and pawing of the buffalo as he rode into the thick of the herd. Around him other men were drawing their weapons and the killing began.

Rifle fire cracked through the suffocating haze and a dark hump disappeared beneath the cloud of clay powder. Bridger aimed and fired. His ball struck a cow from behind just under the right shoulder, a lethal shot. Riding at full gallop he tore open the pouch around his neck containing his powder and poured a fresh charge into his rifle. Guiding his horse only by the pressure of his muscular thighs, Bridger loaded another ball. It was madness and he knew it—and loved it. All about him men were doing the same thing. From the corner of his eye he saw Milt take a tumble from his horse, probably the result of a gopher hole. At once the man was on his feet again, yelling at the top of his lungs for his mount.

Bridger turned toward him, ready to go to Milt's side before he could be trampled, when Ear-of-the-Fox galloped past him. The brave made straight for Sublette, wheeling sharply at the last moment to dodge a charging bull. He jerked the animal about again, the horse pawing the air in protest, then sent him flat out, catching up Milt on the fly.

"Well, I'll be," Bridger murmured in surprise and, a moment later, returned to the hunt.

The hunt lasted until every man was drained of shot, drained of energy, or had a horse under him that was ready to drop. The silence, when it came, was deafening.

Bridger remained in his saddle, gulping long breaths of air, his sides swelling like a blacksmith's bellows. Between his legs his horse's sides swelled greatly, its head hung low between splayed legs and its muzzle running freely with spit and sweat. The stench of dung and sweat and blood mingling with the trampled dust nearly overwhelmed the men with its power. But for Bridger and his men, the work was only half done.

Bridger pulled his sweat-soaked hat from his head and waved it to signal Fitz. "Round up the boys for the butchering. Every man eats his fill tonight!"

Like every brigade, this one had its master butcher. Bridger looked around for Dupree. An independent by nature, he had joined the protection of Bridger's brigade. "Start with that one!" Bridger yelled to him, pointing to the young cow nearest the man. He turned his weary horse in that direction and rode over to watch.

"Do ye listen up good, you damned brownskin," Dupree began, talking to the Mexican, Loretto. He had brought him into the field to teach him the skill of butchering buffalo. "Ye got to prop the carcass on the belly. That's it. Git your skinny ass 'round the other side and shove, you greenhorn. Now, which o' ye boys brought this 'un under?" When Fitz raised a hand, Dupree unsheathed his knife and used it to sever the tongue, the trophy due the hunter. Then he made an incision along the spine, separating the hairy hide from the meat underneath. He cut from backbone to underbelly on either side at the shoulders and at the butt.

"This hyar'll make a dandy cloth for the meat," Dupree told his protégé as he lay the skin in the dust. "This hyar is the boss cut, boy." He jabbed the exposed rump. "Ye never take nothin' till ye got that. You take it." He thrust his razor-sharp blade into the young man's hand.

"Not like that, ye mealy-mouthed Spaniard," Dupree roared when the man made a hesitant stab at the meat. "Ain't they teached ye nothin'? Cut *down* the grain, I tell ye. Gimme that Green River 'afore ye lose a finger. Damned Mexican! Never know'd a one worth 'ee's shit."

The cuts soon piled up on the rawhide: the boss, the hump and hump ribs, the fleece (the three-inch layer of fat that covered it), the side ribs, and the lower belly fat over which the men smacked their lips in anticipation.

"Hand me over a length of that there *boudin*," Milt called as Dupree dug in an arm into the abdomen and pulled out a section of intestine.

"*Jesus Cristi!*" Loretto recoiled in horror as the butcher handed over several yards of smoking guts to the American.

Seeing the look of disgust on the Mexican's face, Blackjack Henry elbowed Bridger in the ribs and winked. "Hey, Loretto! Ain't you ever hear tell o' the 'great gut gobblers'? No? Well," he drawled as the men chuckled, "reckon it to be a few years back. There was these two poor starving devils near about dyin' when they happened onto a freshly killed bull. They'd been up in the mountains most like all winter and it took 'em some time to get up their courage to crawl down from 'em rocks cause they know'd right away the Utes done kilt that bufflar. Well sir, the smell was gettin' higher and riper 'til they gave up and ran down to the carcass. Trouble was, the Injuns had 'bout picked it clean. Nothin' left 'cept the tail and the guts. Both men reached in at the same time, cut loose a section of *boudin*—you know, them curly insides—and commenced to gobbling. They gobbled and swallowed and gobbled that greasy rope 'til they noticed they's eatin' on the same section. 'Cept they's both too hungry to care and they near 'bout swallowed each other 'afore one man thought to bite his part off. Reckon that's one sure way to get a mountain man to smooch another."

Loretto grinned weakly, while the others roared outright, and turned away from the sight of Milton Sublette gnawing on one end of the raw steaming guts.

For the next few hours the men moved from carcass to carcass until they had dressed all the animals they had killed.

"Looks to be enough to keep us in meat till wintering," Bridger observed as he watched Fitz scribble in his ledger.

Fitz winked. "Measured by eye or number, you're on the mark, Gabe, lad."

Sated with meat, his buckskins slick with blood and grease, Bridger settled back in his robes to watch the sage-green sky deepen into the burgundy of the fall sunset. Nearby the more ravenous of his companions still sucked the marrow from sizzled cracked bones and downed pints of kidney fat at a single gulp. The smell of freshly cooked meat had brought wolves in from the timberland to prowl about in the shadows just outside the camp's fires.

Bridger stretched and belched. This was the time a man waited for all his life. The air with its bitter-sweet pine scents, a full belly bringing a loose-limbed drowsiness to equal the intoxication of good whiskey: it made all the months of privation and hardship worthwhile.

He closed his eyes and listened to the night's murmur of men and nature. It was better than rendezvous, in its own way. The Indians said a man must know the earth before he could understand himself. On a night like this, Bridger thought, he came a fair way to knowing both.

Fitz came to mind. He thought he was overly worried about the competition from the East. The American Company partisans weren't likely to survive a winter in the Rockies, let alone beat out a band of mountain-reared sons of bitches like the men about him. Hadn't they shaken off Vanderburgh like a buffalo shakes off flies?

"What you thinking, Gabe?" Fitz asked at his elbow.

"How long we been together, Fitz?" Bridger asked.

"Oh, lad, you and me and Milt and a few others have been on the Missouri close to seven years. Why?"

Bridger rose, shook himself and looked down at the Irishman. "Just wondered, that's all. Reckon we've seen a spot of living in that time." He looked away. "A spot of living."

The last of the ember red had vanished from the night sky when Bridger felt his robe being lifted up. He thrust out a hand, expecting to catch the thief. Instead, he caught a handful of long hair. The figure fell down onto his chest. Eager fingers reached under his shirt to tickle his ribs. It was too dark to see her properly but he did not much care. All that mattered was that she had wriggled out of her dress and was thrusting her hips against his. Soft, pointed breasts burned his skin as he lifted himself to meet her grinding. Then he was on top, slipping into a warm, wet darkness. Briefly he wondered whether she had mistaken him for another man. But the heat of their rutting took no account of the notion as he raced her to the goal, both grunting and panting in time.

Next morning he awakened alone. A casual perusal of the camp produced no squaw among the camp willing to identify herself as his companion of the night, so he forgot about it. He had taken what was offered. If she returned, well and good. If not. . . .

Less easily shrugged off was the matter of Ear-of-the-Fox. Bridger had seen him watching while he made the round of the mess fires. The boy wanted something. What could it be?

"May as well get it over with," Bridger grumbled as he started toward the Indian. "Morning, Ear-of-the-Fox," he greeted him heartily in English.

Ear-of-the-Fox nodded. He knew the white man expected him to learn his tongue, and while he hated the idea, he could not fault Bridger, for the white man knew the Shoshone language well. "How-dee," he said stiffly. "I bring you horse. You lie. Say horse bad for buffalo hunt. Him hunt good."

Bridger was about at the end of his rope. Nothing moved Ear-of-the-Fox from his stubborn, tight-faced disapproval of anything white. Bridger had promised Washakie he would make a warrior out of the boy. It was too late to go back on his word. "You couldn't be calling me a liar," he tested. "So you musta heard me wrong. I said the horse was a mite skittish during rendezvous. Could be he's gotten over it. Ain't tried him out at the hunt since last spring." He paused, glancing up through narrowed eyes to gauge the effect of his words. The stone-faced silence was no more than he expected but he went on doggedly. "Maybe I'm a size too big for the horse. You keep him a while."

The young Shoshone's face darkened. "You think Ear-of-the-Fox too small to ride a proper horse!" His defensive tone revealed his embarrassment at being compared to the six-foot, two hundred pound frame of the American. His black eyes, swarming with youthful anger, stung Bridger. "I need no white man's pity. I am Shoshone. I am warrior. I am—"

Bridger cut off the Indian's words with a short curse. "Never said the horse was yours and, by damn, he ain't!" he roared in a voice that drowned out the other's sputter of protest. "Now you listen up good, boy! You promised me you could bring that horse of mine into line. I aim to see you keep to the boast. You keep him till I come for him. And when I do he better be in first class condition or I'll be hammering you out into a plowshare. You got that?"

Bridger swung away in fury, his long strides taking him out of the tempting range of clobbering the youngster. "Damn sneaky Indians," he muttered under his breath. In his anger he had gone and given away his horse. "You owe me a buffalo pony, Washakie. Damned if you don't!"

Chapter 5

Western Montana—Spring 1831

Bridger pushed his hat to the back of his head and raised himself in the stirrups to check the clearing ahead. With Fitz gone East to collect supplies for the next rendezvous, the full weight of responsibility rested on Bridger alone. He had no complaints. The frigid spring streams were yielding a bounty of pelts. Bridger smirked. If only he could teach that young Spaniard Loretto a thing or two about trapping beaver. One brisk April evening, he set out to try.

The young man tagged along while Bridger set his traps at sundown. Attentively Loretto watched as Bridger baited his traps and set them carefully in the stream. At dawn, he hauled out the traps and hoped one or two were full. Sounded simple but it wasn't, as poor Loretto learned.

"*Madre*, it is cold!" Loretto yelped repeatedly at Bridger that first evening as he stepped thigh-high into the mountain stream. They waded upstream for a quarter of a mile to keep their own scent from contaminating the riverbanks and alerting their prey. It also provided an opportunity to read "sign" from upstream.

If beaver were working the stream, gnawed bits of debris would be floating down towards them. One needed the eyes of an owl and the patience of Job, and Loretto had neither.

When Loretto's muffled curses and bitter words rose to a pitch to threaten Bridger's concentration, he reached back and grabbed the greenhorn by the front of his shirt. Hauling him forward, he pitched him headfirst into the stream. Bridger hung onto him, but held the young man under the icy water until Loretto gave up struggling.

"That oughta take the edge off'n your temper, boy," he snickered, drawing the man out. "Shut your trap or go back to camp." Immediately Bridger set forward again, his five traps jingling in their sacks.

After that, they were the silent partners the profession demanded. Bridger set the traps himself. He looked for the spot on the bank where the beaver prints moved into the river and disappeared. These were the natural runways he used to set his traps. A beaver moving from his house to his source of wood followed a set path.

Night after night Loretto watched as Bridger set to work. The place selected, the mountain man opened the first of his spring steel traps and set it on the river bottom. Then he drove a stake into the bank and connected it to the trap with a five-foot chain so that, if caught, a beaver could not drag the trap out of the water. The beaver, caught by the leg, was not killed by the capture, but the weight of the trap usually caused him to drown. If the animal reached the safety of the riverbank he could escape by chewing off his trapped foot. If not, the trapper faced a madder-than-hell, fifty-pound beaver the next morning.

Bridger chuckled. This morning was the first time he'd sent Loretto out alone to collect the traps. He had shown the boy how to bend a supple twig and tie it so that it stood just over the trap's trigger. Smearing the musky castoreum on the branch attracted the victim. The scent drew a male beaver as quickly as the smell of a bitch in heat would beckon a hound dog.

Of course, there were limits to his generosity. He had not given the Spaniard his secret formula. No other man, not even Fitz, knew that he doctored the secretion from the beaver's preputial glands with the oil of juniper and gum of camphor. Some things a man kept to himself.

Bridger moved his mount ahead a pace or two. He had volunteered for scouting a new campsite since his morning was free. In the distance a gully cut obliquely between Bridger and a stand of cottonwoods that looked promising. If they were sweetwoods the bark would serve as fodder for the mules and horses. His breath formed a small white cloud as he debated riding the distance to check for signs of a recent Indian campsite in the vicinity. He glanced over his shoulder to where Milt Sublette, his scouting companion, had disappeared over a rise. "No sense bothering him," he murmured and reluctantly urged his horse into a canter. The brigade was not far behind and there would be fresh snow before dark. The sooner he found a safe camp the sooner he would be warmed by a fire.

Bridger half expected trouble but it came with a swiftness he was not prepared for.

They leaped up from the narrow gully as he approached. Four knife-brandishing Blackfoot warriors grabbed for his horse's reins, while two more reached for him. Bridger jerked his mount into a rear and the six men twisted and wheeled. The warriors bore markings of vermilion and ocher paint across their faces. Yelling like madmen, they drove the terrified horse wild.

Bridger managed to slip a finger into the trigger of his rifle. The shot he squeezed off went out only as a warning to his fellow trappers. At any moment, he expected to feel the blade of a knife slip between his ribs. When the deadly blow did not come, he realized with sickening clarity that they wanted him alive to face a slow death by torture. Spurred by terrible memories, he let out a terrifying war cry. They would not take Bridger alive. He would take as many of them as possible to hell with him.

Kicking out with moccasined feet, he sent one man sprawling in the dust. With a roar, he drove the butt of his rifle into the face of another. A jerk on the reins tore viciously at his animal's mouth. The horse spun around amd leaped into a full gallop.

But there was a seventh Indian lying in wait. Grimly Bridger bore down on the man. The warrior, holding his ground, aimed his rifle and fired a shot. Bridger heard the explosion, then felt his horse buck violently as it took the shot meant for its rider. Mad with pain, the animal kicked and jerked, nearly unseating Bridger. Several more shots split the air from behind and the horse screamed.

Aware of the death that awaited him if he did not escape, Bridger dug his heels mercilessly into the horse's sides, urging it forward. The horse whinnied in fear and pain, fighting his rider until forced into a gallop—but not before a final bucking plunge jolted Bridger's Hawken from his hands. In desperation Bridger drove his dying animal up the side of the gully. Deciding he was not in a position to choose too carefully, he headed for the ridge over which Milt had disappeared. Blood and sweat streamed from his horse's chest and flanks and Bridger was forced to jump when the horse crumpled.

He hit the ground hard, his Green River in his

hand. He turned to meet his enemies. They were yards away, on foot, but there had been enough time for the warrior with the rifle to reload. Bridger saw him lift it and take aim. A ball in the head was better than capture.

The warrior fired and unexpectedly lowered the rifle, a stunned look on his face. He moaned, staggered forward a step, and fell forward onto his face, an arrow quivering in his back.

Thundering up behind the fallen man, his bow gripped in a fist, came Ear-of-the-Fox. Without a backward glance at the screaming Blackfoot warriors, he rode up to Bridger and offered an arm as he passed. Bridger grabbed it and swung up onto the horse's back behind him.

They rode in silence. The warriors would know that they were part of a brigade and would not want to risk meeting a full-scale retaliation. Bridger heaved a sigh of relief when the caravan came into view and slid from the horse to the ground.

"Reckon I owe you my life, Ear-of-the-Fox. What the hell were you doing out there?"

Ear-of-the-Fox slowed his horse to keep pace with the man walking beside him. He gave Bridger an impassive glance. "I follow you to learn." The English words came slowly. "You lose rifle. You lose horse. I not there, you lose life. How I learn?"

In one smooth action Bridger whipped out his knife and brought it up against the Shoshone's ribs. "I've enough blade left to lay your guts out on the ground," he said softly.

No emotion moved in the boy's face; he kept perfectly still. Black eyes bored down into gray. After a moment, he shrugged, saying in Shoshone, "Good thing you keep something to lose next time." Then he smiled, a cocky, boyish grin. "Maybe you show me how you make dead horse run. Your medicine too strong for Blackfoot bullets."

Bridger grinned back and sheathed his blade. "Sure thing, son. I owe you one."

Immediately the guarded look came back into the younger man's eyes. "You give me horse. I give you your life. We each have what we want."

Bridger nodded and smacked the boy's mount, sending them ahead. He blew out his cheeks and wiped his cold, sweaty brow with the back of his hand. He would never understand Ear-of-the-Fox. He thought he had finally reached him. But the boy would not let it be. He had thrown the "thank you" back in his face. "Wonder what Washakie really had in mind?" he questioned aloud.

"By Gott, Gabe! Vere yu been?"

Bridger looked up to see Henry Fraeb lumbering toward him. The big, round-shouldered Dutchman was one of the oldest men in the Rockies, his temperament and cunning a match for anything on two or four legs.

"Ve got trouble," the man announced. "Dem Company booshrays again find us. Camp t'ree miles away."

"Vanderburgh again?" Bridger grimaced in annoyance. He had not thought to see the greenhorn again till rendezvous. "Figured I'd left him stranded north of the Yellowstone, Frapp."

The Rocky Mountain partner shook his grizzled head. "Ain't him. Dupree say 'ee's dat damn Frenchie from Nu'Orleans."

"Fontenelle?" Bridger's face lit up at the prospect of seeing the Creole again. The smile died just as quickly. "They got Indians with them? I just had a little set-to with a gang of Blackfoot warriors spoiling for a fight."

"Nagh? Dat so?" Fraeb's frown made his face look

like a dried apple sporting a beard. "Dey got Delevare and Iroquois trappers. No Ute. No Blackfoot. Know vat ve do? Set our Dung-on-the-Riverbank Crows on dem. Vipe out whole gottdamn brigade!"

Bridger groaned in mock despair. He liked the Sparrowhawk People, as the Crow Indians called themselves. People of a better disposition never lived. But they were inveterate horse thieves. It was a matter of honor among them. And nothing, short of tethering every animal in camp to a man's ankles, was going to keep them from sneaking off with a few. Still, the Crow were good fighters and allies. They did not take white lives if they could help it. After all, the white man brought with him the horses they coveted.

"I need a horse, Frapp. See if you can't get an engagé to rustle one up for me." Damn Indians, Bridger thought as he plodded into camp. He had lost one horse to a Shoshone and a second to the Blackfoot. At this rate he would be spending his share of the year's catch just to replace his transportation.

Bridger's sharp eyes cut through the campsite as he passed. The spring hunt was nearly over. Loose bundles of uncached pelts filled the center of their makeshift village. The men were busy constructing the crude presses that would pack the skins tightly into one hundred pound bales. After rendezvous, the pelts would be carried back to St. Louis. The brigade had done well. He congratulated himself. Every pack animal had earned its keep in the weight of pelts it bore.

"We'll break camp at the end of the week," he decided aloud. The last of the beaver he had trapped had been shedding, a certain sign that summer neared. The flurry of snowflakes spinning past his nose were more than likely the last of the season. "Fontenelle, I'm most particularly curious about *your* season," he murmured to himself.

Fontenelle knew his camp had been spied upon earlier in the day and did not care. He could not be persuaded to leave his tent when he heard the clamor of incoming riders. "Let M'sieur Bridger come to me," he said to his companion, Andrew Drips.

Darker, shorter and cut of roughhewn timber in contrast to Fontenelle's polished lines, Drips made an unimpressive second-in-command. But, this veteran of the Mississippi trade held his place with respectable ease. "If that's the way your stick floats. I hafta say you're bein' a mite hasty. That Bridger feller ain't short on wits. A pretty smart lot o' boys with him, too, I'd say. Cut loose from Vanderburgh quicker'n a beaver trapped in shallow water." Drips picked at his nails with the tip of his Green River. "Reckon 'em boys aim to set ūs adrift right along. Watch 'em close, Frenchie. Real close."

"I'm well aware of the cunning of our prey, m'sieur. You have lost Messieurs Gervais and the Dutchman enough times to know the sting of failure also," the Creole shot back.

Drips continued to pare his nails, carving a wicked point on the inch-long nail of his left forefinger. It was the sort of trick that could make all the difference in a barehanded fight. "Reckon we're in for more snow?" he drawled. After a short pause he hunched his shoulders defensively. "Leastways, we ain't gonna give up our pelts and horseflesh to 'em wolf-bait Blackfoot."

Fontenelle smiled brightly, his white teeth glistening against his darkened skin. "M'sieur Bridger made the fool of Vanderburgh. I'm not likely to forget."

Drips looked up from his work. "Reckon Cap'n Bridger had a bit o' help in that department. Never know'd the likes o' that Vanderburgh. A high piece o' meat if there ever was one."

"Mr. Fontenelle, sir. Reckon you'll be wanted outside." A young trapper had stuck his head in through the tent flap. "That Cap'n Bridger done ride in askin' where you's at."

"After you, *mon ami*." Fontenelle indicated the way to Drips. "But keep your yammer shut, as you would say. The conversation shall be above you."

Bridger stood with one foot advanced, his left hip cocked and his right arm thrown negligently over his horse's saddle. The fingers of his right hand playfully caressed the barrel of his rifle. Around the campfire forty or fifty men ate their evening meal. Two others paced the edge of the camp facing the open prairie, their rifles slung over their shoulders. The camp was set against the riverbank, a natural barrier to protect its flank. This tactic earned Fontenelle a favorable point in Bridger's eyes.

"Welcome, *mon ami* Bridger," Fontenelle greeted him when he emerged into the evening air. "But what is this? Have you not been offered the hospitality of the camp? You, there," he demanded of the man nearest him. "Get M'sieur Bridger a plate of stew and a cup of whiskey."

Bridger swung his arm from his saddle and extended it. "Right neighborly of you, Fontenelle, seeing as how you're poaching in my backyard."

Fontenelle chose to ignore the remark. "Your season, it was a good one, *non*?"

Bridger lifted his shoulders. "Rheumatism giving me a pain. Must be all them mountain streams I been wading in these last months." He rubbed his neck, the corded tendons rigid in the only betrayal of his anger. "Appears like you ain't done too well yourself."

Fontenelle followed the man's gaze to the meager

stack of pelts at one end of the camp. "It is, how you say, in the hands of the gods." His smile erased the frown from his brow. "*Mais*, did I not invite you to dine? Where is that—" And he veered off into a string of French curses. Bridger's deep chuckle brought the Frenchman's glance his way. "You know the French tongue?" he asked in disbelief.

"Well, I wouldn't go that far," Bridger hedged. "Most likely I couldn't hold a polite conversation. But I've known a Canadian trapper or two in my time and you learn right quick when a man's abusing your good name. Where's that stew? I'm hungrier than a two-day-old cougar cub with a three-day-old appetite."

When the plates were empty and the cups full once more, Bridger brought the conversation back to business. "When you fellers figure to be heading back East?"

Fontenelle caught Drips' eyes as that man opened his mouth to speak. "Why do you ask, m'sieur?" He allowed the twinkle to show in his dark eyes. "Are you in need of supplies that you would hope to purchase from us?"

Bridger's gray eyes traveled with indifference around the faces ringing the campfire. "I'd say our supplies are running fair to even with yours. For instance, this here whiskey's so watered down it'd drown a goat 'afore it'd pickle him."

A quirk of annoyance pulled at the corners of Fontenelle's mouth, but he said nothing.

Bridger drained his cup and stood up. "Better skedaddle on back to camp. Be seeing you fellers in the morning?" He turned away, then, as if remembering something, turned back. "Ain't seen Vanderburgh in camp. Reckon he's nearby?"

Fontenelle rose, a grin twitching, "*Mais non, m'sieur*. The gentleman suffers from a most peculiar

sort of embarrassment. They tell how he wandered into
Blackfoot country last fall only to stumble upon an entire village of Piegans unprepared. Lost two men, we
are told. And worse, he lost all his pelts and nearly every horse in camp. Made it on foot back to safety. But,
of course, you would know nothing of this."

Bridger wagged his head. "In pure truth I didn't.
Every pelt? Hoo-wee! It don't take much of that kind
of education to tell a man he's in the wrong business."
The look of guarded interest on the Company men's
faces showed he'd made his point. "One more thing
you ought to know. Ran into a band of redskins about
midday. Blackfoot sure enough and packing rifles, too.
That's a fact. Any you boys lost your rifles? I'd a
sworn the one that was leveled at me bore the mark of
McKenzie's outfit."

"They ambushed you?" Fontenelle's voice rose in
amazement. "How did you escape?"

Bridger's gaze bore down on the Frenchman.
"Rode out on the back of a dead horse. Reckon the
poor old animal didn't cotton to the feel of a blade
slipping under his scalp any better than me. Could be
I'm gushing at the mouth 'cause of your sorry booze
but I might as well warn you children that this here is
Crow country. Ain't never been no better horse
thieves. Keep a sharp watch out or you'll be dancing
back to St. Louis in the same step as Vanderburgh. By
the by, you're welcome to hitch up with my boys for
the ride down to rendezvous. We've a caravan coming
in two months. Trading will be real fine."

"What do you think?" Drips asked when Bridger
was out of earshot. "Be darn fools not to listen up.
Bridger's got old grit in him, any way you lays your
sights."

"And that is why, as you suggest so pointedly, we
will start back for Fort Union at once." Fontenelle

smiled. "Oh—la, la! Would I not love to play poker with that one!"

As he rode back to his brigade, Bridger sensed something was wrong before the camp came into view. The night was too still. The rustling in the underbrush, the call of the coyote, the night cry of the owl—all of it was hushed. Someone or something stirred the night, cautioning all living things to silence. Except for the whispering descent of the snow, Bridger knew he was alone. He rode along the valley floor in readiness.

The fires at the campsite burned higher than usual and Bridger spotted immediately the source of the trouble—an empty corral.

"Goddamn, goddamn!" he swore as he kicked his horse into a gallop. While he had been warning his enemies, the Crows had paid their respects to his own camp by running off with nearly every horse and mule.

To his further consternation, a council of Crow chiefs was waiting for him when he pulled into camp. "Tell them to clear the hell out!" he shouted at Dupree who hurried over to meet him. "Ain't got time for no more tricks!"

"Gabe, wait!" Fraeb put out a hand to his friend "Dey got some news, maybe good, for yu. Don't talk to nobody but de Blanket Chief, dey say. Dat is yu, no?"

Bridger stopped in his tracks. He had earned the comic title of Blanket Chief when just twenty years old. The Crows loved jokes and would consider the stealing of their host's horses a wonderful jest.

"Okay, okay, I'm getting my temper hauled in," Bridger mumbled. "Tell them thieving, low-down, no-gooders to stoke up the peace pipe. There ain't no use in trying to track horses in the dark. Tracks'll keep in the snow. If not, it'll be 'cause the snow's so heavy, and then the thieves won't get far. Either way, we got till morning. Might as well hear lies as grind my teeth."

Chief Kicked-in-the-Face wore his name well. The heavy-jowled, pug-nosed face gave him the appearance of a soft clay mask that had been bashed in by a booted kick. The Crow were taller and slimmer than the other Plains tribes, but beauty was not their strong point, as this man demonstrated.

"What for is the face of our favorite white friend, the Blanket Chief, so solemn?" the chief inquired with what sounded like sincere concern.

Bridger passed the pipe to Fraeb before replying. Indian councils required a lion's share of patience. An hour had passed since he had entered the chief's lodge. "Chief Kicked-in-the-Face must know that the Blanket Chief is sorely grieved by the loss of his horses," he responded in the Crow tongue. "Especially when the pain comes from a people for whom he holds great affection."

The chief's great cheeks waggled in sorrow. "It is a terrible thing, this stealing of our friend's horses. We would warn you but who is to say what He Who Hates Women will do next?"

"Who?"

The chief nodded in sympathy to his own thoughts. "It is a bad time for He Who Hates Women. He becomes a Crazy Dog in the wintering season. Soon it will be summer. He does not yet find his death. It is a sad thing for a man to be shown a fool to his neighbors. A sad thing."

"Hell!" Bridger muttered under his breath. It would have to be the work of one of them damn fool Crazy Dogs. Crazy Dogs Wishing to Die was their full title. They were only one of many intratribal societies of the Plains Indians and they made the least sense to the white man. Sometimes a warrior swore to avenge the loss of his honor, vowing to become a Crazy Dog. He was easily recognized. He wore his clothes backwards or inside out as a sign of his new status and he talked "crosswise"—said the opposite of what he meant. A Crazy Dog was said to be without fear. He courted death, looking upon it as an honorable, redeeming moment of glory. Usually a Crazy Dog's life was short. If He Who Hates Women had lived out the season, Bridger reasoned, he must be so fierce a warrior that no other warrior dared challenge him. Insults were the usual method of provoking a fight. He Who Hates Women had made off with a brigade's worth of horses. That was insult for him, Bridger reckoned grimly. The Crow brave was about to reach his goal. "Which path does the Great Spirit tell you these Crazy Dogs have taken?"

Chief Kicked-in-the-Face drew the head warriors into a brief whispered council. "We do not hear the voice of the Great Spirit in the wind this night. Perhaps the morning will change that," he answered in regret.

"Don't suppose you'd be willing to take a wild stab at it?" Bridger grumbled in English to face a half dozen blank stares. "Never mind. Pass me a bowl of that there dog stew. Might as well eat it as be in it."

By morning a party of volunteers had cleaned their rifles, loaded their possibles with powder and shot, and packed enough provisions to last them several days on the trail. Bridger had little trouble recruiting men.

"There's one as took my mule Sal," one mountaineer had confessed. "Like as not I'll have her back."

"Bein' as how it's my fault for not takin' a arrow so's I coulda warned the camp—and here I sit livin' to tell of it—I'm for goin'," vowed another.

Across the valley, Bridger watched the white, misty clouds rolling down the mountains, their undersides ragged from being dragged over jagged peaks. "Ain't gonna snow forever," he offered.

"Best you wait for the sign," came the unexpected reply.

Bridger turned to find that Ear-of-the-Fox had walked up behind him. "Hello, son. Ain't got time to wait for signs. The boys know what's got to be done. Can't get our cache to rendezvous without horses. Simple as that."

Ear-of-the-Fox looked puzzled. "Do you not believe that the Great Spirit guides the paths of all men, and that to begin a task without asking his blessing is to court failure?"

Bridger smiled at the simple logic. The time it would take to court the Great Spirit would find his horses beyond hope of recovery. "The mountain man's way is not to ask the way of anybody when it's as plain as the nose on his face. Why lose valuable time pondering what you already know? Whether it's a hunt, a fight or a wedding, man does what he must. Now get ready if you're going. Medicine chants can be sung on the trail. Otherwise you can stay behind. We ain't got time for pipe-smoking and dancing."

Ear-of-the-Fox was seething with anger. "They tell in the Shoshone villages that you are a powerful man. They talk of your skill and your respect for our ways. I have seen for myself that you make good medicine when you ride the dead horse. But now I wonder if you are as powerful as they say. You mock our god when you do not want his help. Maybe next time you call upon him he will mock you. I will go with you. For myself I will see how the Great Spirit answers one who spurns his counsel."

Before Bridger could think of a suitable reply the brave had walked away. "Damn Indian! Can't keep on the right side of him."

He shook himself, scattering the fresh dusting of snow from his shoulders, and turned back toward the camp. Later he would apologize. He was not used to having his every decision questioned, and Ear-of-the-Fox seemed uncommonly able to find every chink in his armor. Sure he respected the Indian ways. But, hell, why sit in council and beat a dead horse with the rehashing of last night's attack when you could be half-way towards recovering your property? There was a time and place for everything, and their place was running the trail—the sooner, the better.

By evening of the third day out, the snow had turned to rain, making each man's load twice as heavy. Gullies and ridges began to emerge from old drifts, but most of the treacherous terrain remained covered.

"Leastways we got an advantage over them Indians what's herding our beasts," Milt voiced optimistically as he sidestepped a small avalanche of slush from the top of an aspen. "This quick thaw is liable to mean some trouble, though. Swollen rivers could cut them off from us."

"Yu talk fool's talk," Fraeb roared back. "Ve vill get our mules. Ain't to be outsmarted by dem Crazy Dog Dung boys."

Bridger was beginning to wonder just how long it would take them to catch up. Skirting the rise, he caught a whiff of smoke in his nostrils, then rushed back down the incline to warn the others.

"Where are they?" Milt questioned later when they both lay on the rise, their stomachs in the mud.

"Up ahead. Camped by that narrow stream. Must be sixty of them, judging by the size of the camp. That damned Kicked-in-the-Face. Only Crazy Dogs steal horses. Hah! Half his village is down there."

Milt squinted to catch the last gleam of daylight. The brigade had come upon the Crow camp from the opposite side of the stream, their advance covered by the thicket through which they had crept. "What do you think? Rush 'em for all we're worth? 'Course, we could lose a few animals in the dark if we do that."

Bridger crawled backward in the mud until he could sit up unobserved. "Tell you what's to be done, Milt. You take most of the boys and spread out along the creek. Keep well back till I give the signal. Send Dupree and . . . What the——?"

Ear-of-the-Fox slithered up beside Bridger as the trapper turned the barrel of his rifle upon him. "One of these days it's gonna cost you, boy, being an Indian," Bridger mumbled and lowered his weapon.

The grin on the brave's face reflected his amusement at having gotten close enough to touch the two trappers before they were aware of him. "Peeja-towahooten must not fear me. I come to help you steal back your prized horses." He held up his bow.

The fading light made the brave's war paint appear gray and brown on his cheeks but Bridger knew the young man's face would be a brilliant rainbow in the bright sun. "We can't use . . ." He paused. Maybe the boy was only spoiling for a fight like any boy his age. The experience of battle would earn him the title of warrior. That, Bridger thought, might at last put them on a better footing. Washakie expected miracles. Well, he would give him a warrior.

"If I take you with me, you will follow my word to the letter. One tiny mistake, one nervous twitch I don't ask for and you'll find more enemies behind you than you ever got in front. You understand me?" He had long since given up speaking Shoshone to the brave, but certain matters might need qualification.

The black eyes were bright in his face as Ear-of-the-Fox answered, "I understand. I count many coup tonight."

"You'll count them to my call," Bridger warned, then swung around on his partner. "What you grinning at?"

Milt chuckled low. "I'm only thinkin' how you do the job of pa real nice. Could be you should get yourself a squaw and a few little 'uns. 'Pa Bridger,'—I do like the sound o' it."

"Settle with you later," Bridger shot back under his breath. "Now get back to the others. Send Frapp up to me before the rest fan out. This here's a three-man operation."

The three men forded the shallow creek, five hundred yards downstream, then crept up on the Crow camp through a thicket of ice-covered barbs that tore at their clothes and faces. A cottonwood log corral held the stolen mules and horses. Bridger noted that the taking of the pack of animals had been more than a harebrained scheme of a desperate Crazy Dog. A corral like that took time and planning to build.

"Frapp," he whispered low. "See if you can get inside that corral on the creekside. Wait for the first shots, then knock them poles down and get yourself a mount so's you can drive them back across the creek to our boys. We'll cover you."

"By Gott, ve got them," the sturdy Dutchman muttered happily and moved forward on hands and knees in the soggy ground.

"Think you can hit a man from this distance in the dark?" Bridger inquired casually of Ear-of-the-Fox.

"You point him out. I drop man like stone," the Shoshone replied.

"Okay." Bridger smiled in the dark. The boy was game. "See them two Indians a-pacing before the corral? You take the one on the left." Bridger rose up on one knee to give his rifle a better perch and aimed it at his target.

The first shot was followed by the swift whoosh of an arrow, setting the battle in motion. The gunshot scattered the Indians about their campfires, but it was too late. An answering volley of fire rained in on them from across the creek as white war whoops mingled with red.

Bridger rushed forward as the first Indians fell. Ahead he saw the dark form of Milt and his men splashing across the stream in pursuit of the retreating Crows. Rising above the battle were the frenzied screams of caged animals. Bridger searched frantically for Fraeb, but he was nowhere to be seen. Out of the corner of his eye, Bridger saw the movement of a shadow. He set off for the corral alone. He jumped the barricade just as a Crow warrior raised the head of a man by a handful of his long hair. His skinning knife was in his other hand. Bridger lifted his rifle, and remembering it had been fired, turned it around. Swinging it by the barrel like a club, he bore down on the Indian with a terrible "Whoo-aughh!"

The butt fell with a dull thud on the warrior's head and Bridger felt the skull give way under the impact. "Frapp?" he cried, pushing aside the limp form of the dead Indian. "Don't want to know if you done under," he blared, shaking the bloody body of the Dutchman. "Frapp?"

Fraeb moaned, his lids twitching as he struggled to open them. Bridger quickly lifted the man's head gently into his lap and wiped at the blood running into the man's eyes from a scalp wound. "By damn! By

Gott!" the older man grumbled after a moment. "Dat curst Injun got my hair, ja?"

Bridger smiled, his heart giving an uncertain lurch he would have denied to anyone. "What you think you're doing, you old grizzly, a-laying about while the rest of us are fighting? Got your scalp! God Almighty, who'd want the sorry piece? It's still where God planted it and there's the varmint who hankered after it." Bridger nodded his head toward the dead Indian.

The Dutchman struggled to his feet and reached into his leggings for his knife. He bent down to the Indian and then stood upright again. "By right, de scalp is yours."

Bridger shook his head. "Don't want it. Rather have these horses. You all right?"

"Ja, ja. Got wind knocked out when Injun jump me from behind." The Dutchman touched his head. "Scalp tickled by knife. Nothing more."

Bridger reached for a handful of the mane of the closest horse and swung himself onto the animal's bare back. "Hee-ya!" he cried, sending out the cue to the rest of the herd.

They were pack animals by trade, used to following a lead. Bridger's familiar voice sent them plunging over the barrier after him without hesitation.

He led them through the edge of the camp to let as many of the trappers as possible capture a mount. Already the battle had begun to fade. Indians did not, as a rule, like pitched battles. The Crow were excellent warriors in their own hit-and-run style. Caught unprepared, they had scattered. He looked about, counting seven dead men, all Crow. He paused when his eyes fell on Ear-of-the-Fox. The Shoshone was crouched over the prone body of an Indian whose clothing had been worn inside out. The Crazy Dog. As he watched, Ear-of-the-Fox collected his dripping trophy and tucked it into his waistband. He Who Hates Women had found his fate at last.

Chapter 6

Cache Valley—Summer 1831

Bridger did not recognize them at once. He had ridden out ahead of his brigade, hoping to spot Fitz and the pack train. In the distance he heard the whooping cries of more than a hundred warriors. They raised behind them an opaque cloud of dust that trailed out of sight. They had been more than two miles away when Bridger's horse pricked up her ears and began dancing nervously as the thunderous pounding of hooves grew louder.

"Easy, Capote," he cautioned, but a muscle jumped in his own throat. Cache Valley was the rendezvous site, but a man could never second-guess who his neighbors might be. The thick cloud enveloping the advancing party made recognition impossible.

Bridger readied his rifle when they came into range, but held his fire as a dozen arrows whizzed by. None found a lodging in his flesh. He raised his head, a yowling cry of victory rising in a wellspring of joy. These were friends, most likely Shoshone, who had ridden out in a warrior's welcome to a friend and equal.

At the head of the warriors rode Washakie, his

heavy black hair powdered light brown with dust. He held his lance aloft in greeting. The mounted warriors split into two sections as they reached the trapper, riding around and coming up behind him, their cries rising in a deafening crescendo.

Bridger held his horse steady until the salute died down, while under his breath he cursed the immaturity of his mount. "If you throw me, you lily-livered showoff, I'll skin you right here and now and wear the only useful part of you into camp."

"Seems like Fitz ain't here yet." Bridger scanned the villages behind the sagebush plain where Crow, Flathead, and Shoshone had gathered to share the trappers' holiday. All was in readiness, the trappers' villages forming the crux of the settlement. "Where the hell can he be?"

Milt kicked his horse ahead, yelling back over his shoulder, "I'll find out." But Bridger only shook his head. If Fitz had made it, there'd be a whole caravan of mules and men to be seen from this distance. The sounds of rendezvous would be reverberating along the canyons of the stream where they were camped.

As Bridger led his men along the green banks of the canyon overgrown with red birch, mountain alder, and hawthorn, suspicion gnawed at his gut. Fitz should have arrived before him. They had agreed that Fitz would ride back to St. Louis to inform Jed Smith and Bill Sublette that rendezvous would be held in Cache Valley. When a man did not show up at the appointed time. . . .

On sudden impulse Bridger waved his men off toward the main camp, then headed for Washakie's village. He did not have the heart to think about the possibility of Fitz's death yet. The Irishman was a tough one; he would get through. Besides, if he were to show concern, his men might become edgy. They were already tuned tighter than a two-dollar fiddle, and randy-footed to boot. No need to rile them with the news of a delay in the beginning of their celebration. As long as the booze showed in a week or two they would keep.

He did not even look back when he heard a horse behind him. After eleven months of dodging this shadow he knew the sound of Ear-of-the-Fox. The realization struck him as humorous. At last the boy was following him to some purpose. He would give Washakie a full report of the boy's progress and slough him off all in the same breath. "No more redskin skulking 'round my robes. Now that's what I call a proper beginning to a vacation."

Washakie's lodge was near the center of the settlement, indicating that he held status among his people, though he was not yet a full chief. Bridger dismounted and walked though the village, greeting those he knew with words of friendship. The more gregarious Indians fell into step behind him, and by the time he reached Washakie's lodge he had gained a following. Word had gone ahead of him and Washakie waited at the entrance to his tepee.

"The Great Spirit finds favor with you, Peejatowahooten," the young chief said when the sign of welcome was exchanged. "We see many packs of pelts ride into your camp today."

Bridger nodded gravely. "We are fortunate in our seasons, Chief Washakie. We lose no men though we travel far into the land of the Blackfoot and the Crow."

Washakie smiled. "It is good. We are glad for our friend. But what is this? You take a boy from us and return a man."

Bridger looked over his shoulder to where Ear-of-the-Fox stood, his bow and quiver case slung over

his shoulder, his mount's reins dangling from his hand.
Bridger had been so used to comparing the sight of the
young man to trouble that he had failed to fully appre-
ciate the growth that had taken place. But here among
his people it was impressive. No longer a skinny youth
with awkward limbs and oversized bones, the sixteen-
year-old had widened in the breadth of his shoulders
and had gained considerable weight.

A smile bloomed beneath the cover of Bridger's
scraggly moustache. He had not done poorly by the
boy after all. If Ear-of-the-Fox had not already had his
first taste of women, he was not likely to remain in ignorance much longer. Bridger noticed a giggling clutch
of squaws sizing him up, apparently finding worth in
the young warrior.

Boldest of the group was a buxom girl of about
seventeen, who stepped out in front of Ear-of-the-Fox,
swinging her hips and murmuring husky words that
turned the young man's face red.

Absorbed in thoughts of what the night would
bring, Bridger's mind was brought back to the present
when he caught sight of a particular Shoshone girl. He
did not recognize her by name. But the sight of her
slim, girlish body with its proud thrust of young breasts
against her sleeveless buckskin dress sent a flame rush-
ing through his bowels. A smile quivered on her lips as
he took in the full sight of her fine-boned face, and
then she was past him, running with outstretched arms
toward Ear-of-the-Fox.

Bridger watched as she passed, seized with the
desire to reach out for her, but he did not. She ran
against the young warrior and flung her arms about his
neck in one swift motion. The boy remained stiff in her
embrace, but Bridger noted wryly it did not still the
sudden jealousy he felt. He could imagine vividly what

his own reaction would have been had she touched him.

The gesture provoked jealousy in more than one heart. Little Fawn had hardly spoken when she was grabbed by the arm and swung around to face the squaw called Yellow Bird That Sings. The older girl shoved Little Fawn away. Little Fawn returned the shove, but was immediately stunned when Yellow Bird That Sings delivered a stinging slap to her face.

The slap drove Little Fawn back a step, her eyes filling with tears. Yellow Bird That Sings turned away with laughter, threading her arm through Ear-of-the-Fox's. Shrieking with rage, Little Fawn sprang forward, extending both arms, shoving Yellow Bird That Sings. The older girl squealed and tripped, falling into the dust. The roar of laughter from those nearby impelled her to scramble to her feet. Her teeth bared in anger, her fingers curled like talons, she pounced on the younger girl, and the two tumbled to the ground, rolling over and over in the red earth. To the delight of their audience, who offered encouragement to both sides, the two ripped one another's clothing until little more than rags covered them.

Bridger moved in close, unashamed to watch the spectacle of exposed breasts and thighs as the two girls tugged and shrieked at one another. He only hoped that there would be enough left of the loser for him to solace. The winner would share Ear-of-the-Fox's robes.

Breathless and streaked with dirt, the two girls finally rolled apart. Only then did a warrior detach himself from the crowd of onlookers and, reaching down to tangle his hand in her topknot, hauled Yellow Bird That Sings to her feet. He spoke to her in an angry hushed voice and pushed her toward the edge of the circle. Not bothering to retrieve the torn bits of her dress, she marched out of sight with her husband.

Bridger watched with amused regret the departure of the wagging hips. She would have been worth a handful of foofaraw, he thought. Too bad her husband had seemed bent on an uncharacteristic observance of fidelity.

He turned back to Washakie. "It would seem that Ear-of-the-Fox proves himself to be a man in many ways. Not only has he killed his first man this past year, but he knows the way to the hearts of women who will fight for the privilege of sharing his lodge."

Washakie's serious gaze went to his daughter who was still sitting in the dirt. "My daughter is impulsive. Her actions are those of a whore. But of one thing I am certain: I, myself, will kill the man who takes her to his lodge against my word."

Bridger spun on his heel. Little Fawn, with a hand from Ear-of-the-Fox, was rising to her feet. In spite of her torn dress and bloody lip, she was still the most beautiful woman in the village. Once more he felt the heat simmer in his veins. She had changed in a year. He wanted her. He looked toward the distant mountains where the cool breeze stirred the spindly tops of the tall firs. He believed Washakie's words. If he wanted release, he must seek it elsewhere. "By damn, but she's a fighter," he muttered softly.

Washakie saw the look on Bridger's face when the trapper looked on his daughter, and he sighed inwardly. Little Fawn had better be careful, he thought, or her father might be forced to seek the life of a man he called friend. "You will stay with our people for the summer?"

Bridger hauled his thoughts back to the man before him. "I would be honored to share the lodging of Chief Washakie. Until my partner, Broken Hand, tops the canyon with his pack train, I will remain with you."

He tossed the reins of his horse to one of the youngsters about him and followed Washakie into his tepee. If Fitz, called Broken Hand by the Shoshone, were a few more days in coming it would give him a chance to gain the favor of the young wildcat Little Fawn. Bridger grinned. What a pleasure she would be stretched out beneath him, her nails turned to sweet agony as they traced his naked spine. He could teach her to purr and moan at his touch. Just thinking about it made him hot and raw, like a bull on the downwind draft from a heifer in heat. Damn! Wouldn't he make a picture, setting up to Washakie's fire with a hard ache in his britches for the shapely little behind he had glimpsed in that scuffle! Hell! What did it matter? One way or another he would find some squaw to ease his cramp.

Little Fawn sat on the fern-strewn floor beneath the shelter of the cottonwoods, her chin propped in her cupped hands. "I did no wrong two days ago. But my father is displeased. I understand this. But how could that slatternly cow, Yellow Bird That Sings, tear me from the arms of the one I call brother?" She looked up pensively into the face of her companion.

Ear-of-the-Fox shrugged. "It is unseemly that you fight like mares over the affections of a stallion," he retorted gravely, only to have it thrown back in his face with her melodious laughter.

"Am I, then, a mare to be mounted by a stallion who leaves her behind for more than a year without even a good-bye?"

Ear-of-the-Fox turned his head away to hide the look that leaped in his eyes. "I did not speak the words because I knew that I must return." His emotion mastered, he looked back with a grin. "Did I not come back? Did I not tell you what I have seen and done?

Does your heart not swell with pride to know that while I left an untried brave, I return a warrior with a scalp hanging from my arrowcase?"

"So!" she concluded, rising to her feet. "Now I am the watery-eyed squaw who must sit at home and wait for the return of her warrior while he goes out to see the world and the wonders it holds." She dusted her hands together to remove bits of leaves and bark, and propped her fists on her slim hips. "I will tell you a secret. I will stay behind for no man. Oh no, I do not think myself a warrior; women are too small and weak. But I can and will see something of the world outside our small valley. I will travel to where our people have never been."

Ear-of-the-Fox rose to his feet, daring to touch her shoulders with his hands. "Your father has promised you to another?" His voice was harsh, crackling with anxiety.

Little Fawn dropped her eyes before his insistent stare. "I must tell you something. But it weighs heavily on my heart. The words are hard for me."

Ear-of-the-Fox looked down into the lovely face so near his own and yet a thousand miles away. He wet his lips, tracing the curve of her soft mouth with hungry eyes. He sought the new fullness of her breasts that seemed to rise beneath his stare. Two days before when she had run out and flung her arms about him, with all the village to see, he had thought he would burst with pride over her not caring who knew that she belonged to him. Then, afterwards, she had held herself apart, refusing to speak with him alone. But today she had sought him out in his aunt's tepee. She had begged him to walk with her in the cool shelter of the trees. And he had come, his heart and mind full. He had even slipped her away from the village when no one was looking so that they might not be disturbed as they learned the secrets of one another. She would be his first woman as he would be her first man.

His eyes fell to the silver bell bracelet about her wrist. "You wear the white man's foofaraw!" he cried in accusation. He lifted her arm and held it between them. "Who dares to give my woman gifts?"

"I wear the gift of Peejatowahooten," she replied simply. But a new wariness crept into her face.

"I do not understand," he remarked sharply. "When last we spoke you swore you would never share a white man's robes. All this has changed?" Anger and jealousy tore at him but he swallowed back the sorrow in his voice.

Little Fawn stepped back, out of the reach of his hands. "Twelve moons is a long time," she explained slowly. "Many things change, for you, for me."

"Nothing changes for me!" he shouted, then clamped his teeth shut in anguish. He was a warrior now, a man of the village, who did not beat his breast like a squaw. "I do not understand. It is a changed Little Fawn, indeed, who can mouth sacred oaths and cover herself with shame."

She hung her head. "You will not allow me to explain."

"I do not need your lies," he said in a voice devoid of feeling. "You do not have to tell me anything. You go to the Golden Beard and sell yourself so that you may adorn your body and gaze at your wicked face in a tin mirror." He raised his fist and saw her flinch away. Slowly he lowered it to his side. "I am ashamed. But perhaps it is not your fault. Maybe Washakie makes you do this. But I warn you"—and his eyes grew pitch dark—"I will have no wife who spreads herself beneath another man. Never must this happen again."

"No," Little Fawn agreed calmly. "You will be

so great a warrior that no woman you love will ever turn from you. But"—she raised her head, her face agleam with tears—"you must believe me. I am not that woman. It never was to be between us. Only in our childish desires but never in our hearts."

"That is a lie. You must know that the feeling I hold for you is no small thing." Ear-of-the-Fox's voice turned pleading. "You must know this."

Little Fawn nodded, pushing aside her tears with a hand. "And the love I bear for you is no small thing. But it is different, this loving, than that which a woman may have for her man. To me you are a brother. You are kind and wise, never one to brush aside my childish questions. You make me see the beauty and mystery of this world. For that I thank you."

"Better that you should love me," he returned bitterly. "Your father is wrong to get the white man, Bridger, for you. Do you know what the Sparrowhawk People call this man? They call him the Blanket Chief. They laugh when he is near. I wonder at the wisdom of our people to give him so powerful a name. He is only a man." He had to think of more words that would turn her interest in Bridger to contempt. "Did I not tell the village counsel how five Blackfoot warriors attacked Peejatowahooten? If not for me, he would be in the sky with the Great Spirit. If he is so powerful why did he not save himself?"

Little Fawn realized she was the cause of his anger. It did not matter. Her feet had been set on another path. "I do not know why this is so," she said. "He is a man. We do not not deny him a mortal form. But his medicine is powerful. And if my vision is a true one, he holds my life and the lives of many others in his hands."

Ear-of-the-Fox was suddenly moved by her

words. "Your vision? You have been visited by the Manitou?"

Little Fawn threw him a frightened glance. "This is what I would tell to you. I waited for your return that I may unburden myself to one who would understand."

Ear-of-the-Fox's selfish concerns vanished. The visitation of a spirit from the shadow world held more significance to a Shoshone than any other expression in life. "Come, sit beside me. You will speak and I will listen that I may help you understand. Perhaps you misread the signs. You are a mere woman, untried in a world where powerful medicines bring victory and death."

Little Fawn dropped to her knees before him. "You must not say a word until you have heard everything."

Ear-of-the-Fox nodded. "I will listen. When the Great Spirit speaks through one of us, we must not question the words."

Little Fawn folded her hands, her slim body trembling slightly. "Soon after you went with the trappers, I knew that my time had come to seek the truth in the mountains where the wind sings. I told no one, not even Blue Feather. She would tell my father and they would hold me to them for fear of my life. But I was not afraid. I heard in the wind a song that filled my soul with the knowledge that I would learn of my fate in the Blue Mountains.

"Our people left for the warmth of the southern hills soon after rendezvous. The dust on the prairie was thick and when I turned back to the mountains no one saw me. I carried only a buffalo robe, a pouch of sacred wood, and tobacco.

"Morning came to the land as I walked in the long grass. I journeyed far that day, resting only when the

sun hung above my head. As I walked, the wind urged
me forward in sweet song as it sought the sanctuary of
the mountains before me. For two days I walked.
There was always water for my thirst and a bird to lift
my eyes ever toward the Great Spirit.

"On the third day of my quest, I reached the foot
of a steep hill. Its peak was so far above my head, I
could not see it. I began to climb, weary from lack of
meat and the long, cold nights without fire. But as I
climbed, the weariness fell from my shoulders until I
felt as light as the eagle who soared above my head.
The sacred bird seemed to cry out to me, 'It is good
that you come to us, daughter of Washakie. The Great
Spirit waits. It is good.'

"The earth seemed to speak to me of the wisdom
and goodness of the Great Spirit. Each rock was
touched by his hand. A warm breeze cheered me as I
climbed, bringing the rich smells of the earth and the
buffalo.

"Finally I came to what I thought was the top of
the hill. But it was nothing more than a ledge where
once an eagle nested. Sagebrush grew in a corner near
its steep, smooth wall. I knew in disappointment that I
could go no further. Too weak to climb down or even
to weep, I fell asleep.

"Darkness had crept upon the earth while I slept.
When I awoke, the whole sky quivered to a rhythm
like that of the buffalo crossing the prairie. It was not
buffalo. It was a great cloud, blacker than the night
sky, rising out of the west. Silver-white horns leapt
from its head. I was afraid. I had no protection from
the coming storm. Quickly I dug into my pouch and
brought forth the sacred twigs and tobacco. I built a
small fire, all the while singing to the Great Spirit that
he might listen and remember Little Fawn.

"In a little while a fire was born, but the winds

agitated it like the fluttering wings of a prairie bird. Nearer and nearer the storm came, its powerful breath a wild shrieking in my ears. I began to think that I had been wrong, that it was vanity and not the urging of the Great Spirit that sent me to seek him. I cried out against the darkness, begging forgiveness for my pride, that I might live to be a witness to the vanity of self-love.

"But the storm came upon me, tearing my prayers from my lips and scattering them across the empty prairie below. I huddled down in my robe, pulled it over my head and waited.

"The winds howled. The rain splashed down with the force of a flood until I thought I would be swept over the side. I thought of my father and mother who would never know what had become of me. Never had I felt more alone.

"Then, suddenly, I knew that just beyond me was something large and fierce. So great was my fear I nearly scrambled to the edge of the cliff. But a great silence had descended upon the night. There was nothing but the trembling of my limbs and the beating of my own heart. I flung the robe over the ledge, thinking that I had been dreaming and that the storm was gone. But I was not alone and neither had the storm fled."

Little Fawn's eyes penetrated deeply into those of her adopted brother, Ear-of-the-Fox. "I must tell you exactly what happened. You will not believe me. Often I have wondered if it was all a dream. But that is not so. You will understand afterwards.

"Before me, with its back to the cliff wall, was a great grizzly bear. He stood seven feet on his hind legs. I fell to the ground before him, certain that this was my death.

"But the bear did not touch me. As I stared at him I realized that he was not real—or if he was, he was unlike any other I had ever seen. He was golden, his fur as bright as a newborn buffalo calf's. Then he spoke to me.

"'Because your heart is good and your desire to seek a vision for your people real, you will come to no harm, daughter of Washakie.'

"He stretched out one huge paw toward the prairie below. Across the land the storm still raged, the light and winds more fierce than before. Yet I heard nothing. The clouds blazed with a fire that turned them red. I cringed away from the sight, remembering that below were my parents and the people of my village.

"Something touched my shoulder. The touch was gentle. 'Do not fear for your people,' the golden grizzly assured me. 'Just as I protect you, I protect them. For this is the way of your people, my path the one you will follow. Many dangers will beset you. But life will change soon on the prairie. There will come a new creature to the land. He will drive before him the beaver and the buffalo. A new beginning will rise from the ashes of the old. You must help your people seek the new way. It is not for everyone. Your way will take you far from your home. You have sought the will of the Great Spirit. The message I bring is that you must see your future through the eyes of the man who comes.'"

Little Fawn shivered, her eyes lowered to the ground. Ear-of-the-Fox had listened in silence as she requested. At first, his face was engrossed, then wide with amazement, and finally touched with the awe of one who believes.

"Truly you have had a vision," he concurred. "And it is as you say. You are charged to a new path, one untaken by those before you." Ear-of-the-Fox realized that he was feeling relieved. The vision had not held the name of the man he disliked. Little Fawn had been mistaken in her interpretation. "This great vision tells you to seek the one who comes, not the lodge of Peejatowahooten. He is a man who becomes more Indian with each moon that passes. You must look elsewhere for the one to come."

Little Fawn breathed deeply, her silence long. She had hoped Ear-of-the-Fox would laugh at her and send her back to the village less sure that what she had witnessed had truly taken place. But he believed her. She knew that when she spoke at the next council of elders that they, too, would believe her. "There is something else. The next morning I climbed down from the ledge, where not even a single sign of the magic had been left for me. I was very weak, and in my heart I began to mistrust the vision that had come. When I reached the prairie, I started toward the trail left by our village. That morning I saw three riders coming toward me. One of them was my father. I raised a hand and cried out in joy as I ran toward them. But when an eagle swooped low before me, I paused and looked up. Something shone like a shaft of light in the eagle's beak and then he dropped it at my feet." She held out her wrist. "It was the silver bracelet Peejatowahooten had left with my father for me before he departed last fall."

"It proves nothing," Ear-of-the-Fox replied quickly, the struggle within him betrayed in his voice. "It does not link you to that man. You refused the gift. You told me so."

Little Fawn shook her head. "You would know it was a sign from the Manitou as surely as I if your vision had come to you before now."

The look on the young warrior's face made Little Fawn draw away. "So, you shun me because you share the knowledge of my failures when I sought out the blessing of the Great Spirit." He sprang to his feet, rage and humiliation contorting his face.

She scrambled to her feet, his pain mirrored in her eyes. "You know that is not so!" She lay a hand on his bare shoulder, seeking to comfort him in a way her words could not. "Each of us travels a separate road. I can do no other than the Great Spirit bids me." Little Fawn bit back the words of love she knew he needed to hear. In the end it would only give them both more pain. But she continued. "I know one thing. If it were in my power I would refuse this alliance."

Ear-of-the-Fox swung around to her, his lips parted as if to speak, and she hurried on. "I have seen Peejatowahooten again and I do not understand why he is the chosen one. I see nothing in him that makes my heart sing nor my woman's body burn. Yet I know the will of the Great Spirit must be obeyed."

Ear-of-the-Fox caught her by the arms and crushed her against him. Her eyes opened wide, her lips parted in shock as Ear-of-the-Fox crushed her mouth with his. He kissed her long, the power of her touch leaving his inner world in flames. She did not struggle against him, nor did she melt into him. He took from her what she would not offer and then pushed her to arm's length. "I will kill the one called Bridger."

The words were simply said but they struck terror in Little Fawn. "You cannot disobey the will of the Manitou," she whispered through bruised lips.

Ear-of-the-Fox's eyes glittered with desire, both for the woman so recently in his arms and with blood lust for the death of the man who stood in his way. "I will seek the guidance of the Great Spirit first. I will purify myself and seek a vision in the mountains where the wind sings. Then I will return, bringing you the offering of my fate. If the one called Bridger dares to touch you while I am gone I will kill him upon my return. His life is in your hands."

He was gone before she could speak. She believed his words. Never before had she seen such a look on a person's face. He was changed in ways she could not understand and the changes frightened her. "I will trust in the Manitou," she encouraged herself. "He will show Ear-of-the-Fox his fate and it will not include me."

She put a hand to her lips. No man had kissed her before. She had felt astonishment in his kiss. She felt nothing when she looked upon the Gray Eyes. Perhaps she was unable to kindle the heat in a man's blood. Ear-of-the-Fox was angry because he could not have what he desired. As a boy he always had been greedy. She was a prize he wanted. He would forget her soon. But Gray Eyes—what did he feel when he looked upon her? She would find a way to discover that.

Chapter 7

Bridger entered the lodge he had been given in the Shoshone camp with a black frown on his face. In desperation he had sought out the services of a Shoshone medicine chief, Eyes-of-the-Hawk. He had to pay the old shaman two horses for guidance as to the whereabouts of Fitz and the supply train. If Fitz were dead—and each passing day increased the possibility—that did not explain why Bill Sublette had not come ahead to rendezvous with the caravan as planned. Unless the entire caravan had been attacked and both men murdered.

"Hell and damnation!" he muttered and ran a hand through his newly trimmed shock of hair. The sun-streaked mane scarcely brushed his shoulders these days, and while he liked the comfort of shorn locks, he knew he had shocked his hosts. Indians customarily grew their hair as long as possible. To willfully cut even an inch was likely to bring bad luck upon a man if he were not in mourning. Some of the white trappers were already grumbling superstitiously about the evil spirits brought into camp by the deed. So he had been

forced to gather up the hair clippings and burn them
ceremoniously with the help of Eyes-of-the-Hawk. It
had cost him twenty dollars worth of pelts.

"Costliest damned haircut a man ever got," he
commented aloud.

Bridger noticed that he was not alone but he ignored the girl sitting cross-legged before the smoldering
fire. The dew cloth had been lifted at the back of the
tepee to allow a breeze to blow through. The pleasant
aroma of the ever-simmering stewpot filled the air. He
pulled off his shirt and pushed a straw into the embers
to extract a light for his pipe. When the blended tobacco caught fire, he sat down opposite the girl and
leaned against a leather-thong backrest. He inhaled
deeply, enjoying the final bit of tobacco in his possibles, and concentrated on keeping his eyes from
straying to the girl who spent far too much time in his
lodge for his comfort and her safety.

Little Fawn chose carefully among the trimmings
of bead, porcupine quills, ermine tails, feathers and
yarns in her workbasket. She had been told to prepare
a buckskin jacket for Peejatowahooten. But her mind
was not on her task. When her father had asked her to
keep the lodge of the Gray Eyes she had been secretly
pleased, thinking that the contact would allow her to
learn more about him. Now, after nearly three weeks,
she knew nothing more of him than before.

Her dark eyes roamed over his bare chest where
the thick pelt of golden hair reminded her again of her
vision. She felt certain that he was the one her vision
portended. He growled like a bear when angered and
roamed the lodge like a caged beast when she was
present. He never gave her more than a brief acknowledging glance when he found her here. She
longed to question him but Indian custom forbade such
conduct. Still, his own people talked constantly about

themselves. Maybe she would find the courage to speak to him today.

Silently, she rose to lift the stewpot from its tripod and offered it to Bridger. "You are hungry?" she urged, without looking directly at him. "The stew was replenished this morning by my father who killed a mountain goat. I have added fresh herbs and roots of the prairie turnip and wild onion. I hope you find pleasure with it, Peejatowahooten."

Bridger looked from the pot to the girl's averted face. "The name's Bridger, Jim Bridger! Don't want to hear that other name in this lodge again, understand me?"

Little Fawn jumped back, startled by the anger in his booming voice. The stew sloshed over the side of the pot, dripping down into the hot coals where it bubbled and hissed. "Oh!" she stuttered, looking anxiously from the fire to the reclining man.

Bridger saw fear register in her face and frowned. He had meant to shake her out of the complacent shell in which she clothed herself, but he had not meant to frighten her. "Let's have a taste of that." He motioned her near with a hand. Using his knife he fished out a bit of meat from the pot and popped it into his mouth. The morsel was surprisingly delicious and he fished out several more before reclining once again.

"Thank you," he said when she had replaced the pot over the fire. "Washakie is fortunate to have a daughter who is both lovely and who cooks as well as you." He had spoken in Shoshone, and to his compliment she smiled shyly and blushed. The smile made him want to keep her near him a moment longer. "What are you doing?" and he pointed to her sewing.

Little Fawn picked up the buckskin shirt and held it before herself. The leather shirt had been fashioned of smoked doeskin, the softest and most supple of the various hides used for clothing. Its seams were heavily fringed and beaded. To the rows of beads running along the shoulder seams she had begun attaching ermine tails, the most prized decorations in an Indian woman's workbasket.

"It is a war shirt," Bridger concluded, his voice full of approval for her work. He fingered the seams, all tightly sewn with short, neat stitches. "Is it for Washakie? Or—" and he drew out the syllable in a teasing manner—"is it for your young warrior, Ear-of-the-Fox?"

A blush blazed across her cheeks and she immediately averted her eyes. A year ago she would not have thought to gain this man's favor by holding the barbs from her tongue. But she was older now and uncertain of all that had passed since then. "It is not a shirt for either, Pee— Jim Bridger."

"Just Bridger will do," he supplied. "Then who will wear your wondrous shirt?" he pressed, greatly enjoying the beautiful color in her lovely face.

"It is for you," she said simply, and resumed her cross-legged position as if the matter were closed.

Bridger shot her a disbelieving look. "For me? Why?"

"Because my father requested it of me," she answered in a tone that did not offer encouragement.

But Bridger was enjoying her responses, and teasing her took his mind off his problems. "I have not seen Ear-of-the-Fox in many days. Did he go to hunt buffalo on the prairie?"

Little Fawn shook her head, keeping it bent over her work. "He goes to the mountains, where the wind sings, on his vision quest."

Bridger pondered that news a moment. That would be the Wind River Mountains, a fair journey. He grinned. And one not likely to bring the young

Shoshone back before the brigades set out for the fall hunt. "That's a serious business, a vision quest. I wish him joy and success," he said sincerely.

"Do not your people do the same when they reach a certain age?" Little Fawn bit her lip. She had not meant to question him. Yet, to her astonishment, she heard him answering the question without a second's hesitation.

"Things are done differently in the white man's world." He paused briefly, seeking the correct words to explain things in her own language. "A boy becomes a man when he trades his short pants for long ones." He made a slashing motion across his thigh and then ran it down the side of his buckskins to his ankles. "A white girl puts up her hair when she's of marrying age."

He saw her frown in perplexity and came up on his knees to reach across the fire and gather the thick black fall of her hair in one hand. "Like this." He twisted the locks into a topknot.

Little Fawn smiled in understanding and he reluctantly removed his hand from the smooth velvet texture of her hair.

"And your women, are they not like the Indian woman?" she asked. Little Fawn sought to learn the one thing no member of her tribe could tell her. None of her people nor those of any of the other tribes who lived in the Shining Mountains had ever seen a white woman.

Bridger grinned and sat back on his haunches, fishing with his fingers for a succulent piece of meat floating at the top of the stewpot. "I would say there are no important differences. Of course, they are more delicate, softer. And they are different in coloring."

Little Fawn's eyes were intent upon him now. "In what way?"

Bridger swallowed his catch and leaned back

against his backrest, licking his fingers. It had been some time since he had conjured up the image of a white woman. Then, most times, it was the image of his mother, as faded and fleeting as a prairie mirage.

"Well, many white women have hair the color of the prairie in the fall—pale and golden. And eyes like the sky above the Shining Ones just after a summer rain. Their bones are as fine as a bird's and their skin is smoother, whiter than the finest bleached doeskin." He grinned suddenly. "They smell nice, too. Like a valley of summer flowers sprung fresh from the soil."

Little Fawn's dark eyes flashed the bearded man a curious look. His voice had grown warm, like the summer breeze at their back. Her lips thinned in scorn, prompted by the natural jealousy of a woman who hears the praises sung of another of her kind. "Your women sound cold. Are they all like this?"

"Not all," Bridger answered.

He remembered his mother, for example, as a plain woman, sturdily built with gnarled, calloused hands and a perpetual droop to her shoulders. She had loved her family and in that loving had lost the beauty and joy of youth that had first attracted his itchy-footed father to her. He remembered, with the eyes of a small child, her seemingly undaunted acceptance of the loss of their tavern in Fredericksburg, Virginia when he was six, and then the farm two years later. Finally he recalled the long wagon trip halfway across the continent to Six-Mile Prairie just across the Mississippi from St. Louis. She had stood firm with James Bridger to wrest a marginal existence from the indifferent wilderness. But one of the migrant fevers common to the territory claimed them both, as well as Jim's younger sister. It was a life not meant for beauty to endure.

Bridger frowned, unaware of the soft black eyes regarding him. From where, then, had come the description he had given Little Fawn? It came to him slowly, the remembrance of a lady he had once glimpsed in the yard of the blacksmith shop in St. Louis. She had been dressed in pink and white striped silk. The copper curls beneath her bonnet had reminded him of the sparks glowing from the heated iron. Her waist was cinched small and the curve of her breasts . . .

Bridger shifted, brought to reality by the stirring in his loins.

"Are they pleasant to mount?"

The question caught him up short. He had been wondering the same thing but how could the girl know it? Bridger's head swerved toward the girl, whose eyes were lowered to her sewing. He hesitated, wondering what to answer. "I don't know," he admitted finally.

Little Fawn's head came up. "Then how can you know that they are no different from the Indian woman?" She laid her sewing aside and came to her knees before him, an earnest look on her young face. "You say your women are beautiful. Is not the Indian woman beautiful? You say your women have eyes the color of the puma's." She shook her head. "A puma is a powerful, dangerous animal. A man should not invite such danger to share his robes. You say these women have hair the color of the dying prairie." She wrinkled her nose. "I do not like the summer's end. It brings with it the bitter cold from the north lands. What man wishes to embrace a norther?"

She smiled, unconsciously drawing Bridger's gaze to her berry-red lips. "You say your women are delicate." She held out a slender wrist, which his gift of silver bells encircled. "Am I not delicate like the fawn for which my mother named me?"

She reached out and gently stroked the red-gold bristles at his chin. "Am I not smooth and soft?" Her

strayed and caught on her that she was the daughter of
his friend. But no more. He had never refused a
woman yet.

He lowered his head, engulfing her mouth with his
own. He tasted the sweet breath of her youth and it set
his belly a-quiver. But she was not experienced at kiss-
ing and the smooth mouth offered back little in return.
So little that he rolled off her at once in suspicion, his
hunter's eye alert for a thief or other invader in his
lodge. There was none.

Assured of his safety, he dropped the knife he had
caught up and lowered himself back against the girl eagerly. But his gaze chanced to meet hers and the look
in them hauled him in, his mouth just short of a tender
breast.

Little Fawn stared at him, her eyes enormous
black pools. There was fear there, and, he would have
sworn, a glimmer of natural passion. But underlying the
usual confusion he expected in a young girl was an
emotion he could not read. She did not struggle
beneath him. She had not resisted even a moment. Yet,
she looked . . . he searched his head for a comparison.
When he found it, it startled him. She looked like a
child whose game had suddenly been turned into serious business. She was playing. The taunting display
and provocative talk had been a silly, childish game!

Bridger rolled over and onto his feet in one
smooth move. "Git up!" he yelled in English. "Serve
you right if I'd a rode you from here to next week.
Only I don't bed babies!"

He swung away from her and ran distracted fingers through his hair, sucking in air to calm his racing
blood. The clamor in his loins changed quickly into anger. She'd asked for it, wiggling her proud tits under
his nose and . . . Hell! What did he care if she was

voice was a whisper, caught in her throat by her daring. Yet she would know once and for all. Swiftly she reached for the top of her strapless leather dress, held up by a thong tied under her arms, and loosened it. "Am I not as beautiful as your white women?"

Bridger's stomach muscles contracted hard as he stared at her young breasts. He could not speak and did nothing when she reached for his hand to guide it to her exposed flesh. "Am I not as soft?" she whispered faintly.

He brushed the dark tip with his fingertips and felt her shiver at the touch. The quivering increased when he gently squeezed.

Little Fawn held his light eyes with her dark ones, afraid to look at the hand moving on her breast. Strange, wondrous feelings sped through her, widening her eyes and stirring her loins in an unfamiliar way. As she watched, his gray eyes turned dark, like the smoke that curled from the wood just before a flame leapt into being. She knew that Peejatowahooten worked his magic upon her flesh. It was not what she expected. It had no match in the easy, playful couplings she had witnessed in the cottonwood groves. This was like the prairie fire that blazed suddenly on the horizon, sweeping all before it as it devoured the land.

Bridger groaned softly when the warm flesh beneath his hand swelled. It was what he had waited for. He took her quickly by the shoulder and lifted her against his chest. He wondered fleetingly why she had not asked for the usual present. It did not matter. Nothing mattered but the gift she was offering him.

His embrace was fierce and without preliminaries. He forced her back onto the earth floor, stretching out full upon her in case she decided to change her mind or stall him. He had deliberately held himself from her these weeks, reminding himself each time his eyes only joking? She'd been strutting before him for weeks now like some puckish mare awaiting her first stud.

"Got to get out!" he grumbled and swept aside the door flap.

Those villagers who saw the shirtless white man stomp out of camp followed his progress with unabashed stares. For a man who earned his living by subtlety and lightness of tread he put on a singularly novel show. The more curious went along as he left the village for the riverbank where he shucked his trousers and moccasins and flung himself full length into the crystal clear mountain stream.

Bridger remained on the riverbank until hot yellow stars beaconed the night. The passion had long stilled in his veins but he could not yet return to camp. In the brisk wind he found all the companionship he desired. A momentary shadow sailed before the stars and disappeared. Beneath him the ground vibrated, a movement more imagined than felt. He knew that far beyond the valley migrating herds of buffalo thundered toward the open plains to the south. A nighthawk's nasal call sounded nearby. At his feet the Snake River flowed by in near silence.

He removed a hand from behind his head and slapped casually at the wriggling thing that had crawled into one pants leg. Inhaling slowly, he filled his nostrils with the turpentine odor of sagebrush, the sharp sting of crushed pine needles, and the acrid smell of the distant campfires.

This is what I live for, he thought. The peace and serenity between the daily battles to survive one more year. But things were different this year. It was the first rendezvous when no supplies had reached the men. Powder and lead were running low and the trail he planned for the upcoming season would require more than the usual amount of shot. It was back to the land of the Blackfoot for the Rocky Mountain Fur Company boys.

Bridger sat up, his eyes roaming the purple humps of the distant range. He had not wanted to admit it but beaver were becoming scarce in the familiar streams. Add to that the competition dogging their trail . . . Bridger snorted. So he had gotten rid of Vanderburgh twice without much effort. The man, for all his city attitudes, did not seem to be the kind to take a besting without seeking a rematch. Most likely he could expect the Company man to be roaming the hills come fall. Then there was Fontenelle and his partner Drips. Good men, men more suited to the profession, and tenacious as ticks.

Something else made him edgy. The Blackfoot now had more rifles than they should if they took only what came with the white scalps they had collected over the years. Where could they be getting them?

"Vanderburgh ain't that dumb," he muttered aloud. No man in his right mind would trade rifles to the Blackfoot in hopes that the Indians would use them only at the trader's bidding. "If that's what they're doing up at Fort Union, God help us all."

Bridger lay back. No sense fretting over matters he could not control. It wasted precious energy and spoiled a man's appetite.

He sighed and cursed. Now why did he have to go and think of appetites? It wasn't buffalo meat he craved. The image of Little Fawn came stealing into his thoughts. She was not tall, even by Indian standards, but straight and slim as a willow sapling. Her rounded breasts and narrow waist were unforgettable. If only she had not made him touch her—first her velvet hair and then a soft breast. Damnation! How much provoking could a man stand?

He jumped to his feet, his mind half made up to finish what he had begun. Wasn't no squaw gonna tease the eyeballs from his head and not know the feel of the rearing and plunging of the bull she had tormented to action.

He crossed the grass in long, purposeful strides, his trousers rubbing urgently at his growing need. A whisper brought him around sharply and he expelled a curse. He had left his lodge so addled that he had forgotten to bring even his knife. A movement, an indecisive sway of a shadow among the veiled cottonwoods, stirred at the corner of his eye. Human. His senses were never wrong. Young, slight of weight and— woman! He was beyond thought by now, the only reverberation in his brain the lusty, snorting scent of a male on the trail of a female.

She moved in on him at the edge of the woods, her face a silhouette marked by a wide, inviting smile. "You look for Yellow Bird That Sings?" she questioned in a muffled voice.

Bridger slowed his stride but not his purpose. If a new heifer had cut out of the herd in front of the one he had marked out, then so be it. "You looking for me?" he shot back.

The womanly figure shrugged, reminding him of the ample flanks and full hips she had displayed in her fight with Little Fawn. Yep, he thought warmly, she'd do right nicely for what he had in mind. Didn't hanker after the prospect of trouble with Washakie anyhow. "You come on back in the woods with Peejatowahooten and we'll see what song the night wind sings."

Later, the odor of their coupling mingled with the pungent earth and sharp smell of sweat. Bridger lay on the bed of leaves he had hastily gathered for them and stroked her face with his fingers. One side was fatter than the other and he wondered for the first time why she did not speak more. "Something wrong with you?" he asked after a moment.

"It is nothing," she responded in a slurred voice. "My husband, Hooting Owl, does not like that I fight with Little Fawn. He is jealous." He felt her shrug against him. "He takes lodgepole to me. Hurts plenty terrible." She reached for his hand and pushed it between her wet thighs. "But you make Yellow Bird That Sings feel much better. Peejatowahooten's medicine more powerful than Hooting Owl's. I tell him so maybe."

"Be obliged if you didn't," he requested dryly. "You tell Hooting Owl you prefer Mysterious Medicine Chief, I never come to you again. Understand?"

The woman nodded vigorously. "Yellow Bird That Sings no fool. I quiet; you come again. Where, now, is my gift?"

Chapter 8

"Don't give a damn what Cap'n Bridger done said! Them doin's don't shine with this crowd, boy. Thar's many a trapper here wants what he's got comin'. Tell that to your booshway!"

Milt Sublette faced the angry knot of men calmly. His eyes never left the face of their speaker, a gaunt, greasy-haired trapper with a face cut into hollows and canyons by the wind. Rendezvous was almost over and Fitz had yet to show. Whiskey now gone from the spring season, Milt and Bridger had little to offer the expectant trappers but the worn-out promise that next day, for certain, the caravan would arrive.

Milt sized up his tormentor. There wasn't much Milt liked better than a fight. Whether knives, fists, or pistols, it mattered little to him. Besides, with the squaws holding back for lack of the persuasive merchandise foofaraw, there wasn't any other kind of release to be had.

Milt grinned. "I've trapped beaver on the Platte, the Missouri and the Yellowstone. I've trapped the Snake and the Three Forks. But, by damn, if I ever seen one o' them rascals rear up on his hind legs and talk back 'afore."

The man's brown face reddened. "You talkin' 'bout me, boy?"

Milt shrugged, and pulling his Green River slowly from its place on his hip, began to pick his teeth with the tip.

"Whoo-ee doggee! Thar's a fight a-brewin'!" yelled one of the crowd.

The word spread like wildfire through the camp and men came running from every direction. The crowd doubled in size within a few minutes.

All the while Milt continued to poke at his teeth with his knife. Bridger had forbidden him to pick a fight, knowing how he loved a good brawl. The Rocky Mountain Fur Company could not stand to lose the friendship of the free trappers, Bridger had explained, and the lack of whiskey and supplies had done nothing to endear them to the men. Well now, thought Milt. He'd not started this one, not exactly. His lips twitched. He reckoned he'd already done enough to judge by the heaving chest of the old man. Besides, he could do with a little recreation and he didn't plan to kill the man, just tickle his ribs a bit.

As he expected, it didn't take another word between them to settle the quarrel. The older trapper's Green River caught a shaft of light as it came into his hand. The two men crouched and circled one another in the space provided by their audience.

"Gonna make meat o' you, boy," the older man taunted. "Reckon you ain't hear tell 'bout this old coon. Got the hair o' a couple Blackfoot in my possibles right now. This here Green River dug in the vitals o' more'n one old goat. Reckon it'll take on one more."

"That's tellin' him, Doc!" urged a man in the crowd, to be quickly shouted down by Milt's friends.

The two trappers made two more full turns before the older man thought he saw an opening under Milt's left arm. He slashed with a wicked stroke. Milt saw it coming and circled his body out of the way. Swiftly, Milt dropped to one knee, gouging upward with his blade toward the man's midsection.

The man screeched and fell back, a long bloody streak appearing on his shirt front. Maddened by the pain, the old trapper lunged forward, one hand out to take the bite of Milt's blade, and the other brandishing the knife for a downward stroke at his victim's neck.

But Milt had not spent his entire adult life in the mountains for no purpose. He crouched down and launched himself at the advancing figure. His fist slammed into the man's crotch with all the force he could put behind it. Finally they fell apart, Milt's breath a long rasp and the older trapper's a screech of agony.

Just like that it was over. Milt raised himself from the dust, pocketed his knife, and sauntered off. He had kept his promise. He had killed no one. If he had fought dirty it was nothing more than what any man could expect. There were no rules to fighting in this territory. Milt smiled. He must remember to say that to Gabe when he had finished cussing him out.

Milt shook his head in disgust. "How you suppose you're gonna make them whiskey-dry, woman-hungry sons of Satan listen to that hogwash? That's what I'd like to know. Gabe, you're plumb queer when it comes to things Indianfied."

In a cooler moment Milt would later wonder why Bridger had not thrown him with his rifle or sent him up Green River for mouthing off like that. But right now he was too worked up to think of much. "Listen to a sensible man talking. If Fitz was here he'd tell you the same. You want to believe what that old faker Eyes-of-the-Hawk told you, that's your business. But you're asking a powerful lot of men what don't set much store by such hocus-pocus, me included."

Bridger sat cross-legged before the campfire, whittling a wooden flute for Yellow Bird That Sings. "Milt, boy, you spout off like that much longer and I'm gonna have to dunk you in the river." He looked up at the man pacing near him, his gray eyes serious. "I ain't got the benefit of book learning like you, that's true. But I ain't no fool neither. I paid two prime bits of horseflesh for my information and I sat and watched every one of the four days of dancing and singing and praying it took to get it. If Eyes-of-the-Hawk says that Fitz ain't dead but on the wrong trail, you can depend on it being so. That's right, go on and snort. I'll lay odds of whatever size you'd like that the old medicine chief still knows his business."

"You're joshin' me." Milt tried to sound offhanded but he could not keep the cynicism completely out of his voice. "You're serious, right enough?"

Bridger chuckled at the break in his friend's voice. "Must be something you want of mine awful bad, Milt. Ain't seen you this frisky since you tickled 'Doc' Newell last week."

Milt ducked his head at the mention of the forbidden fight. "You bettin' or not?"

Bridger peeled a long curl off his work before replying. "Reckon you could tell me what it is you expect me to lay up? Ain't got no ready cash. Ain't got no more tobacco or whiskey. Just what have I got so precious I can't lay name to it?"

Milt shrugged, his eyes daring any man about the fire to speak out of turn. "Reckon as how most of us ain't had the wherewithal to purchase a night's release the whole damned month, and you laying up there in the Shoshone village with more squaws to tickle your balls than you need, you'd be a little shy about what I want. So, I'll tell you. I want a whole, honest-to-God night with that Shoshone princess, Little Fawn!"

The declaration brought howls of laughter and general agreement from the brigade camp.

"Lord love us, don't I wish I'd o' thought o' that myself!" cried one of the men.

"Don't know as how a man can back down on it," chimed in another.

"Well now," Bridger drawled in his slower-than-molasses voice of amusement. "Seein' as how it's you, Milt, I'm near about tempted to oblige. Thing is, the little sweetheart ain't mine to give. Reckon her pa, Washakie, would have a word or two to say about the matter, anyhow."

"You're backing down," Milt charged.

"Now, I wouldn't put it quite like that but . . ." Bridger let his voice trail off. Despite his calm exterior he was fighting mad. Milt had pushed him into a narrow canyon with no way out. If he backed down, reasons notwithstanding, his men would think he set less store by the Shoshone medicine man's words than he swore he did. Then how could he cajole them back into the field for the fall hunt? On the other hand . . .

"Tell you what, Milt. Seeing as how I'm so bet-be-dogged certain that Fitz'll find us 'afore wintering, I'm prepared to bet every man what takes to the field with us a half-pint of whiskey on it. And if that buffalo pony of yours I been coveting is on your side of the scale, you're on with Little Fawn."

"Now that's a bet I don't mind takin'," a trapper shouted. With that began betting and counterbetting that took up the rest of the evening.

When Bridger returned to his lodge later that night, he cast the small figure huddled by his fire a curious glance. Little Fawn had never, in any gesture or word, referred to the afternoon he had tried to take advantage of her. She had kept his lodge clean and his stewpot full. But she did not talk to him anymore, which was just as well. He thought it would be hard to explain to her how he had gotten his men to agree to traipse back out into the wilderness without a rendezvous on the possibility of seeing her delivered into the hands of his partner for a night of public lovemaking. She would not understand that he did not expect it to come to that. It was a sham, like baiting a trap with a choice tidbit. They'd take the bait, his men, same as the beaver, thanks to her.

"Bless your sweet little body, darlin'," he murmured as he dozed off.

Bridger watched through narrowed lids the preparations for the day's march. They were moving on through the Snake River Valley, their catch a good one and complete. He had packed his mule with the company records and the articles of agreement signed by the men, both company and free, who made up his brigade. By rights these matters were the province of the company clerk. But Milt cared so little for his new position that Bridger had compromised by offering to keep the journals if Milt would carry on at the rear of the column.

The packing up of a full company of men took hours, and they began before sunrise. Looking around the camp he estimated that the brigade would be another hour before breaking camp. The miserable trickle of frozen rain on this early fall morning did not help dispositions. He observed a cantankerous mule kick out suddenly at the man who was drawing tight its cinch.

The mule bucked and flashed iron-shod hooves, littering the ground with an assortment of pans, traps, and pelts that had rattled loose from the half-secured packs on its back. The camp tender made a grab for the rope around the animal's neck. He received a glancing blow in the head for his trouble, and drew his blade with a mighty roar, as if intending to murder the beast.

Bridger sucked in his jaw to stop a guffaw of laughter. The poor devil had probably tried to kill the animal on more than one occasion and the added humiliation of drawing the booshway's laughter might goad him to succeed.

"Ain't no sign of nothing," Milt hailed as he rode into camp. "Been as far as the first set of hills and can't see a thing. Reckon, though, this weather'll be turning right unpleasant come nightfall."

Bridger cast a knowledgeable eye to the ashen sky. "I'd lay odds you're right, Milt."

Milt grinned and struck his partner's leg a friendly blow with his rifle butt. "You already laid me the kind of odds I fancy. When you gonna pay up?" He chuckled and winked. "Wintering's gonna be better this year than ever before. Only question is, when you gonna send for the girl?"

Bridger shrugged his shoulders in annoyance. Both he and Milt were deeply worried about the future of the company, but Milt chose to tease him with the promise of Little Fawn. "You know you owe me the fall hunt to prove that Fitz ain't gone under," Bridger reminded him. "You feeling a might randy, you might like what's up ahead. Looks to be we'll be wading thigh-high in ice water by the end of the week. That ought to take the edge off your hunger."

"Aw, I'll keep warm just thinking of soft tits and warm—"

"Ain't you got a job to do?" Bridger interrupted

in an irritated tone. "Well—ain't you?" he insisted when Milt gave him a funny look.

"Sure, Gabe, old feller, sure enough do." Milt turned his horse and cantered away past the camp tender, who had managed at last to slip a noose over his mule's head.

Bridger swore and gave a vicious tug on his mule's rope as he kicked his horse forward out of the camp. "What the hell's the matter?" he muttered to himself when he was out of sight of the brigade. It wasn't as if he were concerned about Fitz. He missed the jovial Irishman; needed his eagle eye in hostile Blackfoot country.

Bridger's grip tightened slightly on his rifle, packed with powder and shot. He had made it a practice to hold surprise inspections from time to time to make certain that all rifles were being kept clean and loaded. It was amazing to him that a man could work these hills for more than a week and not hold his rifle more precious than anything else in his possession.

Nope, it was not fear for Fitz that made him unaccountably irritable. They were running low on shot and powder. They also needed warm woolen blankets to augment their buffalo robes, not to mention more traps and just plain ordinary supplies. But these things were secondary to the unwelcome knowledge that a chance encounter with another well-supplied brigade could well cost him the pelts and business of his free trappers. He could almost smell Vanderburgh in the wilderness. At rendezvous a few of the trappers were talking about the extraordinary wages the Company was said to be offering. But so far his men had been patient, moving with him at his command. Hardly more than a dozen skirmishes had broken out since leaving Cache Valley. But let them fellers get wind of Taos Lightning and trouble would surely follow.

Fraeb had volunteered to head back east to St. Louis with the cache of pelts they owned outright. With luck, he would return by spring with fresh supplies. Bridger shook his head. He hoped Fitz was experiencing some of that luck about now.

By midafternoon Bridger had chosen a campsite and dismounted to wait for the brigade to catch up. He rounded the area, a cottonwood oasis along the bank of a stream, searching for Indian sign. The search yielded nothing. For the present, it seemed, they were safe.

That did not prevent him from inspecting the horses and men when they arrived. The camp was set according to his design: its rear snug against the riverbank, the mules tethered inside the wall of packs and saddles that made up the bulwark at the camp's entrance. At nightfall, he went from camp to camp, listening to the day's complaints from the mess captains.

His face was grim when he entered the last mess. The men were notorious grumblers and shirkers. The last to break camp, they invariably found themselves at the back end of the brigade.

"Cap'n Bridger," began Mahoney, tonight's spokesman. "Seein' as how these here fellers is sick to death o' swallowin' a whole brigade's worth o' dust and dung, we'd like a place right behind you come mornin'."

Bridger gave the man a long look before he declared, "You want to ride in front, you get your lazy asses out of the bedroll sooner! Ain't nothing about sleeping in the open worth swallowing dust for." He moved on quickly, unwilling to hear more of that sort of self-pity. "You, there," he said to the man who had turned away at his approach.

The man turned back, his shoulders hunched defensively as he tried to shield his rifle barrel along the length of his pants leg. "Let's have it, Jacques," Bridger demanded, holding out his hand for the weapon.

Jacques, a tall, rawboned Canadian, broke into a rotten-tooth smile. "M'sieur Bree-ger, you ask ol' Jacques, him part with ee's rifle. Ee say *non. Mais,* I tink ee's not right."

Nothing changed on Bridger's face. "You will hand it over or you'll walk straight out of this camp."

The man shrugged, his smile wider. *"Mais, m'sieur. Jacques, il ne comprend pas."*

"You goddamn well better cawmprand," Bridger burst out and added a few words in the Canadian's own tongue. "Well?" Once more his hand shot out toward the Canadian.

The man sidestepped Bridger. "Jacques, ee don' tink you make him go." When the cajoling tone brought no reply he shrugged a second time and abruptly threw his rifle at the bourgeois.

Bridger caught it handily, knowing what he would find. The barrel was filthy, so clogged with spent powder and dirt it might have blown up and killed its owner if fired in that condition.

"What did you expect to do with this if Blackfoot attacked us tonight?" Bridger interrogated him.

The Canadian smirked. "Jacques do like the booshway; ee throw it to dem and run like hell, same like you last spring." The jibe did not rouse the laughter he hoped for, and he flushed in anger.

Bridger did not look at the man again, but turned to the trapper nearest him. "Can you clean a rifle?" he asked the Mexican Loretto.

The man rose to his feet, his eyes darting from Bridger to the visibly angered Canadian who stood with fists balled at his sides. "*Sí, Capitán.* I clean rifle like new."

Bridger tossed it to him. "Give you ten dollars to do it by daybreak." He swung back to the Canadian, his eyes flinty in the firelight. "You got some objection to that?"

The Canadian saw Bridger's hand slip to the hilt of his skinning knife. He did not doubt that if jumped, the big man would take him under. "Ee gives rifle back to Jacques?"

Bridger let his hand fall from his knife. "He'll give it back when I'm satisfied that he's done a good job. By the by, the ten dollars it's costing me will be deducted from your account. Understand me?"

The Canadian ducked his head once in assent before Bridger strode off.

Chapter 9

Vanderburgh swirled his wine glass in idle contemplation as he listened to his host reiterate his plans for the Rocky Mountain area.

". . . must be plain to a man of vision that we are well under way toward snatching the entire western trade out from under McLoughlin's nose." Kenneth McKenzie leaned back in his dining-room chair until it teetered on two legs. His fleshy face was flushed with self-congratulation and his whiskers bristled in the light of a dozen tapers set in the silver candelabrum before him. "The idea was brilliant, if I may say so myself. And don't know why I shouldn't, come to that." He patted his ample stomach, superbly covered in a tailored uniform of his own design.

Vanderburgh downed the last of his wine as if it were the watered whiskey he had become used to on the trail, rather than the rare French import it was. "Aren't you forgetting something, Mr. McKenzie?" he ventured, rising to his feet.

McKenzie reached out to pinch the cheek of the young Nez Perce girl seated next to him. She giggled, the agitation of her shoulders drawing his eyes to the deep décolletage of her fashionable European gown. "What's that?" he replied as he popped a dried fig into the girl's open mouth.

Vanderburgh drew a long breath, unable, after some months in his employer's company, not to resent the offhand manner with which he was met. "I mean, sir, have you not forgotten the Rocky Mountain Fur Company?"

McKenzie's forehead wrinkled, tilting his hairy brows forward. "The who? Ah yes, of course. The ragtag bunch of ruffians who persist in believing that we shall get tired of the play and return home like good little boys. Ha! Look at your face, Henry. One would think I'd called your sainted mother a lousy tart!" Booming laughter rattled the china. "There, there, boy. Don't take offense. 'Tis a joke, Vanderburgh, you prig. By God, no wonder them rough and tumble Rocky Mountain goats tore your britches when first you tangled with them. It's your attitude, you know," he continued, wagging a chicken leg at his lieutenant. "So much a prig you make yourself contemptible. Not that *I* find you so," he amended quickly, belched, and guffawed again. "By damn if I don't like my company better than anybody I know!"

"If you find these mountain people so contemptible," Vanderburgh ground out carefully between clenched teeth, "why, then, do you propose that I should resume trailing them this fall?"

The front legs of McKenzie's chair slammed down on the floor. He had been drinking heavily, he knew it, but that did not give any man the right to question his tactics as a businessman. He heaved himself to his feet and swung out an arm, just missing the Indian girl who had risen beside him. "You dare to question the decisions of your superior? What kind of discipline are they teaching at West Point these days? By all that is holy, I owe you no explanation of my thoughts!"

He gave the younger man a withering glance, resumed his seat, and then casually waved Vanderburgh back into his. "Sit, Henry. We'll talk, man to man, if you wish. Where's the wine? Yes, yes, fill both glasses," he directed the steward who came running at his call. "Now, you think you have a right to know what I have up my sleeve, huh? Tell you what it is. What's been my aim since the beginning in '29? To build a system of forts on the Missouri, that's what. Forget them long hauls to rendezvous and back. Bring the goods upriver. Make them bug-ridden white savages come to the forts to trade, same as they have for years in other parts of the country. We built Fort Union for just such a purpose. Right here at the mouth of the Yellowstone. We'll gather business from the Yellowstone and the Missouri. Right this very minute my man Kipp is building our second base at the mouth of the Marias. Going to call it Fort Piegan. Right smack-dab in the middle of Blackfoot country, it is. We got them red devils near ready to sign a peace treaty. Bet that'll keep McLoughlin awake nights. He and his Hudson Bay Company boys thought all they had to do was wait till them unleashed savages had done their dirty work, and then resume trading with the Blackfoot themselves."

He winked at Vanderburgh and then at the nubile girl at his side. "Outfoxed them there. Them Canadians ain't the only folks who can trade with the Indians. And bless my soul if young Fontenelle hasn't done us a good turn by talking them Nez Perce Injuns into going back to St. Louis with him this summer. Glorious publicity. Can't you just see the headlines in the St. Louis papers and, better yet, back East? 'American Fur Company Initial Exploits Include Indian Missionaries!'

Sounds so good to me I wish I'd thought of it. Time enough later to get my full share of the glory. You and me, Vanderburgh, we have to keep our noses to the old grindstone. Did I tell you I'm trying to raise the funds to buy a steamboat to work the Missouri between here and Independence? Don't look so took aback, man. It's a river, same as any other. If they can manage the Mississippi they'll conquer the Missouri in due time. Well, what do you think?"

Vanderburgh had permitted himself the liberty of lighting his pipe. "You are asking me what I think of your lack of concern with the Rocky Mountain Fur Company, I take it. I must reply that I haven't the slightest idea. I've heard all about your plans for the building of forts and your wild scheme—" He halted to give the older man a direct look. "Your scheme for a steamboat line to run supplies and pelts up and down the river. What I haven't heard is one confounded word about Bridger, Fitzpatrick and the rest."

McKenzie studied the man through whiskey-bright eyes. "Give you this, Henry: You ain't a man to mince words, even if it's to your host and at his table."

The jibe hit home as McKenzie intended, knowing that Vanderburgh liked to think of himself as the gentleman personified. "Don't much like traipsing after a bunch of crafty devils like Bridger's crowd, do you? Well, can't say as I blame you. Must smart something terrible to be led by the nose into a trap, especially when you been warned up front. If I was you, I'd be anxious to even the score."

"Don't try to cozen me, McKenzie," Vanderburgh burst out, once more forgetting his manners. "You know as well as I that you have some purpose in my leading a brigade south into Indian territory. And I feel I have a right to know what it is I'm risking my neck for. You allude so carefully to my humiliation at the hands of the Blackfoot last fall. It would never have come about had those Indians not been armed with weapons equal to our own."

"Mr. Vanderburgh," McKenzie said in a soft voice, "I do believe the evenin's imbibing has gone to your head. Surely I do not hear you right when you suggest that we, the American Fur Company representatives, are breaking the territorial law by selling weapons and ammunition to the Indians."

As a member of responsibility in the fields, Vanderburgh would be held to account for any breach of governmental laws. "I don't relish being shot at with American rifles," he avowed, keeping his eyes on the smoldering bowl of his pipe. "A man says things in the heat of the moment. Perhaps they were Hudson Bay rifles, after all."

"Good man." McKenzie nodded in approval. "Now, I'll tell you exactly why I'm ordering you back to the field come daybreak. Yes, tomorrow, Vanderburgh. You've been holding ready for weeks. Can't be a surprise. And here's why: we must learn the territory. That Bridger crowd has access to more unknown streams and mountain fords than any other folk, excepting the Indians themselves. Now that don't represent much of a threat in and of itself. But they're stubborn men, like their mules. Beating them with a stick is the only way to make them go. Of course, it helps if you got a nice, juicy carrot hanging before their eyes. And that's where you come in. Flash your money under their noses, Henry. Talk big. Up the wages to whatever is necessary to pry those squaw men away from Bridger's side. Loyalty's got no friend who can't be had for cold hard cash. Just between you and me, I don't give a damn if you lose every man, mule, and pelt you collect this next year. Just bring in the Opposition's free trade and they'll fold up as naturally as a tent without its stakes."

"*Écraser toute opposition?*" Vanderburgh offered.

McKenzie grinned. "You got it straight at last, Henry."

" 'Course I'm listenin', Gabe. It's just that I don't like what I'm hearin'. You're askin' me to go over to the Company's camp and parley, like we was bosom friends." Milt shook his head, the squirrel tail on his fur hat swinging in sympathy.

"It ain't like that at all," Bridger replied as he dusted snow from the shoulders of his capote. "The word is out that Drips ain't been resupplied neither. As long as he's following us I'd like to know if that's true. Wintering in the mountains ain't the same as wintering on the Mississippi. Thought we might invite them over for a spell. Offer to trade them pemmican and buffalo meat for pelts."

Milt winced. "Now I know you're snowstruck. Feed them when we're near starvin'? Of all the addle-headed, poor—"

"Milt, Milt," Bridger broke in calmly, "you're wasting a heap of heat over nothing. Don't expect them to accept. I sure wouldn't if I was them. You go, make the offer like the fine young gentleman your mother raised you to be, and come back with their 'no thank you' and a fair knowledge of their size and supplies."

"Spy out the land, so to speak?" Milt's expression brightened considerably. "We need to know if they're worse off than us. That bein' the case, what we gonna do about it?"

"Can't say right off. A man never knows when the signs will point out a new trail." Bridger pulled the hood of his Navaho capote up over his head. "Damn cold weather for the Salmon River Valley. Reckon we'll be knee-high in snow before morning. Better ride on out, Milt, so's you don't have to travel at night."

"As if I . . . Hey!" Milt grabbed Bridger by the arm and thrust him around. "Ain't that—? By damn! It is! That's Frapp comin' into camp!"

Up along the treeline Bridger's eye made out several dots moving against the white of the fresh snow. "It's Frapp, all right. I'd recognize his God-awful red bandanna in hell. God Almighty, he's got the mule train with him!"

Their ringing voices tumbled the rest of the men out of their tepees. Soon the valley echoed with the "Hee-ayyahh-aagh!" of an Indian war party as the trappers swarmed up the steep hill to greet the incoming men. Bridger told the men who remained behind to rouse the camp cooks and squaws to prepare a feast. "Rendezvous!" He bellowed with a wide grin. "A sure-fire, raise-some-hell rendezvous starting now!"

Fitz must be with them, Bridger thought in relief, though he hadn't seen him. That was the only thing that would explain the old Dutchman's early return.

"Ve got no farther dan Platte River 'afore ve sight dat redhead Irish, Feetz," Fraeb announced between large gulps of the first round of Taos Lightning. "Dat crazy potato farmer, know where he got to? He goes not to St. Louie, ho ho. He goes south to Santa Fe with Smith and Big Bill. Goin' to try de markets in Nu Mexico and Chee . . . Choo . . ."

"Chihuahua?" Milt asked through a mouthful of pemmican.

Fraeb nodded emphatically. "*Ja.* Dat's de by-damn place. Dey tell Feetz him come with dem. Credit, he's hard to find in St. Louie."

"McKenzie," Bridger grumbled. Word through

the mountain grapevine said the Company man was up to all kinds of tricks.

"*Ja.* Maybe. So de Irish, he goes. He tells great story of . . ."

But Bridger had stopped listening. Instead he lay back and closed his robe, letting the whiskey warm the hard to reach places. Never again would he let anything shake his faith in ol' Eyes-of-the-Hawk. Damn if the old shaman wasn't right on target. Not only was Fitz alive as he predicted, he had been on the wrong trail, going south instead of east. Luck had put Fraeb and Fitz at the Platte River at the same time. Too damn bad Fitz had not made the full trip. But he guessed his friend had done the right thing in taking their pelts to Santa Fe to make good the company debts.

Bridger's gaze swung to Milt, who was on his way to becoming stone drunk. Milt was a good partner, and better than most in a fight. That was his trouble, too. Milt was a hothead, given to provoking a fight just for sport. Bridger tried to avoid that kind of thinking. His smoldering temper was already flaring up due to the dirty dealings of McKenzie's dogs.

Fitz had said at the beginning that their doings with the Company boys would be a battle of wits. So far a couple of old Indian tricks had put them off. But Drips was an old hand at tracking, and things were different this fall. Every time he shook off Drips he was just a hair short of walking into Robidoux, a new Company partisan McKenzie had stuck on his trail. Only a few miles to the west, a company of Hudson Bay trappers had set up their wintering. Things were getting tight all around.

So deep was he in his own reflections that Bridger did not realize the voices about him had petered out.

"What's wrong?" he grumbled when the silence penetrated his daydreaming.

"You better tell him again, Frapp," Milt said quietly, giving Bridger a sympathetic look.

The old Dutchman scratched at the grizzled stubble on his chin. "Ain't no easy way to tell yu, Gabe. Feetz say 'spit it out.' Knows yu don't . . . Here is. Jed Smith, he goes under de summer back."

Bridger sat up and grabbed the older man's shirtfront. "You know that for a fact? Jed's gone under?"

The old man's face wrinkled over in pain. "By Gott! I tell Feetz he's for to tell yu. But is so. Comanches ambush him in the Cimarron desert."

Other than a few muttered curses, silence held the company. Fraeb continued, "Feetz say to tell yu, Jed goes under in fine style. Takes three Injuns with him. Chief is one."

The news brought hoots of delight to the men and soon the party was toasting, laughing, and remembering old times. This was the true and fitting memorial to one of their own. They never doubted for a moment that the most reverent man ever to enter these mountains would expect anything less.

But Bridger could not listen. He stood up, took an unsteady step or two, then found his stride and left the warmth of the lodge for the winter outside.

He walked for a long time, his moccasin prints in the snow marking his passage. The wind howled in his ears till they stung with frostbite, but he was not aware of it. His hands grew stiff and his beard crusted over with icicles. His lips cracked and bled as he parted them for breath. Not until his face hardened with ice did he realize that he was weeping.

He left the village and made his way up the southern slope of the mountain, down which Fraeb had come that morning. Tall spruce sheltered him from the sting of the wind, but nothing eased the wound Fraeb's news had made in his heart.

Finally, from sheer exhaustion and exposure, he looked for a place to rest. He spied an overhang jutting out from the hillside and quickly made his way to it. He dropped to his knees and shoveled out the accumulation of snow. After a few minutes, he crept into the hollow that would house his frame. He wrapped his robe about his body and lay down, his back to the rock wall.

Memories swirled past him, tossing him back in time as lightly as a bullboat on the Missouri rapids. As a rawboned boy of seventeen, his face was perpetually reddened by the heat of the blacksmith's furnace. How he had longed to escape, never able to endure the smells of tar and oil and smelted iron. He had yearned for the country, for wide open spaces where a man could stretch out his arms and his imagination. Oh, maybe that was not what he had had in mind in the beginning. Like every boy growing up at the edge of the American frontier, he had longed for adventure. And the notice tacked to the post near the blacksmith shop had offered just that. Recruits were needed to embark on the first full-scale expedition to trap beaver on the Upper Missouri.

He had not stopped to ask himself if this was what he really wanted or how he expected to trap beaver. He had never trapped anything more difficult than a rabbit in his entire life. The only thing he knew was that it offered him a chance to escape. No one questioned him. They were desperate, signing on any man who managed to place an X on the roll. It had been the beginning of a new era, the opening of the Rocky Mountain Territory. He had been the youngest and greenest of a brigade composed of runaway slaves, mulattos, half-breeds, army deserters, and criminals. And then there was Jedediah Smith.

Jed was six years his senior. But to Bridger, he was the embodiment of all the boy ever hoped to be. Jed was different in more than the obvious ways, such as preferring to be clean-shaven in a world where men sported beards. He could quote from the Bible and discuss the pursuits of Greek and Latin scholars with ease. Rumor said a man of Jed's qualifications must have been running from something to bury himself in the wilderness.

Bridger had not cared. He saw Jed as a quiet, dignified man who could stand in hand-to-hand combat with the toughest fighters the West ever spawned. And he was convinced that it did not matter what Jed might have done.

Jed had taught him how to lay traps, where to place his floating stick so that the beaver would set into it, and where to look for signs of the equally dangerous foes: Indians and grizzlies. Jed had taught him to improve his aim with the company rifle he had been issued. He had showed him how to cut off the bottoms of his first pair of buckskin trousers so they would not shrink around his ankles. Mostly, Jed was always there with a comforting word in the midst of a midday when the mosquitoes were so thick they darkened the sky, driving men and mules to madness.

Bridger shivered with cold. Sleep was quickly overtaking him now. Memories were turning into dreams, and the one he dreaded most moved before his eyes as he struggled against it.

It happened his second winter out. Nineteen and full of good intentions, he had never seen what a grizzly could do to a man. Old Hugh Glass was as ancient as the hills even in those days. Glass had been careless, allowing himself to be surprised by a grizzly and

her two cubs. When six men finally killed her and
dragged her off Glass, there was little left of him. His
right arm and left leg had been busted. His ribs had
been crushed and his scalp had been ripped, a long flap
of it hanging over his left ear and down on his shoulder.

They had done what they could, going through
the motions of sewing him back together with sinew
and setting the broken bones. Nobody expected the old
man to live. By nightfall they were restless. They were
a small detail out from the main camp and Arikaras
were nearby. Yet a dogged scrap of humanity kept
them by the dying man's side while they argued over
what to do.

Bridger had wondered all the rest of these years
why he had opened his mouth that day. The older
men, veterans, were unwilling to risk their necks for a
dying man. Bridger knew it was not his place to speak.
Yet he heard himself volunteer to remain behind to
wait for Glass to die. The leader demanded another
man stay with the "baby" of the brigade and Conners,
an army deserter, agreed to—for pay.

Then the trouble began. Hugh Glass would not
die. One day dragged into the next as he lay unconscious and barely breathing. And it went on—two,
three, four days. Conners was for leaving. He caught
up Glass's rifle and knife, saying they would prove he
had not left before the old man died.

Soon Bridger left, too; left the old man to die
alone in the wilderness with no one to hide his bones
from the wolves.

It might have been something he could have gotten over. When he came back to the camp subdued
and silent, the men merely shook their heads and
mumbled about a man learning to accept the realities
of life. He might have forgotten and convinced himself

that Glass was beyond help. But hell would be waiting for Bridger six months later.

They were wintering on the Upper Missouri when the fort gates swung open on a strange visitor. Dripping ice and uglier than the worst nightmare was Hugh Glass.

The story quickly became legend in the mountains. The old man's ordeal in the wilderness—his walk over one hundred miles of barren ground with a broken leg, with neither rifle nor knife to aid him—had become a standard tale at every rendezvous. The memory of his betrayer receded into the forgotten edges of myth. But Glass knew.

Only Jed had said a word in his favor. Glass wanted Bridger's life, but Jed stood between them. "He's just a boy, Hugh. What'd you expect? Nobody else even volunteered to stay with you. He got scared; listened to bad advice. He's only a boy. Reckon he has some growing yet to do."

And now Jed was gone. The only man who had ever understood—and forgiven—his torment.

Bridger shivered uncontrollably. Jed had forgiven him but he had not forgiven himself. That was the reason he dreamed of his own death so often.

Winter sunlight filtered through the pines. Bridger rolled over, his ice-crusted robe crackling as he peeled it away from his body. Groggy and with a sour taste in his mouth, he drew himself up and crawled out from under the ledge where he had slept.

Then he realized where he was. He remembered the familiar nightmare that sought him out in the weakness of sleep. He rubbed his hands briskly through his hair and let them fall to his sides. Something was different this time. Usually after the dreams visited, he awakened with shame fresh in his mind. So strong was this feeling that he had often gone off for several days to convince himself that his courage had not deserted him. Today he felt nothing.

Bridger shook himself. He felt like returning immediately to camp. He had mourned Jed's death as best he knew how. And while he could not quite figure why, the grief left him feeling more content with himself than he could remember.

He bent and scooped up his robe and slung it over his shoulder. "Damn it all, Jed! You already gone over five months back. You can stop looking after me now. I'm all growed up!"

Funny how he thought Jed might hear him. Seemed likely he would, though. A man like Jed, he would always find time for a friend, even with the heavenly harmonies to distract him.

Chapter 10

"Gabe oughta hear this for himself. Most like he'll—Hey! Here he comes now. Over here, Gabe! There's a feller here what's got a message for you." Milt waved a vigorous greeting to the man walking into camp.

Measuring his bourgeois' walk as well as his bloodshot eyes would allow, Milt decided that whatever Bridger's personal feelings were about Jed Smith's death, he looked fit to take on the more immediate problem that had just come to light.

"Howdy," Bridger greeted the pintsized stranger standing next to Milt. "Don't know if we've met. My name's Bridger. I'm bourgeois of this outfit." He put out a hand, the small man surrounding it in a bear-trap grip.

"Name's Carson," the young man announced. Towheaded and bandy-legged, he did not reach the height of the other men's shoulders. Nonetheless, he seemed at ease in their company. "Come in with the Dutchman, Frapp," Carson continued. "Been trapping down Taos way last few years. Least I'd aimed to keep at it till I ran across a friend of your'n." Carson grinned, the ruddy complexion of a true blond crinkling up like old leather. "Heard about them fellers from back east who're hoping to run off the last of you old mountain goats. Sounded like you could use some help."

"That's mighty big of you," Bridger remarked in a flat voice. "Seeing as how we're doing just fine you might figure to offer your services where they're needed most. A few of them Eastern Company boys is camped not far from here."

"Already been there," the cocky young man said. "That's where I went first light."

"Now ain't that interestin'," Bridger drawled in a voice that made Milt shoot him a speculative glance.

"Sure enough was," the stranger agreed mildly. "Right after I left 'em boys I moseyed on over to the Bug boys' camp."

The news that Carson had been all the way to the Hudson Bay Company camp startled Bridger, but he managed to remain respectably noncommittal. "You do get around, don't you, son?"

"Yes sir, that's a fact. Keeps a man from joining up sides too quick." He scratched his sandy moustache while eyeing Bridger closely. "Ain't you interested in the news Milt says I got?"

Bridger shrugged. He was hungry and not much given to playing games with a sawed-off runt who looked like he'd been born astride a horse. "You got something to say, Taos, you spit it out. I'm gut-sore and whiskey-dry. Aim to right both o' them troubles right off."

The little man's grin stretched full on his bearded face. "Fitz said you was an ornery, bear-cross bastard. He didn't say you was a fool." He paused and shrugged easily under the razor-sharp stare Bridger gave him. "Should have known Fitz wouldn't lie to me. Now, you up to hearin' my news or am I gonna have to pass it out piecemeal to your boys?"

Bridger's mind had been at work. "What did you say your name was?"

"Carson—"

"Yeah, yeah, I heard that part. That ain't what folks call you, is it?"

The little man roared with laughter. "Reckon you're fishing for the given name. It's Christopher. Ain't that a sorry-assed bitch? Folks what know me call me Kit—Kit Carson."

Bridger's brows lifted in recognition, but before he could get out a word Milt jumped in with, "You're the feller we hear tell was one of them six trappers who held off a full two hundred Comanches in the middle of the open prairie and got away?"

Kit looked down his length. "Appears so."

"Hoo-ee!" Greatly impressed, Milt looked to Bridger to share his enthusiasm.

He was doomed to disappointment, for Bridger merely grumbled, "A fair piece o' work. You ready to tell what you got to say, or am I gonna have to commence to gnawing on my moccasins while you warm up to the subject?"

"Don't you want to know whose side I'm choosing?" Kit asked, greatly enjoying himself.

"Tell me your news. Then I'll decide if I care."

"Don't it just break your heart?" Kit murmured to Milt, who sniggered. "Okay, Bridger, have it your way. This here message comes direct from the booshway of the Hudson Bay Company. He extends his respects and—"

"Shit!"

"What's that?" Kit looked up at the big man in innocence. "Oh, you ain't interested in that part, huh?

Okay, okay. This here is the gist o' it. The man says he's had a most peculiar wintering. Blackfoot been doggin' his every step. Only they're a mite uglier than usual. Been tauntin' his boys and the Pend d'Oreille folk with the news that McKenzie's built a new fort on the Marias. Says they're bein' outfitted by the American Company with rifles and powder. Says they've given the word to run every Flathead, Nez Perce and any other kind o' Indian off their land—just as soon as they kill every white man."

All three men were silent for a moment. "What do you make o' that, Gabe?" Milt asked finally.

"Sounds like the Blackfoot have declared war and all hell's about to break loose." Bridger hitched his trousers and lifted a foot to inspect one moccasin. "Don't look too appetizing after all. There's vittles and whiskey inside. What do you say?"

Vanderburgh blew out his cheeks to relieve the sting of the bitter March wind against his skin. Maybe he would abandon his clean-cheeks policy after all. There was something to be said for the insulation of whiskers. He raised himself in the saddle and traced the length of the caravan behind him. Beyond his own brigade stretched a second—Drips'.

Vanderburgh snorted and settled back into his saddle. He supposed he should be grateful. Drips had finally caught up with them in the Snake River Plateau. But he wished that Fontenelle had been the one to bring in supplies. Not only was Drips a man of few words, most of them curses, but he stank! How could Fontenelle stand the man? As an army man he was used to the smell of horses and laboring men. He had even acccustomed himself to the pungent aromas of castoreum and buffalo chip fires. But Drips . . . Well, there was nothing to compare to the throat-gagging presence of the man.

"You thinkin', sir, maybe that Mr. Drips done caught a skunk in his britches?" Fletcher had wondered.

Vanderburgh sighed. Skunks probably tracked a wide path about the man. It was a miracle the man could trap anything that breathed the same air as he. Upwind he was barely tolerable. Downwind . . .

"Mr. Vanderburgh, sir? We found 'em!" A young man came riding down the broad slope of the prairie, his yell startling several of the old-timers who reached instinctively for their rifles. But the man was grinning and Vanderburgh rested confidently in his saddle. If it was not Indians the scout had found then it could only mean he had sighted the Rocky Mountain brigade.

"Where are they?"

The scout pulled in alongside. "They're camped beside a creek bottom not three days' journey," he reported, pointing out across the barren terrain of the Idaho lava beds.

Vanderburgh scanned his surroundings. For two months they had been crisscrossing the level plains of the Snake River Plateau. Treeless sagebrush plains seemed to extend forever, interrupted occasionally by a broad lava dome or butte. He had been near giving up hope of finding the Opposition before the season was out. But McKenzie's jibes were still ringing in his ears. He would have to lose more than a dozen trappers and scores of miles before he turned back. Finally his goal was within reach and he would move heaven and hell before losing the Rocky Mountain brigade again.

"Ride on back and inform Drips of your discovery," he ordered the scout. "Tell the men they rate an extra ration of whiskey when we make camp tonight.

And tell Drips I'll have a word with him now." On horseback, and with Drips downwind, Vanderburgh thought he'd stand a better chance of conversing without gagging. He wasn't going to let anything trouble him after the news he had just received.

The Rocky Mountain brigade man watched in silent frustration as the Company men rode down into the narrow canyon of Willow Creek.

"You shoulda struck camp and showed 'em a clean pair o' heels," Kit murmured to Bridger as they watched their competition approach.

"Yeah." The single word carried all the finality of his conviction. Bridger raised a hand to shield his eyes from the sun, swearing when he recognized Vanderburgh. Pulling up stakes would have meant leaving the area half-hunted and, worse, free for the Company boys. His eyes flickered back toward his campsite where hundreds of scraped pelts, their fleshside up, lay stretched on willow hoops to dry. Hundreds more were folded and packed away for the trip to rendezvous. It would have meant a hurried scramble across difficult country to escape Vanderburgh. "Anyway," he said aloud, "they knew we were here. Don't like the idea of them thinking they scared us off. We'll lose them soon enough."

Bridger had not thought to see the Company people again before rendezvous. Fraeb and Gervais had sent word that they were having a difficult time shaking Robidoux and his Hudson Bay folks off their trail. "Mountain's getting so damned crowded a man can't take a leak in private," he muttered. He knew Vanderburgh would be along soon. Couldn't blame the man for wanting an audience for his bragging. Let Vanderburgh have his say, then they would get rid of him.

Kit Carson turned to look after Bridger. He did

not think much of the man he had seen leading the American partisans. His eyes surveyed the brigade he had been traveling with since December. An independent by choice, Carson had not signed on with the Rocky Mountain camp. He was free to trade his pelts at rendezvous for whatever price he could get. "Wonder what they'll be offerin' up at Fort Union?" he muttered softly. There was one good way to find out.

Bridger was surprised that he had to wait so long for Vanderburgh. It was past nightfall before he heard the lookout's cry indicating an approaching rider. Vanderburgh rode into the opposition camp with two of his scouts and a pack mule. Bridger decided the packs contained whiskey and tobacco. "Come to trade?" Bridger called out in his bass voice.

Vanderburgh dismounted and threw his reins to one of his men. His hand was extended as he walked toward Bridger. "Hello, Captain Bridger. Imagine our surprise when we learned whose camp it was we'd stumbled upon this day."

"Stumbled on us, did you?" Bridger retorted, disregarding the hand Vanderburgh shot forth. "Where're you headed?"

Vanderburgh's lips twitched at the man's deliberate slight. "Don't know actually. Out to tour the country, you might say. You appear to have done well this season."

Bridger shrugged, his face stony. "Leastways we managed to keep to one side of them Blackfoot."

Vanderburgh's mouth tightened but he kept his tone civil. "You're fortunate. I've lost eighteen good men this year alone."

The news amazed Bridger till he reminded himself whose fault it was the Indians were doing so well. "It must hurt double bad, a man being hunted with his own rifles."

Vanderburgh ignored the snickers surrounding him. "Is there somewhere we may talk privately, Captain Bridger?"

"You got something to say my boys can't hear?"

"You needn't be rude," Vanderburgh said in annoyance. "Neither of us requires an audience for what we have to say. We might as well get it over with."

Bridger eyed the man a little longer. Vanderburgh was leaner than he remembered, his face a deep tan over a perpetual red burn. There were new wrinkles and lines, carved by the wind and long days of exposure. There was still the dandy in his tone. But the man now had the look of one who had spent enough time in the wilderness to have a right to his say. "Suppose we mosey on over to the tepee I've pitched." Bridger hunched a shoulder in that direction and walked away. Vanderburgh followed after a quick, meaningful glance at his two scouts.

"Now, what do you think we got to say to one another?" Bridger had settled himself on the floor of his lodge.

Vanderburgh looked around, his eyes pausing a moment on the young Flathead squaw who stood by the door flap with arms folded. "She belongs to you?"

Bridger's gaze swung to the girl. "Her name is Wind That Sighs. Her pa loaned her to me for curing his lame horse during wintering. She ain't mine. You want her?" A wicked look accompanied the question.

"Thank you, no." Vanderburgh looked to the pot of simmering stew, determined that it was the source of the strange smell surrounding him, and politely looked away.

Bridger saw the look. "Hungry, are you? Hey you, get the man a knife," he directed the girl. "You're in for a real treat. Ain't every day a man gets a fresh pot of dog stew. And Wind That Sighs, she's a first rate cook. Might change your mind about wantin' her after you had a taste."

"Dog stew?"

The look of horror on the partisan's face made the mountain man roar with laughter. "Ain't up to city standards? Sorry. The Company man says he ain't got the stomach for real mountain vittles. Reckon once when we're hungry enough to eat a raw bear, hair and—"

"Captain Bridger! Spare me your yarns," Vanderburgh interrupted with a shudder. "I've come to talk business."

"Don't know nothing much about business." Bridger shook his head slightly. "Have to talk to Fitz or Bill Sublette, if you want to talk business."

"Very well. Play the mountain fool. You can pass on a word as well as the next, I suppose. Tell whoever is in charge of this company of yours that we, the American Fur Company, wish to purchase controlling interest in your business. We will be generous to all concerned and mean to hire as many of your people as are willing to come to work for us. You, of course, would be welcomed most generously. With your superior knowledge of the country and our capital to back you, we would soon control the fur trade from Boston to the Pacific Northwest. You could go back East, make a name for yourself. Perhaps even marry and settle down—after you've produced a map of the beaver streams in this part of the country, of course. You'd be famous, possibly rich. Tell Fitzpatrick and Sublette that. Or—" and he leaned close—"has it occurred to you that you know a bit more about business than you were first willing to admit?"

He sat back with an expression of satisfaction. "You could be the first, you know. I've just so much money given over to me for this purpose. The first to sign up will get the biggest share, stands to reason."

Bridger drew out his knife slowly, a gesture that made Vanderburgh draw in a quick breath. With a smile, Bridger jabbed a bit of meat floating at the top of the stewpot. He chewed it slowly, licking the juice that dribbled out of the corner of his mouth. "They got dog stew back East? Reckon not," he said in a slow drawl. "Seems to me like they should though. Ought to be plenty of dog meat to be had, seein' as how they're raisin' them to be businessmen and partisans."

He swallowed the meat, his eyes locked on Vanderburgh's face. "Yeah, there must be plenty of dog meat around. Folks what'd sell out their own for a few bones, even nice juicy ones, ain't nothin' but a pack of lousy, fartin' dogs.

"Now take me," he continued with no variation in his flat tone. "I wouldn't know how to get on in that kind o' society. Some bastard come around telllin' me how's I could skin my friends and sell their hides to profit, know what I'd do?"

Vanderburgh made a slight movement with his shoulders, his eyes fastened on the razor-honed blade flashing dangerously in the man's hand. "I'd be like to skin that bastard and sell his hide instead. You take my meanin'?" Bridger said softly.

Vanderburgh pulled himself together with supreme effort. "I understand that you are, indeed, a very poor businessman. However, I am content to wait until you have passed the word on to the others. Some of them might not see things quite the way you do."

"You're a cold son of a bitch," Bridger drawled in what sounded like humor. Vanderburgh gave him a sharp look. "Yeah, you tickle me right fine. Ain't scared of nothing and willing to sell out your granny's grave to get what you want. I could cut you up, dump you in this here stew, and serve it up to your boys. They'd never know the difference. Only," Bridger drew out the word, swirling the knife on his fingertip, "I'm gonna let you walk out of here like you ain't said them things to me. I'll beat you, Vanderburgh. Ain't a doubt in my mind. You ain't got forever in these mountains. The Shining Ones, they don't like you and you don't like them. This here is my home. Aim to die here, given the chance. That's why I'll be here when you're gone."

Vanderburgh rose to his feet. "You had your chance. It makes no difference to me. It'll all be over come the end of the summer." He gave the mountain man a pitying look. "They'll sell you out in a minute for the right price. Hate to see you lose out. I like a fighter."

Bridger rose to his feet, his gray eyes sharp with anger. "You make the idea of killing you sound better with every breath. But I got a feeling it wouldn't be worth it. The way McKenzie's supplying rifles to the Blackfoot, I figure it won't be long before you're gone under anyway. Killing you wouldn't stop McKenzie and that's all I'm hankering to do. But I ain't inviting you into this camp no more. You ain't welcome."

Vanderburgh picked up his hat. "We won't need to talk again, Bridger. As I've said, your time's about run out. We've got men in the Flathead camps making up a trade treaty. Fontenelle took a party of Nez Perce back to St. Louis last year. We've even got a caravan setting up to make rendezvous this summer. We'll outbid and undercut you at every turn. Too bad you didn't take my offer. Could be you won't be able to find anybody to buy pelts from."

Bridger eyed him squarely. "You're forgetting something."

"What's that?" Vanderburgh asked in amusement.

"You got to get the caravan to rendezvous before you can buy us out. We get there first, you lose."

Vanderburgh shrugged in annoyance. He had not meant to speak of the caravan led by Fontenelle that would be leaving Fort Union in mid-June. "Good night, Captain Bridger. I won't need your guidance." Satisfied he had gotten the final word, Vanderburgh turned and left.

"Cap'n Bridger! Come quick! Milt's done taken to tangling with one of them half-breeds!"

Bridger slammed down the trap he was repairing. "Hope the Indian cuts his heart out," he grumbled. Nothing had gone right since Vanderburgh had shown up nearly a month ago. Right under his very nose the partisan's scouts had stolen a couple of his free trappers by offering them whiskey on credit against the pelts they had to sell. Now Milt had joined up again with his smaller brigade, bringing along some Iroquois trappers he had been able to spirit away from a Hudson Bay brigade. As usual, Indians meant families: wives, children, and young pretty daughters—in a word, trouble.

He grabbed up his knife just in case and hurried out, thinking to stop the fight before it got under way. The sounds that greeted his ears when he threw back the lodge flap dashed that hope. A cheering, roaring crowd had gathered near the main campfire. The fight was on.

By the time he had fought his way through the howling gang of men, both antagonists were covered in their own blood. Bridger recognized the Indian as the troublemaker John Gray. Gray was notorious for his nasty temper and fondness for the blade. He had laid Milt's brow open just above the left eye, and his own right arm dripped blood from a slash at the elbow.

They circled one another cautiously, their blades jagging out like silver lightning across the space dividing them. Growling like a wild animal, Gray shot out his foot, a vicious kick meant to crush a kneecap, but Milt jumped back in time. Suddenly, the tempo changed. They fought silently, waiting for the final blow.

Bridger gnawed the inside of his lip, anxious that his friend win and conscious of unthinking admiration for the superb, deft movements of these men who were courting death with every gesture.

The end came quickly; a reflexive action more clearly imagined than seen, and the Iroquois was on his back, Milt's Green River leveled across his throat.

"I ain't sayin' you ain't got a right to defend your daughter, Gray," Milt panted. "But don't go listenin' to lies. I ain't ridden her . . . and I don't aim to." So saying he swung a leg off the man and lifted his knife. The men all started forward at once, some to congratulate the victor and some to console the loser. But it was not soon enough. Before Milt could complete the act of sheathing his knife, Gray lunged up, his body twisted toward his opponent, striking Milt full in the chest with his blade.

Bridger heard Milt's startled gasp of pain and knew he had caught a bad one. A cold, hard pounding started in his own chest. As if awakened from a dream by the hissing of a rattler, Bridger reached for his Green River. Letting loose a bloodcurdling war cry, he launched himself at the Iroquois, and sunk his blade to the hilt in the man's chest.

The Indian jerked once, his weight toppling both men to the ground. Bridger tossed the dead man from him, and swirled on his knees in the dust, expecting to face an attack from one of the Iroquois' party. But none came, aside from a single female cry that splintered the night.

"It looks bad, Gabe."

Bridger turned his head at the touch on his arm. Kit was crouched down next to Milt, his efficient hands staunching the flow of blood caused by the removal of the knife. "You mean he ain't dead?" he asked in surprise.

Kit looked curiously at the big man who had killed quickly and saw that his face could barely contain the emotion he struggled to hold in. "Reckon it don't make much difference, but he ain't dead—yet."

Hope flared briefly in Bridger's eyes. Milt was one of his closest friends. He had killed the varmint who'd jumped Milt. He had done all he could. "You, there. Give us a hand," he ordered of the men nearby.

He rose, keeping his eyes purposely away from Milt's bloody face. "Loretto? You get them other Iroquois folk out of camp come first light. Don't want to see them ever again."

"It ain't gonna do him much good," one of the trappers said of Kit and Bridger's attempts to bind Milt's other wounds. "That deep one, cut lung or spleen most like. Breathin' funny, ain't he?"

"Shut up!" Bridger shot back. "Get outta here. Can't a man die in almighty peace?"

"Easy," Kit counseled softly. "It's gonna be a long night."

Milt groaned and, anger forgotten, Bridger turned from the onlookers and hunkered down next to the wounded man. "Take it easy, Milt. You got a bad cut."

Milt's lids jumped, then rolled back as a wan smile worked the corners of his mouth. "Gabe?" he breathed unsteadily.

"Don't talk," Bridger warned. "You got it in the

lung?" Milt nodded a fraction. "Damn. Thought so. Can I get you something? Whiskey? Water?"

Milt's slender smile grew. "You make . . . a damn . . . sorry mama, Gabe. Didn't see him." His eyes closed briefly.

"He ain't gonna try that devil's trick on anybody ever again," Bridger volunteered grimly.

Milt's eyes reopened. "You got him? Gray?" Bridger nodded. "Al—always could . . . count on you." He took a breath and Kit wagged his head at Bridger. "I ain't got . . . much time," he managed in a raspy voice. "You tell . . . big bro— Tell Bill I'm . . . sorry I missed . . . him this time."

"This mean we ain't moving out come morning?" asked a man at the back of the crowd.

Bridger swung around. "What the hell kinda question is that? 'Course we ain't moving out!"

"Now, wait a minute," Kit countered. "Vanderburgh and his boys pulled out yesterday morning. We're finished for the season, too. Ain't nothing to keep most of us here. You aim to continue in the fur business, you can't let McKenzie's man get the drop on you down at rendezvous."

Bridger knew Kit was right. If Vanderburgh beat him to rendezvous, he would be trying to get the free trappers to sell him their pelts. Sweat gathered and ran down his back. He would not leave a wounded man in the field. "Kit, you can see the brigade down to Pierre's Hole. I'll be along in a few days."

Kit sighed, reluctant to cross the man. "That sounds purely fine, it does. Only, who's gonna keep the independents from dealing away their pelts? They don't know me from shit, and besides, I'm a free agent, same as them. The name of the outfit don't carry no weight and you know it. It's you and you alone they'll listen to. Without you going along, we might as well stay."

"He's right." Milt was alert once more. "You gotta, Gabe. Do it for . . . all of us."

"If you figure I'm gonna leave you, Milt, you're plumb outta your skull," Bridger remarked tightly. "What's a few days?"

"You want me . . . to hurry up and . . . die?" Milt's chuckle ended in a spasmodic cough and he choked on blood.

"Shut up, you damned fool!" Bridger commanded angrily. "We'll talk things over in the morning. Nothing more tonight. Now clear out, all o' you."

But when dawn stretched slender fingers of light across the prairie, Milt was no closer to death than in the first moments after he had been stabbed.

"Cap'n Bridger, sir?"

Bridger unrolled from his robe and looked up into the face of one of his men. "Yeah. Who're you?"

The young man doffed his hat, revealing a thick fall of rich brown hair. "My name's Meek, sir. Joe Meek. Me and Milt, well, we've been friends sorta since the spring hunt and . . . well, I'd be right proud if you was to let me stay with him till he goes under. I don't mean I expect him to, I just don't mind waitin', either way. I'd kinda like to show him my thanks for lookin' after me, like." He nervously twisted his hat brim between his long hands with large knuckles. "Look, Cap'n, sir. I know you're important to the men under you. I'd feel it an honor to oblige you in this. Milt said you was a man one would count himself lucky to die beside. I believe that, sir, I do."

In spite of himself, Bridger smiled at this praise. "How old are you, Joe?"

"Twenty-two. I'm a veteran, sir."

"And you're not afraid to strike out on your own after . . . well, if Milt goes under?"

"Well, sir. It's like my pa told me. It ain't being

scared what keeps a man from doing what he might, it's being unwilling to be scared that limits him."

"A fine sentiment." Bridger fell silent, wondering if fear of being afraid had once made him a coward.

"Sir?" Meek looked embarrassed. "Well, do I get the job?"

Bridger gave the young man a gentle pat. "What will you do if Milt hangs on for days?"

"If he hangs on that long he'll be fit to ride in another week," came Meek's prompt reply.

Bridger rose and put out his hand. "Think I like you, Joe Meek. You come and look me up as soon as you make rendezvous."

"Maybe there'll be two o' us, Cap'n. Seems to me Milt ain't about to stay behind when there's women and whiskey to be had."

Bridger smiled. "Hope you're right, son."

Chapter 11

Pierre's Hole—Summer 1832

Bridger rode out across the flat bottom of the central Idaho valley to be alone. He had been at rendezvous nearly a week and no pack train had yet arrived. He slid from his saddle and began to walk, encouraging his mount to do the same. Behind him, spread out along two miles of the valley known as Pierre's Hole, were the myriad lodges and tepees of waiting men. There were over a hundred Nez Perce lodges alone. There were also the Flathead, Bannock, and Shoshone camps. Besides his own brigade and Milt's, there were Fraeb and Gervais' men who trapped on their own, bringing the total Rocky Mountain trappers to just about one hundred. And every day a new group of independents, numbering ten to twenty, showed up. Along the creek banks of the valleys a sizable town had sprung up nearly overnight. Out across the plains herds of horses and mules roamed free to graze. The biggest and most important rendezvous was about to take place.

"Too blessed many folks," Bridger murmured. And if things were not bad enough, Kit had up and ridden out after the first day.

"Thought I'd go and look around a bit for my-self," Carson had said as he packed. "You can't expect a man to swallow whole that story of yours about boiling mud and fire leaping from cracks in the ground without a look-see."

"You going to look for Colter's Hell alone?" Bridger had wondered.

Kit had just smiled and said, "If I was up to fight-ing Indians I might need a friend or two, but since I'm planning to steer clear, it'll be easier to do it alone."

And he had gone, leaving Bridger to wait it out with Fraeb and Gervais.

"Goddamn lot of help they are, too," he sighed under his breath. Gervais had found himself a young Shoshone squaw and promptly bedded down for what looked to be the entire summer. Fraeb, on the other hand, was soon to be a father.

"Damn ol' goat! Who'd o' thought 'ee still gets it up?" Dupree had snickered. "Reckon we'll know it's his for certain if it comes up squalling that God-awful gibberish o' Frapp's."

"Women! They're trouble. A hindrance and a nuisance. Won't catch me shackled to one of 'em," Bridger insisted. "They get too clingy after a while. Sent that Flathead squaw back to her lodge. She'd start whispering about marriage every time I climbed outta my britches. Tends to cool a man down right quick."

Bridger walked on a while, in admiration over what, to his mind, was the most beautiful country in the wilderness. Pierre's Hole lay at the western slope of the Tetons. Dotted with little blue lakes that sparkled in the distance, it was a wild, emerald-green paradise caught between the rugged peaks of the Shining Ones. The air was thin and clear, without the choking dust and oppressive heat of the prairie. Away to the east the nipples of the Three Breasts (as the French had named the peaks) shone a warm golden brown above the timberline.

The memory of other breasts drew Bridger's thoughts from his immediate surroundings. His mind wandered back to that day a year ago when he had held Little Fawn beneath him. She had tasted of honey, her skin as sweet as the fragrant wild grasses beneath his feet.

Instantly his groin tightened and Bridger swore. That's what he got for thinking of females. He wondered what he would do if he ran across her this year. Most likely she would be married. A year's worth of young warriors must have been plenty eager to prove their virility. Maybe she would be a little more pleasant to him this year. Ha! Well, the gal was doomed to disappointment. He would not soon forget how she had led him on. This time let her come begging. He would watch and think it over and then, just maybe, he would change his mind.

"I would speak with you, my father."

Washakie looked up at the sound of his eldest daughter's voice. "Come in, Little Fawn. I, too, would share words with you."

Washakie noted that his daughter was dressed in her best buckskin shirt, pantaloons and moccasins, all embroidered with beads and worked with quills. Her hair had been carefully combed and lightly pomaded. Most surprising to him was the fact that she kept her eyes lowered as she approached him. The attitude of respect was not uncommon for a girl when addressing her father, but Washakie no longer expected Little Fawn to adhere to this Indian custom.

"What would you say to me?" he inquired.

Little Fawn's voice was soft. "I would talk to you of marriage, my father."

Washakie studied her meek attitude and suspected deception, but decided to hear her out. "This is good. I, too, would speak to you of marriage. Come, sit. We must speak of so great a matter at length. What would you say to me?"

Little Fawn sat and folded her arms, her eyes still on the ground. "I would know from you, Father, what a man seeks in his mate."

The chief sighed inwardly in relief. "It warms my heart to hear that you are at last ready to accept the words of your mother who counsels you to wed. You have lived fifteen summers. You have reached the age to bear strong sons and beautiful, industrious daughters. Finally you are ready to accept one of the young warriors who sit and pipe upon their willow flutes until I think I shall banish them from our village or go mad!"

Little Fawn stole a look at her father's stern face and dissolved into giggles. It was true that she had many suitors this year. Each sat outside her father's lodge and played his willow flute in hopes that she would share his robe.

"I am sorry, Father, if the warriors disturb your sleep," she said when her laughter had died. "I encourage none of them, but still they insist on interrupting me when I am at work at the riverbank."

Washakie nodded. "But, surely, there is one you do not wish to discourage. This talk of marriage—is there someone you have chosen?"

Little Fawn cast an eye at the stew simmering over the lodge fire, more as an excuse to turn from her father's inquisitive look than from a desire to keep the promise to her mother that she would watch the pot. "Before I speak of the man, will you tell me what a man expects of his bride and why a man chooses one woman over another?"

"You ask a great deal, daughter. Are you so un-certain of your chosen one that you need your father's counsel?"

"My father, I have never been more certain of anything in my life than I am of my desire. But that does not promise that my desire is returned. It is that return of desire that I would learn to capture."

Washakie smiled at the solemnness in his child's voice. The matter was serious, indeed, for her to be so grave. "I will tell you what I know, but matters of the heart are not settled by words. A man seeks a woman of pleasing appearance—"

"Am I not beautiful?" she broke in, her eyes enormous with hope. "Would I not find favor in any man's eyes, even to those of the white man?"

The question was not one he had expected, but Washakie answered calmly. "You would find favor with any man who breathes."

"What else does a man seek in his wife?" she prompted.

"A man's demands are few. He would return to his lodge at the end of his hunt to find his lodge clean, his buckskins mended, and his meals hot and tasty. There is much work for a wife. The lodge must be fashioned from new hides and kept airtight and water-resistant. Then there are the children that every man desires. A warrior who covers himself with glory by counting many coup and stealing many horses may have much wealth and can afford many wives to see to his comforts."

"Like you, my father," she slipped into the pause.

"Yes, like me, Little Fawn." He reached for her hand. "There are other things you would do well to talk with your mother about. Certain things a mother can teach her daughter that her father cannot."

"You mean the pleasure a man takes from mounting a woman?" she asked in unabashed frankness.

"Yes, my child," he answered without pause. He was not surprised to learn that Little Fawn would speak her mind, whatever the subject. "A man looks for a woman who will give him that pleasure."

"And is the pleasure of the man returned to the woman?"

Washakie reached for his pipe. Their conversation was becoming more difficult than he had anticipated. As he filled his pipe he wondered if the object of his daughter's passion had caught her alone in the cottonwoods. "You are not a child, Little Fawn. I would ask if you have shared the robes of your intended."

"No," she answered quickly, but lowered her eyes.

"I remember a day last summer when you disappeared from your duties for most of the morning," Washakie said. "Your mother sent two of your sisters to search for you. Later I was told that you had gone walking in the cottonwoods with Ear-of-the-Fox." He looked at her as if expecting a reply, but Little Fawn would not meet his gaze. "I thought to receive the first of the betrothal gifts from Ear-of-the-Fox that day but learned, instead, that he would leave us. Is this the warrior who has captured your desire and does not return it?"

"No!" Anger swept her complexion. "I have told Ear-of-the-Fox that I cannot be his wife and that is why he went away. Oh, but I did not mean him to go away forever!" she wailed and threw herself into her father's arms. "I am so sorry to be the cause of the loss of one whom you called 'son.' The fault is mine, only—do not banish me."

"Little one," he whispered gently and patted her

shoulder, "is this what troubles you? Do not despair. Ear-of-the-Fox will return."

"No," she stammered. "You misunderstand."

"Do I?" Washakie gathered her close and let her head rest against his shoulder. "You are in love. You traded strong words with your intended, and he left you. It is not as you think, Little Fawn. Ear-of-the-Fox left us to seek glory for himself. He told this to me before he went away. I have tried to be for him the father he lost but the ways of each man are his own. Ear-of-the-Fox finds my path not to his liking. He would make war on the white man as I have sworn never to do. He has gone south to join our cousins, the Bannocks, whose exploits at war are well known and respected. He now fights the Blackfoot and the Cheyenne. He wishes to return to you a full warrior with many horses and many scalps. For you he does this."

Little Fawn wiped the tears from her eyes with her fingers. "It must not be for me. I have told Ear-of-the-Fox that my path lies another way."

Washakie's brow wrinkled. "Your words confuse me. Is Ear-of-the-Fox not the man you went into the cottonwoods with? Has he not asked you to be his wife? Does he not expect you to share his lodge when he returns?"

"All you say is true, Father, but I have not lain in the grass with Ear-of-the-Fox or any other man." Little Fawn composed herself and looked up at her father. "I have chosen the white trapper, Bridger."

She searched her father's face for anger or approval but found only the mask of a chief who sat in judgment of her. "My father, have I angered you? Please, allow me to explain."

"You may explain," he answered.

Little Fawn repeated the story of her vision quest,

a story known only to Ear-of-the-Fox until now. Her father's expression changed from amazement to consideration.

"I remember the day we found you," he mentioned when she was done. "Your mother was so afraid, thinking you had stumbled and broken your leg and been left behind. We searched two days before finding you. Our hearts were so filled with joy for your safety that we did not think to question your excuses." He looked at her for a long moment. "I see now that is when the change took place. Oh yes," he added, smiling at her look of confusion, "you changed in many ways after we left our summer hunting grounds. You were no longer content to run and play like your sisters, but stayed by your mother's side that you might learn from her. You think a man does not listen and watch his own children?" He laughed softly. "How would I defend myself in a household overrun by women if I did not keep an ear to the ground? I know more of you than you could guess. But not of your vision. Perhaps my mind was too occupied with the problems of our people's journey to recognize the honor the Great Spirit bestowed upon my household."

"Do not think it, Father," she protested. "I told no one of my vision but Ear-of-the-Fox." She looked down. "And only him because he would not believe that I cannot be his."

"You believe that you belong to Peejatowahooten?"

There was an element of doubt in Washakie's voice that confused her. "I do not know. That is why I come to ask you for the way to a man's heart. If my vision is a true one then it will be realized. But, I am no longer a child. I want a husband and children. Must I wait forever?"

"Such impatience," Washakie reproved gently.

"The Great Spirit works in his own time which is not yours to question."

Little Fawn hung her head. "You speak the truth, Father. But I do not wish to wait until I am old and bent with age."

"Would not Peejatowahooten then take you if it is meant to be?"

Little Fawn's lower lip trembled. "You tease me, Father."

"You would have me weep with you?" Washakie shook his head. "You say you are no longer a child. Act, then, like a woman. Patience is the quality of an excellent wife."

"But I have not patience."

He nodded. "Perhaps that is why the Great Spirit holds from you what you most desire. Or perhaps, the Great Spirit waits for you to show your willingness to follow the path he has offered you."

Anticipation leaped in her dark eyes. "How may I show my willingness, Father?"

Washakie drew slowly on his pipe. "That is for every person to learn for herself. You chose to seek a vision. Now you must seek a path to fulfill it. But I must warn you that you may fail. The man the whites call Bridger is not an ordinary trapper who comes seeking pelts and wealth in our land. Never has he bought a woman to keep his lodge." Washakie smiled. "Neither must he pay for a woman to share his robes. He is fond of women. Perhaps too fond for the hopes of my daughter. The man who has grown fond of a variety of meats will often not willingly sit to the same dish ever after."

"Unless he finds in the same dish all the varieties combined," Little Fawn amended quickly, her lips pursed in thought.

Washakie chuckled. "I believe Peejatowahooten

shall find his meals ordered according to the wishes of my eldest daughter before long."

"Do you truly think so, Father?"

"It remains for the future. A man must court that which he desires. For a woman it is the same."

"I will do this, if I have your permission, Father." Little Fawn looked at him hopefully.

"Would it matter if I denied you?" he questioned. "In one thing I will have you pledge. If Peejatowahooten refuses you, you must marry the warrior I choose for you. It is a father's right to choose the husband of his daughter."

Little Fawn jumped to her feet. "He will not refuse me."

"If he does?" Washakie persisted.

She lifted her shoulders in annoyance. "If he will not have me, then it was not the will of the Great Spirit."

"If you ain't a sight to behold! Damn it all, Milt! I ain't been so glad to see——" Abruptly Bridger broke off and swung his partner off his feet in a bear grip. "Hoo-wee! Thought you'd bought a ticket to hell that time."

"Hell? You're more like to kill me than that old Iroquois. Leave go, Gabe, 'afore you break my ribs!"

Bridger set the man back on his feet and steadied him. "You're a mite thin, Milt. And I swear you're uglier without a beard but, by damn, it's good to see you!"

"Well, you can thank Joe for that." Milt turned around and waved Joe Meek toward him. He grabbed the younger man by the hair and shook him slightly. "This here feller was my eyes, ears, and hands them first four weeks. Kept me like an old sow bear with her first cub."

Joe reddened to the ears. "Told you, Cap'n Bridger, I'd bring Milt in for rendezvous. Just kept feedin' him stories about how you fellers was goin' to be up here all alone with them purty squaws and all them barrels o' whiskey, and him stayin' down there with a rip in his chest and nobody to mourn it. He got right upset at that piece o' news. Worked so well, in fact, he about walked out o' that gulch 'afore he'd stopped bleeding. Lucky thing he didn't though. 'Twas forty days 'afore we broke camp and Milt was bare able to ride when we near about tumbled headfirst into a village of Bannocks."

"Yeah," Milt chimed in with an irritated look at his companion. "You tryin' to steal my story, boy? Just find me a place to drop my load and ply my appetite with a heap o' vittles and I'll tell you a story to put the orneriest man here to thinkin' on marriage."

Bridger groaned. "Not you, too, Milt. Is it catching or what? First Frapp. Then Gervais. Now you. Ain't a man in camp got a mind what ain't ruled by his lust!"

Milt grinned. "Look what's talkin'. Don't see you highsteppin' it outta the way of that sweet little piece over yonder." He nodded toward Bridger's lodge.

"What the hell you talking about?" Bridger turned around and stopped, nonplused. There, standing before his lodge with two of her sisters in tow, was Little Fawn. His mouth fell open and he snapped it shut as he walked quickly toward them. No doubt Washakie had sent them to inquire why he had not yet visited the Shoshone camp. He could not very well tell the chief that he kept away for fear he might jump the man's daughter and tumble her in the dust in full sight of the whole village. But as he neared her, he slowed his stride.

She was dressed as he had never seen her before.

Her shirt and pantaloons were fresh and elaborately decorated. Such clothes were worn only for special occasions. He could smell the scent of her perfume, the herbs of sweet grasses and horsemint. All of a sudden he knew a fear he could neither name nor understand. But he sensed that he was the game and she the bait.

"Well?" he demanded when he had come to a halt a few feet from her. "What do you want?" Milt's chuckle made Bridger realize he sounded too belligerent. He had butterflies in his stomach. He would have laughed in contempt if any other man had confided to him such a weakness. His hands were clenched into fists as he took one menacing step toward them. The youngest girl shrieked and hid her face in Little Fawn's shoulder.

Damn, he thought, as embarrassment flooded his sweaty face. He was reduced to frightening children.

"You're scarin' the wits outta your squaws, Gabe!" Milt bellowed. "What's got into you? I ain't after that little sweetheart no more, if that's what's eatin' you. I'll find myself a gal o' my own." He threw a companionable arm about Joe's shoulders and walked away.

Unwillingly Bridger's gaze went back to Little Fawn. In the dark, velvety depths of her eyes he thought he saw a sparkle of amusement. Did she know how she affected him? "What are you doing here?" he repeated more angrily than before.

"I come to keep your lodge," she answered in a quiet voice.

"Don't need no squaw," he shot back. "Ain't got nothing to pay you with, anyhow."

She cocked her head to one side and he realized he had curtly spoken in English. He pulled himself together. Washakie had sent her, of course. "I do not wish a woman to keep my lodge," he said in Shoshone. "I cannot pay three women. Not even one."

A smile appeared on her lips and he felt a strange tug at his groin. "I do not ask that you pay me," she offered. "It is a privilege to keep the lodge of Peejatowahooten."

He could not say why, but the suspicion that she was laughing at him raised the hairs on his neck. Scowling down at her he said, "I do not want the services of a woman. Not you, anyway," he murmured. "My women do not play tricks on me but serve me well in all things."

"I will serve you, Peeja—" She saw his frown deepen and quickly changed to "—Bridger. You know I am a good cook. I will keep your lodge clean and the stewpot simmering. You will not know that I am there. My sisters will help. You will see, you will like plenty much."

Without replying, Bridger stomped off. One more minute in her company and he'd be grinning like a blooming fool and thinking himself a lucky man. "Damn her! Know she's up to something," he grumbled.

"Something didn't smell right, did it, Joe?" Milt reached for another buffalo rib that had just been pulled from the spit. "Between us and the village the braves were fencing in their herd. They no more sighted us than they gave a holler and reached for their bows. Me and Joe figured we didn't stand a chance of outrunning 'em, me ailin' and all. So's we up and made a dash for the center of the village."

Milt whistled through his teeth. "Reckon them varmints didn't count on that. We made it clear into camp 'afore they got wind o' what we had in mind. Rode 'em right down. Spied the chief's tepee, and in a flash we was inside. Reckon we sorta surprised the old feller. Near about dropped his teeth, seein' us two white men a-trampling his breakfast. Kicked up a real fuss. Squaws shrieking and covering their eyes, 'twas a most satisfying sight."

He leaned back and tossed his bone into the fire. "It's a good thing we remembered that Indian law about the hospitality owed any man who enters the chief's tepee."

"Near about cost us our lives, anyhow," Joe volunteered. "Leastways, soon as them braves joined us. Got a bit crowded, what with ever' one o' them determined to speak up."

"Didn't even offer us a sit," Milt picked up as Joe swallowed a mouthful of whiskey. "They just commenced to jawin' 'bout what they was goin' to do with us. Chief was madder 'n hellfire that we got into camp. Didn't understand much of what was said, 'course, but we knew we was in for a bad time. Not one o' them red devils so much as looked our way, 'cept to poke a coup stick at us. Lord, them folks do love the sound of their own voices."

"Not like some," Bridger stuck in.

"Now, don't you go badmouthin' me. Funny thing was, it took them all the morning and half the afternoon to make up their minds. We never figured exactly what sorta dying they had in mind for us. Not that we had much preference. Still, when they filed outta that lodge, leaving just one old buzzard to guard us, me and Joe knew what we had to do. We was about to jump the warrior when he gives us the sign to keep quiet. Pretty soon it was dark. Well, what do you think happens? That old feller signals us to follow him and just then we hear a great commotion at the far end of the village. Folks is runnin' past our tepee like the village was on fire. The chief throws up the flap and motions us to leave. And here we go followin' him like we was out for a stroll while all hell was breakin' loose at the other end of camp. We musta run half a mile once we was out o' camp. Crossed a stream, went up a gully, and landed in a thicket, right behind the old chief. And then, what do you think we saw?"

"The most beautiful sight human eyes ever set themselves upon," Joe answered in a ringing voice.

Milt reached out and thumbed him in the chest so hard the younger man fell over backward. "You might be a fair nursemaid, Joe, but you got to work on your mouth. Keep tellin' you, this here is *my* story. Now you bait that trap o' your'n with this here piece o' rump roast and let me finish up." He tossed the meat at Joe and wiped his hands on his buckskins.

"Now, where was I? Oh yeah. We rushed up into that there thicket, thinkin' o' nothin' but hidin' our asses, and ran smack-dab into the most beautiful"— he frowned meaningfully at Joe—"the loveliest bit of womanflesh this side o' heaven. She was standin' there in the thicket holdin' onto the bridles o' our horses but, I swear, she coulda been holdin' the tail of a grizzly and I'd o' not know'd the difference. Glory be, she was fine." He closed his eyes and, lifting his head toward the sky, a half-witted smile spread over his face. "Chief said she was his daughter. Called her Umentucken Tukutsey Unde— Oh, hell, I forget. What you reckon that means, Gabe?"

Bridger scratched his head. He had heard about enough of this mooning. "Sounds like Mountain Goat," he drawled. The men that had gathered about to hear Milt's story roared with laughter. "But most likely you jumbled up the name. I'd say she'd be called Mountain Lamb if she's half the beauty you claim."

Milt stroked his naked chin. "Mountain Lamb. Hell, yeah. I like the sound o' that. Well sir, there not bein' time for talk, I grabbed up the little honey and

landed a nice juicy kiss on her soft little mouth, mounted up, and dropped her into her father's arms. Not, o'
course, before I said I'd be back come the fall. Damn,
if I ain't married 'afore Christmas."

"Sounds to me like too damned many good men
got their minds rotting with foolishness," Bridger announced in a disgruntled voice.

Fraeb raised his head at the bourgeois' tone.
"Maybe for yu, too, der is a woman, no? Little Fawn,
she come to yu without yu ask her. Maybe she got
melting loins for our Gabe. Maybe yu go and cool de
little squaw's fire?"

Milt's eyes glinted in the dark. " 'Course, if you
ain't up to it, I'd be mighty happy to see to the matter
for you."

Bridger pulled himself to his feet with deliberate
slowness, glaring at Milt. "You keep clear of that gal,
you know what's good for you. I ain't gonna tell you
again. You got that?"

"Captain, ee's got it bad," Gervais offered from
the doorway of his lodge.

"Where the hell did you come from?" Bridger
asked. "Thought you was holed up till fall."

The tall, swarthy voyageur shrugged. "A man
must keep up ee's strength. I smell de ribs. Here I am."

"A good thing, too," Milt declared as he waved
the fourth Rocky Mountain Company partner inside.
"I was just about to tell Gabe a thing or two. Was
hoping to find Fitz and Bill here. Anyways, me and Joe
heard somethin' while we was comin' in. First up, we
spied trouble in that Bannock camp. Queer enough we
was attacked without no provokin' on our part. Somethin's set them Bannocks' backs up and I don't like it
one bit. Other thing we saw in that camp was one of
our old brigade mates, and he didn't do nothin' to help
us out neither."

Bridger swung back to Milt. "What are you talking about?"

Milt snorted. "I'm talkin' about that Shoshone, Ear-of-the-Fox. He was in the Bannock camp. Growed a bit, too. Hardly recognized him. Looked to have been through a bad time. Had these festerin' places on his chest, one above each nipple."

"Sun dance?" Bridger asked grimly.

Milt nodded. "Sure thing. Looked like the poor son of a bitch had a nasty time of it, too. Plugs o' flesh was missing where the things worked themselves out. Now, why you figure a fine young buck like that would go for such a thing? The Shoshones ain't much for torture. Musta been bullied into it. Poor devil, his eyes was all glazed over with fever. Reckon I can't blame him for not standin' up for us. Thought for a while I was wrong, thinkin' it was him. Then I spoke your name, Gabe, one time, and the boy almost took my head off with his tomahawk. God almighty, heard it sing past my ears like an angry wasp."

Bridger stared at the campfire with narrowed eyes. This was not good news. The Bannocks were generally peaceful. And while they were easier to provoke, they had posed no serious threat to trappers as a whole. "Think it could be they're being riled by the Blackfoot?"

"I wondered," Milt said. "Thought they looked to be fresh from a battle. Joe and me saw a few scalps hanging out to dry but there wasn't much time to visit." He winked at Bridger.

"If they know the Blackfoot are receiving rifles from whites it won't matter much to them which whites it is," Bridger mused aloud. "Damn McKenzie and that fort of his. He's causing a stir he'll not easily quiet down." A murmur of agreement rippled through the throng of men.

"What do you make of that business with Ear-of-the-Fox?" Milt asked.

Bridger hunched his shoulders. "Can't say. Don't seem to be our business. But I reckon the Bannocks are. I'll check the guards around the camp. Better warn them to keep alert. Bill will be in any day now and we'll be full of enough lead and powder to blast them Indians clear back to the other side of the Divide. In the meantime . . ." He let his voice trail off as he left the lodge.

The clear blue of twilight had faded to violet when he entered the lane leading to his lodge. From a distance the tepees shone in the night like gigantic lanterns, their golden skins glowing from the fires that warmed them. He paused a few feet from his own, resting his hands on his hips. He heard voices coming from inside. "Little Fawn?" he murmured in surprise.

Bridger balanced on the balls of his feet, ready to disappear into the shadows if anyone should emerge from within. Idle fascination kept him rooted to the spot. His better judgment told him, however, he should ride over to the Shoshone village and inform Washakie that his daughter was thinking of taking up residence in his lodge. What did she expect of him? Could she not feel the heat in his gaze when it touched her face? Did she not know the look of a man who had caught the scent of a female, and stood flesh-fired and ready to enter her?

The trembling began in his belly and he growled deeply in his throat. He would not, could not, allow her to move in on him like a frisky colt in the protection of an old mare. He would teach her once and for all the danger of stirring a banked fire.

The movement of his hand nearly tore the flap from the tepee, but Little Fawn merely smiled and rose to her feet when he presented his broad, long-legged form in the doorway.

"You are tired and must be hungry," she soothed in her softest voice. "Fetch Bridger's pipe and a plate of stew," she instructed her two sisters. She smiled at him shyly. "You must forgive them if they are slow. We are unfamiliar with your ways but we will learn quickly. What else would Bridger desire?"

He looked deep into her face, unable to decide if the innocent tone was a clever disguise. If so, she was as cunning as an old cougar. He shrugged and dropped down by the fire. "I will have my moccasins removed," he drawled. If she wanted to play lodge squaw he would see her a good run.

Instantly she was on her knees before him, lifting each foot into her lap as she peeled away the tough shrunken leather. During the year he seldom removed his moccasins. Wading in streams made them shrink and twist until he found that he often could not get them on when they had dried.

"Bridger would like a new pair of moccasins?" she asked when she was done. "My sister, Twin Arrows, will fashion a pair for you. She has only eleven summers but she can make moccasins any man would be proud to wear."

By custom, the squaw seeking the attentions of a warrior offered him a pair of moccasins made by her own hands. But, surely the eleven-year-old had not set her heart on him?

"Where's the stew you promised?" he bellowed suddenly. To his satisfaction the three girls shrieked. Almost at once the satisfaction died. The youngest, Twin Arrows, began to weep, her round little face dissolving behind a veil of tears.

"Hellfire and damnation!" he roared and came to

his feet. He swiped his moccasins from Little Fawn's hand. "Get these children out of my lodge. Now!"

He threw back the flap and disappeared into the night.

Chapter 12

Bridger told himself that he had to go back sometime. It might as well be now. He had rechecked the guards and given enough orders that his men would be grumbling behind his back for days. He simply had to go back to his lodge and sleep.

He hung back from the door to his lodge, uncertain whether his relief was greater than his disappointment at finding his fire so low that the tepee no longer glowed. He hitched up his trousers and lightly pulled the flap aside. She was gone. He could sleep now. That was all he wanted.

The banked hearth had been expertly set, and the hardware and tools of his trade neatly hung from the lodgepoles in the manner of an Indian household. He tried not to be pleased, told himself that he would have done it himself when he got around to it. In fact, he preferred the clutter. A woman was forever trying to set a man to order, disturbing the perfect disorder that was his nature. But when he stuck a finger in the warm stew and carried it to his lips, he had to admit that the girls had done a better job of his rabbit than he would

have done on his own. Still, that was not reason
enough to invade a man's home, uninvited, and he
would not soon forgive the insult.

He subdued the image of himself as the roaring
bear in the midst of a trio of doe as he pulled his shirt
over his head. He had done no real harm. He might
even see his way clear to buying them a string of their
favorite blue beads. Maybe they thought they owed him
something for . . . He halted his undressing, his
trousers about his ankles. What could they owe him?
He owed them, by his figuring.

"Hell! Why couldn't they have just said Washakie
sent them instead of acting all mysterious?" He stepped
out of his trousers and tossed them aside. The nights
were chilly but he preferred the brisk air next to his
skin after months when he never shed his clothes. He
padded around the lodge checking his rifle and saddle-
bags before crouching down and grabbing his buffalo
robes.

The sudden movement and feel of flesh beneath
his hand gave him a nasty turn he would not soon forget. He went down of all fours, throwing himself over
the thing that was tangled in his robes. The squeal kept
him from bludgeoning the culprit with his rifle butt,
which he had reached for. With a strong jerk, he tore
the buffalo skins from his captive.

"You!" he shouted in anger.

Little Fawn sat up, her face a soft blur in the dim
glow of the embers. "Bridger comes home," she whispered in a sleepy voice which trembled slightly as she
focused on his blazing expression.

"Don't call me Bridger like I was a dog," he demanded savagely. "My given name's Jim. Just what the
hell do you think you're doing here, anyhow?"

"You told me to send my sisters away. This I
have done. Did you think that I would leave you, too?"

"Yes," he answered before he could stop himself. "Aw, that ain't what I mean." He reached out and placed his hand against her cheek. "You're so young. You don't know what you're doing and I sure as shooting don't know what I'm liable to do if you stay. Don't you understand, little girl? A man can only stand so much pushing till he gets the urge to push back. And more than push, he needs to pull and shove and drag till he gets the satisfaction of the woman beneath him. You ever lay with a man?"

"Only you," she murmured.

"God almighty, that don't count!" His voice broke on the words. "There's a powerful lot more to laying with a man than trading a few kisses. And don't you go telling me you don't know what I mean." He caught her by the chin and wagged it. "You know what you're doing here?"

Little Fawn turned her face so that her lips rested against the inside skin of his wrist. "I come to be with you, Jim."

Bridger felt his insides leap. "You ought not to say things like that if you're gonna take them back," he growled.

Little Fawn sat up, loosening the robes wrapped about her. His eyes went to the soft flesh bared to the night. "I want you to teach me everything that makes a man find pleasure in a woman." She reached out and tentatively touched his beard. "The Indian is not a hairy beast. The white man is like a bear. When you kiss me I want to laugh and sneeze. Can you teach me not to do this?"

The groan was dragged up out of him by the last effort of his conscience and then he reached for her. She was in his arms, his mouth swooping down on hers in possession. He did not question why she felt so perfectly suited to him, why her curves fit his angular lines. She yielded and molded against his hard, heavy body as though cut to fit him. All that mattered was that her arms could reach about him and her thighs fit the indentation of his waist. The sweet agony of possessing her was like nothing he had ever known. It was a new thing for her and old, beyond reckoning, for him. But her awkwardness melted under his experienced caresses and his senses woke anew under the gentle probe of her tongue.

She didn't cry when he entered her; he did not expect it from an Indian woman. He knew he was the first, and a smile smoothed his mouth until dragged away by the intense assault of their bodies. His cry overlapped her moans in the final moments and he wondered fleetingly if he would be the butt of jokes the next morning. Then she was curled next to him, the sleek lines of her back pressed against his hard, flat belly. He wanted to relive this night again and again in the days to come.

"It ain't forever," he murmured in drowsy denial. "It's only for rendezvous. Can leave anything. Anytime."

"It's them! Bill's a-bringin' 'em in!"

The bellow rolled through the rendezvous camps. Vanderburgh stumbled groggily from his tepee to look out across the valley to where the Opposition camp had gone wild as rifle shots split the silence of the morning. "What's that caterwauling about, Fletcher?" he demanded.

"Caravan, sir. They're saying the Rocky Mountain Company done brought in the first pack train." He eyed the partisan warily. "Guess that means our boys won't be in time to save our contracts."

"Nonsense," Vanderburgh countered sharply. "A day or two won't make much difference. It'll take the

Opposition that long to unpack and organize. Send out a fresh rider to scout for Fontenelle and Provost. They can't be far behind. Fort Union is half the distance Sublette's men have crossed in coming from Independence." He returned to his tent, giving no indication of the frustrations seething beneath his stoic exterior.

"Damn you, Fontenelle," he whispered bitterly. Where could the man be? At least McKenzie's plans were proceeding according to design, judging by the outrider he had sent ahead of the caravan. The Blackfoot were up at Fort Union signing a peace treaty that would take them off his trail in the coming season. Now he had to get supplies in before Bridger.

As he dressed, Vanderburgh reminded himself that it was not his job to beat Bridger at his trade, but to make it impossible for him to reap any benefit from that trade unless he cooperated with the Company. Still, it smarted to know Bridger had beat him in getting supplies. It was as if McKenzie went to considerable trouble to limit the success of his men in the field. Left to his own devices, he would have gone out into the wilderness and, during a conflict over stream rights, would have pulled out a rifle and put an end to the competition once and for all.

Vanderburgh pulled on his boots in short, angry tugs. That is what any military man would have done. The only way to eliminate the enemy was to gun him down. A pitched battle to the last man, that was all it would take. But, of course, McKenzie could not be persuaded to see it that way. He had wanted to incorporate the Opposition trappers into his company, once they were bested.

He spit out a curse as his boot slid over a raw blister. He could not wait to get back to civilization. When his fortune was assured he planned to go back to Indiana, maybe look over the political situation.

At least McKenzie had taught him that much. The man's main objection to an all-out battle hinged on his concerns over public opinion. McKenzie was afraid that word might get back to Congress, where the merest whispers of wrongdoing would be enough to send some senators into spasms of delight. They had a formidable proponent in William Clark, Superintendent of Indian Affairs, who, along with his partner Meriwether Lewis, had first opened up the Northwest to the Americans nearly thirty years before. Clark had gotten Congress to outlaw the sale of whiskey to Indians and a new law would ban whiskey in Indian territory altogether.

Congressman William Ashley, too, had a good deal to say about the conduct of Americans in the Northwest Territory. He had made a fortune in the fur business by sending Sublette, Smith, Bridger and the others out here in the first place. Yes, Vanderburgh mused, every man connected with this business in the last thirty years had come away with wealth and political prominence. Perhaps he would add his own name to the roster.

"Mr. Vanderburgh, sir?" Fletcher stuck his head into the tent. "A rider just come in from the Rocky Mountain Company camp. Mr. Bill Sublette sends his greetings. Says you're invited to dinner. Says you're to bring the men, too. Hospitality from one mountain man to another."

Vanderburgh slipped into his coat. "Tell them I'd be delighted. Don't gawk, Fletcher. I've told you before, you don't understand the subtleties of business. At least this time I'll have the chance to converse with educated men. I've had about all I can stand of that mountain goat, Bridger."

"What do you mean, he ain't with you?" Bridger

glared at Bill Sublette, a tall, sandy-haired man with a long scar down the left side of his face from an Arikara tomahawk.

"You mean he isn't here?" Bill boomed back in surprise. "Hellfire! I sent that little redhead ahead of us more than two weeks ago to tell you to hold out, we were nearly here. Took my fastest mount. Ain't any of you men seen him?" he asked of the independents who had gathered round to join in the celebration of the incoming pack train.

The round of denials brought the two men's glances together in grim understanding.

"Ain't got to be like that," Milt assured quickly. "You know Fitz. That little Irishman ain't about to go under without us hearin' about the mess he made of the boys what made him come."

"Coulda been a mountain lion. Mebbe a b'ar. Ain't gonna know nothin' 'bout that till one of us runs into his carcass," Dupree volunteered. "Poor doin's for certain."

"Must be tired, Bill," Bridger said quietly. "You about wore the hide off your arse making it in as quick as you done. Didn't really hope to see you till the end of the month." He slapped the older man on the back. "I'm right glad to see you, only I wish . . . Well, you're here and rendezvous is begun, official. Milt, get them supplies unpacked. Dupree? You start cutting that alcohol, if you think you can keep your head out of the jugs long enough to do it. Get Loretto to help you."

Dupree screwed up his face. "Them Spaniards, the way they take in liquor, and him worryin' 'bout me! Wagh!"

"Getting mighty tired of this business of losing men," Bridger admitted wearily when Bill, Milt, Fraeb, and Gervais had joined him in his lodge for a partners' meeting.

Bill drew out a bundle of cigars and passed them around. "You heard about Jed, Jim? Real sorry."

Bridger nodded solemnly. "Reckon when it's a man's time, he goes under. Still, Fitz didn't seem ready."

"I know," Bill mumbled as he bent forward to light his cigar from the burning straw Little Fawn held out for him. His eyes ran quickly over the beautiful girl, then he said, "This here loss goes beyond mere friendship. That's not to say that friendship ain't important." He looked at Bridger. "But you boys got a business to run. And I'm here to collect. What you figure to be the worth of your catch this year?"

Bridger had been busy watching Milt's hand, which had rested for an instant on Little Fawn's thigh, but he answered the question after intercepting Milt's gaze and exacting an apologetic shrug.

"We figure to have sixty thousand dollars in pelts. That don't count what we stand to make on the Indian trade and the independents what worked with us. Of course, we got our debts to pay." His mouth twisted in pain. "That sorta figuring was Fitz's line. Reckon Milt'll be taking on the books for us." Milt was once again staring at the back of Little Fawn as she bent over the stewpot. "Or could be we'll be burying your younger brother, Bill. That child don't know when to leave well enough alone."

The remark drew Milt's attention. His gaze flickered to Bridger's hand fingering his Green River. "Now, Gabe. You know better than to accuse me o' stealin' what don't rightly belong to me. Just lookin'. A man can't hold it against a friend for lookin'."

"You got the bawdiest eyes in the territory, Milt," Bridger criticized. "Got the girl looking like she's been mauled and you ain't even touched her. Keep out the way," he warned.

"Sure thing," Milt replied, watching in relief as Bridger's hand moved away from his knife.

"I swear, Milt, you're more trouble than a motherless cub," his brother vowed in disgust. "You figure you can keep your mind on business long enough to help me go over the company books?"

"De question is, who will watch you?" Fraeb asked with a wolfish gleam in his eye.

"You care to step outside with that complaint?" Milt sprang to his feet, knife in hand.

"Sit the hell down!" Bill and Bridger yelled in unison. "Appears to me we got ourselves a problem," Bill continued in a more normal tone, ignoring the two men who were glaring at one another. "Jim, you got any ideas?"

Bridger shook his head. "Not right off, I don't. If Fitz turns up I won't have to. May as well see if Dupree's got the first batch of whiskey ready for drinking. Looks to me we could use a sip. Going to send a man to look for Fitz, too." He got up and left.

"If I was you, Milt, I'd plant my rear back down," the older Sublette cautioned in an undertone. "You look a bit green around the edges. You been fighting again?"

Milt shot his brother a look of disbelief. "You mean to let that ol' weasel get away with callin' us thieves?"

Bill chuckled. "If Ma could see you now, she'd take a bar of lye soap to your hide and a hickory switch to your britches. Frapp's got a right to have his say. Owns a piece of the business. I'd a done the same myself, in his place."

"What will happen to Fitz's share?" Gervais wondered, speaking for the first time.

"Yeah?" Milt threw an ugly look Fraeb's way but sheathed his knife and sat back down. "What happens if Fitz don't turn up soon?"

Bill wiped his mouth on the back of his sleeve. "Didn't want to say nothing in front of Jim, seeing as how he and the Irishman are so close, but there's Blackfoot swarming all over the Divide this year—Gros Ventres to be exact. Shot up our camp two weeks back on Green River, near the South Pass. Them Indians surprised the stuffing outta us, firing into camp with all the rifles of a military platoon. We lost four horses, but no men. Guess they just wanted to flex their muscles. However, if Fitz ain't here by now, he won't be coming. And that means you boys got a problem."

"Yeah." Milt agreed, and threw Fraeb a last dirty look. "If Fitz was the brains of this outfit, Gabe is the heart. And the heart's about gone outta him these last weeks. Ain't sure he won't be hiein' out on a new trail if Fitz don't show."

"*Ja.* Milt's right," Fraeb announced. "Gabe, he don't look so happy. Ve vorry he leave da business."

Bill rubbed his jaw. "That's poor news, indeed. Gabe—is that what you call him now?—don't seem himself, all right. Any of you know the reason why?"

Milt looked at the girl standing by the fire and shook his head. "Beats the hell outta me. He's got just about everythin' a man could want. Maybe it's them Company boys trailin' us that's got him in a fret." He sat forward, an earnest expression on his face. "You know what they're tryin' to do? Them bringin' in a caravan ain't the half o' it," and he went on to recount to his brother the events of the last two years.

When he was done Bill gave a low whistle. "I'd heard some of it but there's worse to tell. Back in St. Louis, Astor's people are forcing the price of beaver so low it won't hardly pay to bring a caravan out here this year. Was thinking I might have to raise my prices."

"Can't do it," Milt said flatly. "You raise anything one cent and the independents will just wait for the Company train to pull in. It's got to be a wide open rendezvous or we go under, permanent-like."

"*Oui*. De price, he must stay low," Gervais added.

"Okay, okay." Bill threw up his hands. "I'll keep things the way we agreed. But when the trading's done and rendezvous is over, we'll talk again. Where do you reckon Gabe has gotten to with that whiskey he promised?"

Little Fawn slipped out of the lodge without attracting the attention of the men. She used her hand to shield her eyes from the summer sun that rode the crest of the mountains. Bridger was not in sight, she noted with misgiving. He had warned her after the first day not to venture far from his lodge when he was not about, but she had felt the younger Sublette's eyes on her all afternoon and doubted that she would be more safe inside.

Wiping her hands on the skirt of her working dress, she started across the camp. She had not understood most of what the men had said but she remembered the one called Fitz. He was a little man with hair the color of a sunset and a crippled hand. Her people called him by that title, Broken Hand. If he were dead then Jim would be suffering, though he would never tell her so. But she knew. He talked of the man with flaming hair often when he held her in his arms before they slept. The bonds were strong between them, like those a tribal brother felt for another.

Whistling trappers made crude invitations to her as she made her way to the south end of the camp. Then she saw him. Standing fifty yards from the camp, staring out across the open valley floor, was Bridger. He stood alone, his rifle draped over one arm. Her heart yearned for him.

Bridger did not turn when he felt a small hand slip through his arm. He had heard her advance, the soft swishing of her moccasins in the grass a familiar sound to him these past two weeks. "Why are you here?" His voice was deep and distant.

Little Fawn leaned her head against his upper arm. "It is not always good for a man to be alone with his grief."

"How did—?" He turned, staring down into soft brown eyes and another familiar feeling came over him. He had come to rely on her. She often satisfied his desires before they had fully formed in his mind. She would know that Fitz was missing and that he might be dead. "You shouldn't have come looking for me. By nightfall every man in camp will have enough whiskey in his belly to make him think he's got the hair of a black bear inside him."

Little Fawn smiled up into his stern face. "You would not want another to mount your woman? I am glad. I belong only to Jim."

He was immediately sorry he had shown the least concern. He shrugged free of her. "You keep sashayin' about, wiggling your arse in Milt's face and you won't have no say so at all. That boy'll hump anything that looks female."

Little Fawn turned away to hide her frown. Whenever she tested his feelings he became angry. "I thought you were pleased with me. I thought you wanted me for yourself alone. I will not be shared by your friends like an old robe."

"Damn right you won't," he insisted feelingly and spun her around to face him. "Not that it matters much one way or the other to me but, if you want to sleep in my lodge, you will do no night crawling. Do you understand?"

Little Fawn's lower lip began to tremble as his cold, gray stare pinned her. Why did he always like to remind her that his only interest in her was that she pleased him when he mounted her? "Sometimes I do not like you, Jim," she said in a whisper. "Sometimes you treat Little Fawn very bad."

Bridger grinned suddenly and pulled her hard against him. "Sometimes I think you are right, little one. I am a hard man. Remember that when it comes time to say good-bye." He pushed her out of his arms. "Now. What brings you—? What the blazes was that?"

Out of the corner of his eyes he had caught sight of a flicker in the underbrush near the river. In one motion he pushed Little Fawn behind him toward the village and swung around with his rifle ready. "Run back to the camp, honey. If that's a scout from a raiding party I don't need no help and you'd just be another thing to worry about. Now git!"

He shoved her again up the path and started toward the riverbank, his Hawken balanced in his hand, ready to fire. He went quickly into the cottonwoods nearest him, ducking down when the underbrush grew too thick. First on his knees, with brambles tearing at his face and clothes, and finally on his belly, he crawled toward the spot where he had sighted the movement.

No sign of disturbed animal life nor flutter in the thicket lessened his certainty that what he had seen in a split second was a man. He could not afford to be wrong about such a thing. In ten years he had learned never to be wrong about the shape of a man. He was sweating from exertion when he reached the place along the riverbank where he had seen the figure. The man he hunted was uncommonly adept at hiding.

Maybe, this time, he thought grimly, he would not see the arrow or tomahawk that could spell his death.

Reflex action pulled the rifle to his shoulder, but memory froze his finger on the trigger.

Naked, emaciated, his skin torn and scratched in so many places the blood made a red crisscross stitchery over his body, a white man stood in the clearing, his eyes glazed over with fever and his legs trembling.

Bridger scrambled to his feet and dropped his rifle as he ran toward the man. "Fitz? My God, Fitz! Is that you?"

At the sound of the voice the man fell to his knees, his arms raised over his head in protection. "I can't run . . . no more. Kill me, damn you! Have done!" he wailed pitifully.

Bridger's belly pitched and bile rose into his throat at the sound of Fitz's voice. In shocked recognition, he realized he should not have known Fitz at all. Every hair on the Irishman's head had turned pure white.

Bridger dropped to his knees beside the whimpering man and threw his arms about him. "It's all right, Fitz. You're safe now. It's Bridger. You hear me? It's Gabe."

Fitz raised frantic eyes to Bridger's face, their blue depths unseeing in their fear. "It's Gabe!" Bridger roared and shook the man by the shoulders. "Got to get a hold of yourself. Can't have the others seeing you like this. Fitz, you hear me?" But the man keeled over into the grass when Bridger let him go.

Bridger scooped the bruised and starving man into his arms and started back to camp.

"Give that man another mouthful of whiskey. Not that cut stuff neither. The unadulterated jugful of the real alcohol," Bill said as he passed over another tin keg of liquor to Fitz.

Fitz sat huddled before the campfire, a blanket thrown over his nakedness. The liberal doses of whiskey were slowly restoring the color to his thin cheeks. His smile was lopsided as his eyes passed around the ring of men. "Faith be praised, I never thought to see you lads again."

"Shut up and eat," Bridger growled. "Damn fine thing you done, wandering off like some greenhorn. What'd you think you were doin', making like that idiot Yankee Bill brought in with him?"

The chuckles were for the Yankee trader, Nathan Wyeth. Sublette's pack train had picked up Wyeth's brigade on the trail just out of Independence.

"Tell us again about the boats on wagon wheels Wyeth had with him, Bill. Was there really four o' 'em?" Milt probed.

Bill wagged his head. "Can't say for certain. Heard that story second hand from one of Wyeth's men. Can tell you they were wearing the damned silliest uniforms I ever saw. All brass-buttoned with fancy leather boots. And carrying little tin horns. Give 'em bugle lessons, a feller told me, so's they can signal one another over the plains." Bill guffawed at his own story, and even Fitz was holding his sides as laughter shook the entire company.

"Shoulda left 'em for the Injuns," Dupree offered.

"What, and have them Blackfoot think that's the sort of critter we got coming out here from now on?" Bill waved his tin cup around. "A toast to the dumbest, greenest Yankee ever to set foot out of Massachusetts!"

"Where's he now?" Bridger asked when the hooting died down.

"Reckon he's trying to convince the last of his

men to stay out here with him." Bill grinned. "Got to give credit where it's due, though. Didn't have to tell that Yankee the same thing twice. He'll shape up just fine with someone to show him around a bit."

Bridger recoiled in horror. "You ain't thinking of me?"

Bill snorted. "Suppose not. But he's had a bad time of it. Suffered a lot of mishaps on the trail. Storms were fierce the first part of the journey. Then came the alkali pains, stampedes, and injuries. And you know, every one of them twenty-four boys caught the mountain fever. Such bellyaching you never heard in your life. Course that was before we ran across the Stephens brigade. Nineteen hungry souls left stranded last season when the Gant-Blackwell partnership went bankrupt."

"Geez, Bill! You tryin' to run us outta the territory by yourself?" Milt cried. "Ain't it bad enough we got to deal with McKenzie's sorry asses without your draggin' in every stray cur what happens to be clinging to life?"

"Have another drink, Milt," Bridger advised, passing his cup. "Truth is, Bill, you do seem to have brought too many boys into camp for our own good."

"Oh yeah, sure," Bill replied. "You would have left them out there. Don't give me that. You can go stuffing every dude from here to Taos with them mountain man stories. Only don't expect me to believe them. Half the men you got under you stay because they know they don't have to worry about being left behind to rot if something goes wrong. They know they count for something with you, Gabe."

"Ah hell! Where's Vanderburgh?" Bridger called out gruffly, hoping to cover his embarrassment at such lavish praise. "Maybe he ain't coming after all. Not that I mind, not with Fitz here." He looked the Irishman over. The trembling had stopped and his wide grin was the best assurance that he was himself again. "Suppose you're up to telling us what you been up to these last weeks? Besides running through the Rockies in your bare-butt birthday suit."

Fitz swallowed a gulp of whiskey. "Sure'n if it doesn't sound like you're glad to see me," he sallied.

"Ain't sure I am," Bridger returned calmly. "I been out here for the better part of two years while you been gallivanting all over God knows where."

"If that don't sound just like my wife h'yars poor meat," Dupree put in from the back of the crowd. "Bless her old rawhide heart, she's the reason this child's out here."

An appreciative rumble of chuckles rolled through the men. "Well, Fitz, I'm waiting," Bridger insisted.

"Blessed be the Holy Mother for I don't remember the whole of it." Fitz shook his head wearily. "But seeing it's you asking, Gabe, here goes." He took a long breath and hugged his robe a little tighter. "Started off right enough. Riding one horse and leading another, I rode out from the Sweetwater to tell you boys that it looked to be Bill was gonna make it in first."

"Yeah, I'm in first," Bill answered.

"Then why's it so quiet over in the other camps?" Fitz asked.

"Uh ... reckon that's my fault," Bridger confessed slowly, his eyes sliding from the Irishman's. "Bill just pulled in at noon, and first thing we know'd was that you weren't with him. It sorta put us off from trading. Kinda like firing shot with damp powder."

Fitz's brow shot up clear out of sight behind a forelock of snowy hair, but all he said was a mild, "That so?"

"Go on," Bridger urged.

Fitz smiled serenely. "I was riding mostly at night,

knew there were Injuns about, sign was everywhere you looked. Made it through the South Pass slick as greased lightning and went on north to Horse Creek, making good time. It wasn't till I got up into the mountains that I ran into trouble, and even so, it was a bad piece of luck things fell out the way they did."

He shook his head in wonder. "I was in a small valley, hemmed in by flat, straight canyon walls, when all of a sudden I looked up and there I was plumb in the middle of a whole migrating village of Blackfoot. Must have fallen asleep in the saddle. I was practically into their camp 'afore I knew anything. Dropped the reins of my lead horse and lit out like wildfire.

"Them braves were right happy to see me. They came tearing out across that plain after me in nothing flat. Dug my spurs into my animal till the blood was running down her sides like sweat. We must have made every ridge around, hoping to find a quick way out of that valley. O' course, I knew from the first it was a lucky break I wasn't gonna get. The horse under me had been ridden hard. She gave out so quick I thought at first a stray shot from them Blackfoot had caught her. Didn't have time to check. Just hied out for the crop of rock up ahead. Them devils behind me was raising such a noise they fairly lifted me up that mountainside on their voices alone. I was tiring about the time I spotted a crevice in them rocks. Crawled in quicklike and scraped together all the loose brush and small boulders in sight to hide the opening.

"Warriors were all over them rocks in a second, chanting and bellowing to the Great Spirit for my scalp." He reached up and touched his hair gingerly. "Reckon my scalp was a bit disturbed by the possibility of leaving home, too."

He shook himself and waved off the offer of more liquor. "Knew my only chance was that them Blackfoot weren't about to move every rock from the side of that mountain. Only I did begin to wonder after a while. They made a camp just feet from my front door, spread themselves with war paint and commenced to offering sacrifices for their Manitou. If I hadn't been so worried about my hide I might have enjoyed knowing I rated such a big to-do.

"The damn business went on all day. They poked and picked and bent every inch of that ground till I gave up hope of them missing me. But when night came, I was still holed up safe.

"I crawled out of that hole when they went back down to their village. Discovered they'd posted a guard. Nothing for it, I crawled back in and waited. Another day went by while I sweated and they hunted. Come nightfall of the second day I decided to take my chances, being so thirsty I didn't much care what happened. Crawled out and got the first bit of luck—the guard they had posted was fast asleep. So I cut a wide path around their village on foot. Come morning I cached in a thicket. Them Indians weren't too dumb, though. They musta found the place where I'd been hiding the last two days 'cause they swarmed out in every direction, following my tracks till nighttime. Took to sucking on rocks to keep my juices flowing. But I'll tell you the truth, I'd rather have had a cup of whiskey. Got any more, Bill? Thank you, kindly."

"That all?" Milt protested when it seemed Fitz had given out.

Fitz lowered his cup. "Ain't it? Well, of course, I had to walk the rest of the way to rendezvous. And them Blackfoot, they didn't give up the chase till I cut across the Snake River. Moccasins gave out after a few days. Tried to cut a new pair out of my leggings but they wouldn't hold together. Reckon I would have made better time, but my rifle got busted when I fell down a gully early on. Just me and my Green River. Ate mostly berries and roots when I could find them. Figured them Indians couldn't be far behind, so I kept moving. Knew when I caught sight of them fat-nippled Tetons I was on the right trail. Took a bit of doin' but I made it."

"Reckon I owe you an apology, Fitz," Bridger said. "Thought you was just lollygagging about, wasting time. Didn't know you was out collecting the best story this rendezvous is going to hear."

"I take that kindly," Fitz returned with his cup lifted. "Here's to the best damn outfit these here Rockies are ever gonna see."

Cheers echoed throughout the valley floor, the men toasting and dancing in an all-out celebration of the brigade's reunion. Bridger added his deep voice to the huzzas. Beneath the laughter, though, he knew what the crossing must have cost Fitz, and his admiration deepened for the Irishman. "Damn fine man," he murmured under his breath. "Not a bad storyteller neither."

Chapter 13

"Goddamnit, Gabe! Does he have to stay through the whole blessed rendezvous?" Milt jolted his sleeping friend, his eyes hard and angry as they watched Vanderburgh down his latest cup of alcohol. "He's been in camp swilling our whiskey nigh on a week. Get rid o' him." Once more he prodded Bridger.

Bridger rolled over and supported himself on an elbow. "What did you go and do that for, Milt? I ain't had a full night's sleep in days."

"Keep outta that squaw of your'n an' you won't be so powerful tired." Milt winked. "Figure you could use some help?"

"Don't try it," Bridger replied and dragged himself upright. "And don't say no more to me about that bastard Vanderburgh. I had about all I can stand of him."

He scrambled to his feet and crossed the clearing. He stopped for a moment to join a circle of onlookers betting and urging on a pair of wrestling trappers. The two muscular men were naked and smeared with bear grease, making their wrestling holds harder to keep.

A little farther on he was nearly trampled by a stampede of riders racing through the camp. He swallowed the dust they raised and cursed, wishing he had his rifle handy to pick off a few of them. The whole camp seemed to pitch and weave before his eyes. He reckoned that most of the figures bobbing in and out of his sight were as walleyed drunk as himself. He passed a game of sticks that had been in progress since the beginning of rendezvous. The current gambler was a broad-bellied Crow who was down to his breechcloth. He took the intricately carved and painted fox bone in one fist and transferred it from one hand to the other, all the while singing a mystical song.

Bridger paused, curious about the stakes. Neither money nor pelts lay on the ground between the gamblers. Finally the Indian flung his arms wide, jerking his head and body in time to his rhythmical song. Immediately a cunning trapper called out and pointed to the Crow's right fist. The Indian looked stunned, his eyes widening as he opened his hand, and the little bone fell to the ground. A great holler went up as the trapper ran into the center of the ring to claim the astonished Crow's breechcloth and belt.

Bridger shrugged and walked on. Another naked Indian did not make much difference at this stage in the festivities. In fact, he would be a lot less noticeable than the trapper and squaw coupling on the ground near his tepee. He looked at the girl's face, decided he did not know her, and moved on. Just so long as it was not Litttle Fawn.

This rendezvous was better than any he had ever remembered. And there seemed to be the fellowship that had been missing the year before. "It's amazing the amount of friends a man can make with a few barrels of whiskey," he had mentioned to Little Fawn the night before as he lay on his robes while she rubbed the stiffness from his shoulders.

He had been participating in a tomahawk-throwing contest that day, taking on any newcomer until his muscles ached. But he retained the title of best in the territory.

"It's in the wrist," he had explained to her while she smeared him with the thick black oil from the Popo Agie River. It was not good for much else, but he and the other trappers swore by it for easing the aches of chilblains. "Like most everything else a man does, he's got to learn how to manage that fine difference that makes his effort count."

Little Fawn had leaned over him then, her bare breasts caressing the side of his face as he lay on his belly. "And you, Jim, do you manage the fine difference in all things?"

He had turned over quickly and pulled her down on top of him to demonstrate the answer to her provocative question. And she had matched him, effort for effort.

Bridger did not enter his lodge immediately but settled down cross-legged before the doorway to try and settle a perplexing problem. He looked out through the noisy camp, his mind centering on the girl in the lodge behind him.

Little Fawn had been with him a month. She asked nothing of him, just mended his clothes and kept his fire burning and stewpot full of delicious grub. At night she disrobed before him, as if she had done it all her life, and climbed into his robes without question or request. Sometimes he purposely held himself from her to see what she would do. But on those nights, she merely turned from him and snuggled her back to his front and fell asleep. Other nights he went too far and the next morning there would be circles under her big dark eyes and bruises where he had been overeager with his hands. She never complained, just smiled at him with a tenderness that made him feel guilty and uncomfortable.

It would have been a lot easier if she had gone at him with a knife the first time he had left a mark on her, he thought. He would have subdued her, slapped her rear a few times, and threatened her with all kinds of hell he had no intention of carrying out. Then she would know her place, and he would be certain of his. He felt he was being slipped into a new harness without knowing where the bondage would lead him. She never asked for anything. Maybe that's what bothered him.

"I'll buy her something and that'll be an end to it," he declared and came to his feet. The Rocky Mountain Company had cleaned up at rendezvous, their pack train of tobacco, whiskey, lead and powder, new traps, foofaraw, and other requirements quickly traded for nearly every pelt in camp.

Bridger headed directly for the Nez Perce camp, his money jangling in the pouch tied about his neck. The Nez Perce had been practicing selective breeding of their horses for years, and their animals were the best to be had anywhere. He had been over to their stockade earlier in the month, selecting replacements for those that had been lost during the year. One in particular had struck him—a pig-spotted rump bay, a breed the Nez Perce proudly called Pelouse. He was not sure it was broken in enough to be a buffalo horse, but it would be a perfect gift for Little Fawn. If he would be paying a fortune when most men handed over foofaraw, well then, he guessed she was worth it.

As soon as he walked into camp he knew he would have to haggle with the herd leader, a portly warrior named Wolf Heart.

"You buy for hunting. Good horse. Go fast," the Indian began when he saw Bridger sauntering about the willow barricade.

Bridger rubbed his jaw in doubtful consideration. "Good for running, maybe. Strong deep chest, yeah. But hunting buffalo, the legs are too delicate. Step in a gopher hole, they'd snap."

Wolf Heart raised his hands in horror. "That animal no hunt buffalo? I kill self if horse prove to have bad heart."

Bridger swallowed his grin. "You kill self over every poor horse you sell, you'd be dead ten times over. I ain't buying it for me, anyhow. It's for my squaw."

The old Indian's expression turned sly at that news. "You buy maybe for Nez Perce girl? Father of Young Sparrow most glad to have fine buffalo horse. Maybe trade daughter for it."

"I ain't buying no wife," Bridger shot back irritably. "Thing is, I'm trying to pay the girl off. She been keeping my lodge for rendezvous. Thought to give her a mount of her own."

"You give horse to squaw who keeps lodge?" The fat jaws of Wolf Heart's face waggled in disbelief. "You got Nez Perce girl? Make plenty good lodgekeeper. Make plenty good ride, too. I send you a granddaughter; you pay out in horseflesh."

Bridger sighed in frustration. "I got a Shoshone girl. Don't need no other."

Wolf Heart shook his head, his lips pursed in disapproval. The Nez Perce and Shoshone were old enemies, enforcing a truce between their sporadically warring nations at rendezvous time so that trading could take place. "You don't need fine horse for Snake girl. Buy her swayback mule. She knows no difference."

Two hours later he was leading the frisky,

spotted-rump horse back through camp. He thought he had not done too poorly. Twenty dollars plus two bolts of scarlet cloth seemed quite reasonable. He was whistling by the time he reached his lodge. And for the first time since he could remember, he was wondering what her reaction would be when he handed Little Fawn the reins and told her the horse was hers. If she was truly pleased he might buy her a saddle blanket and a leather saddle with silver ornaments next summer. But there would be no next summer. That is why he had bought her the present—to say good-bye.

A little embarrassed to present the gift right out in front of everybody in camp, he decided to tether the horse in a stand of cottonwoods. He would go and get her and bring her back.

Little Fawn rose instantly when he entered, her hands still tangled in her freshly washed hair. "You are back," she said in a glad voice. "You are hungry." She began to reach for the pot but Bridger waved her away.

"I'm a grown man. I can look after myself. Besides, I have no hunger." He made a brushing motion with his hand. "You finish your hair."

He sat down, enjoying the chance to observe her female primping. She smelled better than anything he had ever embraced. There were many things he would miss when rendezvous was over. Too bad he was not the marrying kind.

Little Fawn picked up her brush, a porcupine tail section inserted into a wooden handle, and smoothed the tangles away. She dipped a finger into her pomander and the pleasant, fruity scent filled the air as she rubbed it into her hair. She made a center part and reddened it with vermilion. Then she spread a light creamy lotion on her cheeks, and crushed a few herbs which she scattered onto her old dress before tucking it away for the next day.

When she rose, her bare feet and the long fall of her hair over one shoulder caused that familiar tightening in Bridger's groin again. The thought that he would soon leave her behind made his need more urgent. He reached out for her, intent on feeling her writhing beneath him, and remembered the horse. Unaccountably, the desire to put her happiness before his made him change his mind. He would wait until he had given her the gift and then spend a lazy afternoon making love to her in the cottonwoods. That is how he wanted to remember her.

Little Fawn sucked in her lip uncertainly when she saw the desire flare up and die in his eyes. She had come to know, to look for, that light that made her stomach lurch and her loins melt, like snow upon which spring sunshine spreads its light. "You find disfavor with Little Fawn?"

Bridger shook his head. "I find nothing but good with Little Fawn. You look so pretty I want to show you off a bit. Put on your moccasins; we will walk."

She slipped her shoes on and walked over to him. Bridger smiled down at her, slapped her on the rump, and walked out of the lodge ahead of her. He did not turn to see if she followed him; it was the custom that one's woman walked a respectable distance behind. Not until they reached the cottonwood shelter did he turn and wait for her, leaning his rifle against a tree and folding his arms across his chest.

She came quickly over the grass, her presence less disturbing to the animal life than his own. He wondered if that was because she smelled of the woodland herbs, sweet pine and dried summer flowers.

"You say you want to show off Little Fawn.

There is no one to see me here," she teased with a toss of her head.

"Perhaps I should have said I want to show off something to you," he responded. His shoulders came away from the tree trunk where he lounged and he pointed to the clearing in the grove. "What do you see there?"

An exclamation of delight burst from her. "You have bought a new mount! Oh but he is beautiful!" She went right over to the Pelouse and began stroking his arched neck. "It is a Nez Perce horse." She wrinkled her nose. "They have their uses. Their horses breed true. My father says it is the Great Spirit's gift of kindness for making them fat and ugly and very bad warriors."

Bridger chuckled. "Your people have a way of turning a compliment into a two-edged blade. What does Washakie say of me?"

Little Fawn bent her head to the animal's mane, hiding her expression. "He thinks you are a great man with powerful medicine."

"Is that all? Had he no other words for the daughter he allows to come and share my lodge?"

"He says you are a man fond of many dishes," she stammered slowly.

Bridger looked quizzical. "A man of a large appetite, is that what he meant?"

Little Fawn raised her head. "Perhaps so. Will you ride him for me?" she beseeched suddenly, turning the question aside. "What will you call your horse?"

"So many questions. He is for you to ride." He bent and, lifting her by the waist, swung her up and over the animal's bare back. "There," he said, tossing her the loosened tether. "Try him for size."

She dug her heels into the Pelouse's belly and the horse started forward, his strength all but unseating her as he sprang away. Bridger cried out after her in alarm, but she was tearing across the grove and out of sight before she could bring the big, snorting horse to a walk.

Bridger's heart leaped into his throat when he lost sight of the tiny girl bouncing dangerously on the horse's broad back. He cursed up a blue streak as he took off on foot after them, thinking he should have ridden the animal first to test his spirit.

When he burst through the underbrush onto the open plain, he saw, to his immense relief, that she had turned her mount and was coming toward him at a sedate, ladylike pace.

"He is wonderful, beyond the best of my father's herd," she called out to him. "You will be glad of his speed when you trap in the land of the Blackfoot."

The wild ride had hitched her dress up to the top of her thighs and the expanse of smooth brown leg against the darker roan of the animal sent the heat in his body scurrying in every direction. His eyes grew dark in anticipation of getting her back into the shelter of the cottonwoods. It was the only thing on his mind when he yelled out, "He's yours, a gift for you to add to Washakie's herd."

Little Fawn hauled in the reins with a strength that surprised both man and beast. She slipped from the horse's back and ran through the bunch grass, throwing her arms around Bridger's waist. "Oh, I am so happy! I knew he was too fine an animal to ride to death on the plains!" She leaned away from him, tilting her head back so she could see his face, but he kept her arms about his waist. "I will make my father understand that the gift of this one horse is more valuable than a dozen of the usual kind. I will tell him that with eight daughters to marry he must not become greedy with the first. Other suitors will fill his corral to overflowing." She bent her head to his chest once more, her body trembling in excitement. "I love you, too, Jim Bridger. I shall be a good wife to you."

He stepped back, tearing her arms from about his waist. "That ain't no wedding gift!" he shouted in an irate voice.

"Oh, but it is enough. You will see," she promised, tears standing in her eyes. "It is enough for me. You must not worry."

"You got it wrong, girl. It's a personal gift, a thank you, from me to you. We won't talk wedding or marriage. I'm leaving in a few days and—"

He stopped and threw up his hands. How had his plan come so far from the point? He should have known what all her attentions were leading up to. He took a deep breath and looked directly into her eyes. "You been a good woman this summer. I enjoyed your company. You ain't asked for nothing for your trouble. I thought to repay you, that's all. That animal's yours, not Washakie's. My gift to you."

"He's—he's . . . ?" Little Fawn's smile crumbled, her eyes welling over with pain. "You do not wish to marry Little Fawn?"

"Christ!" Bridger swung away from her. "It wasn't supposed to be like this between us. I warned you from that first day." He turned back to her, a plea for help in his eyes. "Told you I wasn't in the market for a wife. You said you came to be with me, nothing about wanting marriage. You tricked me!"

He knew he was being unreasonable, but he felt cheated of his pleasure in surprising her with the horse. She was supposed to be happy and grateful, expending her joy in spending a lusty afternoon in his arms. Instead, she stood before him with tears splashing her cheeks and her face crumpled with disappointment.

"You like me no more?" she sobbed. "You find other squaw?"

For a moment Bridger felt something akin to relief. This kind of reasoning he understood. "If that's what's got you upset, then the answer is no." He put out his hand to touch her but she backed away. "There ain't no other woman."

He stopped, for he had been speaking English. In Shoshone he said, "I have found no other woman to share my robes. It is not a matter of growing tired of you. I have never been happier with a woman." He lifted his broad shoulders in a helpless gesture. "I am not a marrying man. No woman would suit me."

Little Fawn bit her lip, her tears barely controlled. "I do not want your gift. I do not want payment for what I do from love. You keep the Pelouse."

"Ah, girl, you're making too much of this," he groaned in exasperation. "Come on back with me to the cottonwoods and we'll talk some more."

She understood the deeper meaning of his words and backed away again. "You no love Little Fawn?" she asked in an uncompromising tone that would brook no lies.

"I gave you the horse, didn't I? Don't that count for something?"

She had not heard what she wanted to hear and turned her back to him as he started toward her. "You stay back!" she yelled in the first show of temper he had seen all summer. "You think to be rid of me, to toss me aside like an old pair of moccasins. But you are wrong, Jim Bridger. I am in your blood as you are in mine." She tossed her head in an unconscious gesture of pride. "The medicine is strong, the power great. You will not be able to leave me behind. You will come back. You will see. You will not be able to keep away."

Later, he realized that she had done what she meant to do. She had sent him away feeling defeated when he should have been the one to drive her off. But he was too bug-eyed angry to think of anything other than taking a lodgepole to her small, defenseless body.

"All right, dammit! Have it your way! We'll see just how goddamn long I can keep from sniffing about your skirts, and I'll lay the goddamn horse down as ante. You keep him till I come back, you hear me? He's yours till I come a-crawling back on my belly for you. And dammit all, I hope you got the gumption to send me up Green River if I'm so sorry-assed as to turn up!"

He stalked off in a blind rage, hoping some dumb, unsuspecting trapper would look at him cross-eyed before he made it into camp where he would surely pick a fight with a good friend. He needed to break some poor bastard into about a million splinters before he was going to feel any better.

As luck would have it, he met three unsuspecting independents before limping into camp, three unwitting trappers who quickly understood why folks said Jim Bridger was born with the hair of the grizzly in him.

"Lord, ain't you a sight!" Fitz declared when his big friend slumped down beside him. "You been wrestling grizzlies? Hey! You're bleeding on my new buckskins."

Bridger put a hand to his half-closed right eye and it came away with a slick glob of blood. He was missing a patch of whiskers on his left jaw and the knuckles of both hands were like raw meat. "Shoulda seen the sons of bitches when I finished with them," he mumbled through broken lips. He felt around in his mouth to learn that no teeth were missing, though two felt uncommonly loose.

"Caught them peeling their eyes over Little Fawn?"

Bridger took a swing at Fitz, but he was too tired and the Irishman too quick.

"What'd I say?" Fitz roared in affront. "Never mind. Faith, you're a wee sorry sight. Buck up, lad, with a touch of the spirits." He put a cup of Taos Lightning in Bridger's hand. "It won't make you well, but you'll care a lot less about your condition," he advised with a grin. "Besides, when you're done, Bill wants to talk with the partners."

"That's about it," Bill said regretfully. "Sorry, boys, but the books don't lie."

"Are you sure you've figured it right?" Milt's voice was raspy with disbelief.

"Sorry to say, we checked them twice," Fitz answered. "There's no way around it. When all the debts of credit are paid and our part of the supplies, totaling thirty thousand dollars, we've got about seven thousand left to split five ways."

"Ve bin robbed!" Fraeb bawled, thumping the ground with the butt of his rifle for emphasis.

"Now, hold on," Bill cautioned. "Fitz himself hired the only man at rendezvous who don't drink to manage the store. Nothing got past him for want of a sober head."

"That's a fact," Fitz concurred. "That Charles Larpenteur ain't much for socializing, but he's a hardhead when it comes to business."

Bridger had been sitting back, listening passively as the others talked. Now he rose from the floor of the lodge and walked over to the place where Bill had layed open the account books of the Rocky Mountain Fur Company. He looked at the incomprehensible scrawl in disbelief. "You trying to tell us we're worse off than when we bought the company two years back? That don't shine, Bill, and you know it. We done outtrapped, outtraded, and outwitted every other outfit in the mountains this last year. We've sweated blood and given up a few good men to bring in more and better pelts than any man's ever seen at one time. We can't be that bad off."

A wriggle of alarm worked up Bill's spine as he stared into Bridger's silvery gaze, smooth and frightening as a honed blade. He was older than Bridger, had known him since Jim was nineteen. But he saw for the first time what the others had been telling him for years. Bridger was a magnificent example of the breed of men who made the fur trade possible in this territory. But he had no patience for the ironies of life or the vulnerabilities of running a business. If he could not accept the answer he had been given, he would walk out, and none of them would ever see him again.

"Listen up, Gabe. The measure of profit in this business has always been the markup on trade goods. That's where Jed and Jackson and I made our money. So did Ashley, near the end of his years. McKenzie's boss, Astor, has been driving up the wages for the men and forcing down the price a pelt will bring us on the market back East. They can afford to wait it out and take a loss while they're doing it." He looked around the lodge, feeling it safe to leave Bridger's steely eyes and address the other partners. "You boys got to realize that you're running a losing proposition."

"Is that why you sold out to us when you did?" Bridger interrogated.

The question hung in the air while Bill took his time before facing Bridger again. "Are you calling me a cheat?"

"I ain't calling you nothing. That's for you to say."

Bill hesitated, then nodded grimly. "I know what you're thinking and it ain't quite like that. Jed and me figured we'd seen just about everything this part of the country had to offer. Wasn't we the first to open up this territory? Do you remember, Gabe, that God-awful time we had making it up the Missouri that first year? Well, things was looking sorta tame after a few years. I realize that you got your hands more than full with the Blackfoot stirred up the way they are. Only, well, you love a fight better than most of us. Where another man thinks it's prudent to turn back, you go dead center on."

"You know why," Bridger replied softly.

Bill nodded once. He remembered the Hugh Glass incident well. "Thought you'd forgotten that. You should. Proved yourself a long time ago."

"We ain't discussing me," Bridger growled. "Go ahead, keep on explaining why you're rich and we're piss poor."

Bill's face twitched. "I'm not making excuses, and any man who thinks I am can just step outside. I'm not that long out of the wilderness."

"Ain't asking you to do that, brother," Milt cut in. "Just think you owe us that explanation, like Gabe says."

"Okay." Bill shrugged off his anger. "I'll tell you what you're doing wrong, if you want my opinion." He took a cigar from his pocket, thought better of lighting it, and stuck it back. Such tactics might prove useful in a St. Louis boardroom meeting, but he knew it would not set well with this crowd. "Any time a man goes into business he's taking a chance. Jed and I knew we were getting tight that last year. We decided to get out. Gabe, you and Fitz came to us. We didn't force you," he added quickly. "We gave you the same terms Ashley gave us three years earlier. 'Course we knew Astor's men were scouting out the territory. They'd been out here and driven right back in '27. They aren't the only ones with an eye on the territory. Ran across a feller by the name of Bonneville who's on his way out here. He's got Astor money backing him, too. You boys got to come to terms with the fact you're going to be doing a heap of sharing of these Rockies in the next few years. Best thing to do is stop trying to buy out every trapper who sets foot in the area. You're offering wages that's cutting your profit way down. You're paying out tribute to every tribe in the territory and taking great risks up in Blackfoot land. What you need to do is rid yourself of the competition long enough to make one clean sweep of your streams in the coming year. The profit, minus all that trading and bribery, will set up the lot of you as wealthy men."

Bill smiled, satisfied with his logic, and decided he deserved that cigar after all.

"Sounds good!" Fraeb volunteered.

"Me too. I like it," Gervais added.

Milt looked at Fitz and then at Bridger. "Well, Gabe?"

Bridger had drawn out his pipe and was tapping tobacco in the bowl. "I got two questions. How we gonna keep Vanderburgh off our trail? And what are we gonna do for a living when we are rich men with no territory left?"

Bill shook his head. "You're hardheaded, Gabe. With your money you can pack up and go home. Back in St. Louis you'll be a celebrity. There's plenty of folks just waiting to hear about how you lived all these years out here in the wilderness. You can settle down, buy some property, maybe even find a little gal and raise a family."

"You mean set myself up civilized." Bridger drew on his tobacco. "No more dodging arrows and sleeping

with one eye open so's I don't get my scalp lifted. No
more wandering through stretches of unending desert
and drinking mule blood to keep from starving. No
more discovering that just over the next ridge the land
drops off so quick and beautiful it about takes a man's
heart outta his chest. No more valleys so green they're
misted over with silver so's a man won't shame himself
with tears at the sight. No more mountains sticking up
bald above the timberline where the snow covers the
brown knobs most of every year."

He carefully tucked in the flap of his tobacco
pouch before looking up at the older Sublette. "That's
what you suggest I give up. No sir, I don't think so,"
he declared when he had breathed a ring of smoke into
the air. "I'll just stay right here. But I'd be obliged if
you'd tell me how to get rid of McKenzie's men."

"I didn't say you'd get rid of them, exactly." Bill
looked to his brother for help, but Milt merely
shrugged. "Listen here, Gabe. You must have come to
the same conclusion as the rest of us. You can't go on
fighting an outfit the size of the American Fur Company. You'll have to settle with them, that's all. You
ought to think about going over to Vanderburgh's
camp and sitting down with a map of the territory and
dividing it up between you. You take the western slope
of the Rockies—it's still mostly virgin streams—and
McKenzie's fellers get the east. They haven't gotten
their supplies yet and some of their men are getting
anxious to get back into the field. You could make extra money by outfitting them from our store. Good
God! It's there for the taking."

"Bill's talking sense, Gabe, though don't none of
us want to hear it," Fitz put in when Bill was done.

"If none of you wants to hear it why let him say
it?" Anger and frustration boiled through Bridger's
words. "Do you realize what he's asking? Bill wants us

to just walk over and hand our livelihood to men who don't know the first thing about surviving in this land. Money don't give them rights to come out here where they'd have died that first year if they hadn't caught hold of our shirttails every chance they got. And you say cut a deal with them, give them half!" he roared. "I say let them come and take it, if they got the balls to try."

"Hold on," Milt objected, rising to his feet. "You got no right to talk to Bill like that. He's just telling us how he sees it."

Bridger turned on Milt, his expression as hard as granite. "You agreeing with him?"

Milt shrugged, his eyes falling before the man's. "What if I am?" he challenged, his chin coming up. "What did we come out here for if not to make a few dollars? Stands to reason we must cut a deal or go under. Like Bill says, it's the perfect time. Vanderburgh's stuck here till Fontenelle comes in. He ain't gonna wanna be the last to leave the valley. He'll think he's got off with the goods while we'll have the year to make good our debts and line our pockets."

Bridger walked over and picked up his rifle propped by the door flap. "You're fooling yourselves if you think Vanderburgh will keep to the bargain. Even if he would, you think McKenzie will?" He eyed each of them in turn. "Milt and Fitz, I knew you wasn't planning to live out your days here. But Frapp, Gervais, and me, we ain't got nothing to go back to. Everything we know and love is out here and I'll be damned if I lose my corner of it to the likes of Vanderburgh. You go ahead and meet with him if you want. I can't stop you. But I'm planning to hunt beaver come morning. You're all welcome to come. We'll start out for the Yellowstone first."

He turned and walked out. His image as a man alone silenced the others until he was out of earshot.

"He's right, you know," Fitz said finally. "By damn, we know he's right and yet it's the only logical thing we can do."

"How come, then, we feel like a barrel of snakes?" Milt asked in a sour voice.

Bridger was sitting in his doorway when Fitz came striding through camp about daybreak. From his grim expression, Bridger knew where the Irishman had been.

"Looks like summer's about gone," Bridger commented matter-of-factly. Fitz turned, shrugged and dropped down in the dust beside him. "See that mist over yonder?" Bridger continued. "It comes in about this time every year. Won't be lifting till past noon. Aspen's turning silver already. Another week and the cottonwoods'll be golder than a five dollar piece. Yeah, it's about time we was riding out."

"The sons o' bitches said they needed time to learn the territory better so they'd know they were not being cheated!" Fitz burst out. "Cheated! Shit! They wanted to talk about honorable intentions."

"Reckon you can be ready to ride today?"

Fitz turned on his companion with an incredulous look. "Your ears broke or something? Didn't you hear what I just said?"

Bridger chewed a blade of grass. "If you can't be ready then Frapp'll get first shot at the season. Was by a while ago; so cussing mad he was making less sense than usual. Figured he'd been over to the Company camp. Told him to take Milt with him a spell. Ain't feeling right friendly toward the Sublettes right now. Thought it might ease things a touch if they was to go

south to the Snake River a while. Take that Yankee,
Wyeth, with them, too."

Fitz looked away. "What about Gervais?"

"Going it alone with a few men and the Shoshone
nation down to the Bear."

Fitz swallowed over the tight spot in his throat.
"What about me? You aiming to see me off in any particular direction?"

Bridger turned his head to look at the Irishman
slowly. Fitz's bones were again covered with flesh and
his color was good, but there were lines cut deep in his
face that would never leave him. His white shock of
hair still took some getting used to. "Reckon I'll keep
an eye on you myself this time. You keep getting lost
when my back is turned."

A great grin broke out over the Irishman's face.
"You aren't holding no grudge? Then why you sending
Milt away?"

Bridger spit out the grass. "Milt's got business
down south. Seems there's this little Snake squaw,
name of Mountain Lamb. Girl saved his and Joe's lives
last spring. He's been talking some nonsense about
marrying her ever since. Might as well let him hang
himself the way he wants."

"And Bill? You going to say good-bye?"

"What did he say to Vanderburgh?"

Fitz chuckled. "Don't think I ever saw Bill so
damned mad. He cussed them Company partisans up
one side and down the other. Told them they weren't
the only ones with friends in high places. Mentioned
William Clark was a friend of his and warned he'd be
watching, and if McKenzie made one false step he'd
make it known clear to the halls of Congress."

Bridger nodded, a glimmer starting in his eye.
"Knew Bill would come to his senses."

"He said more, Gabe. Told Vanderburgh he

would begin establishing trading forts of his own come the new year. Threatened to beat McKenzie at his own game. Said we were all here to stay."

Bridger rose to his feet, staring off in the distance with a smile on his lips. "Reckon I'll mosey on over and wish Bill Godspeed going home."

Chapter 14

A thin plume of dust signalled the advance of riders cutting across the bottom of the valley. Bridger was just finishing up his turn as guard at the south end of the camp. He peered through the telescope he had purchased from the Sublette pack train this year. His experienced eye told him they were white men. They would be Fontenelle's outriders, he thought. But as he watched them approach, he noticed that neither man seemed in full control of his mount. They were waving their arms wildly, and though their cries were lost to the wind, Bridger immediately sensed trouble. Hoisting his rifle, he let off a warning shot toward the camp.

"Hurraw!" he roared. "Trouble's riding in!" He set out on foot toward the riders. Milt and Fraeb's brigade had ridden out at dawn the previous day. It must be they who were in need of help.

He recognized the younger of the two men first. It was the eighteen-year-old cousin of Wyeth's. A passing moment of chagrin spread over him. The boy had been nothing but one big pain the ten days he had been at rendezvous, complaining and despairing of returning home. If he had merely gotten lost riding out with Milt then Bridger had roused the camp for naught.

"It better be a good one, boy, or you're gonna be sorrier than ever that you come out West," he muttered as he stopped to wait for the rider to reach him.

But his misgivings eased as they neared. The man riding with the younger Wyeth was a veteran of Fraeb's outfit. He would not be along to comfort a bawling brat. There was trouble of a real nature brewing.

"What'd you make of that?" Fitz asked as he came scrambling up beside Bridger, his rifle loaded and ready.

"Looks like Milt mightta run into trouble," Bridger replied. "Best get the boys rounded up. Appears to be we'll be fighting Indians 'afore nightfall."

A few minutes later his suspicions were confirmed when the two men arrived.

"Captain Bridger, sir, we're being attacked by Indians!" the Wyeth boy cried, his breath coming so quickly he could hardly hold his horse. "Mr. Sublette says I'm to tell you it's Gros Ventres, a whole village of them. We're outnumbered three to one. The brigade women and children are right behind us, only we were sent on ahead to get help."

"Must be the same village what's been wandering about these hills all summer," Bridger mused aloud. "Fitz, you think they might be the one's attacked you?"

Fitz nodded. "Can't be too many villages of that size about. Reckon we better get on out there before Milt and Frapp beat us out of all the fun." Smiling, he broke into his brogue. "Sure'n if 'tis not my duty to show at least a few of the laddies a return of their hospitality."

Bridger nodded. "Better send a couple of fellers to

look for the folks coming in. We ain't got time to defend women and children while fighting Indians."

"You aren't really planning to attack those savages?" The Wyeth boy had knelt on the ground and listened to the conversations about him.

Bridger pushed his hat out of his eyes. "What did you expect, son?"

"Well, it certainly seems reasonable that you should at least give them a hearing," he answered promptly. "You seem a good deal too eager to fight it out when a short discussion and compromise might accomplish your goal as easily." He pulled a handkerchief from his pocket and wiped his face, still raw and peeling from the harsh crossing of the arid plains a month earlier. "A war chief, so I'm told he was, rode out ahead of the rest of his tribe with a pipe extended in his hand. It is a sign of peace, even I know that. And you know what happened? No sooner did our two ambassadors reach the poor man than they jumped him and shot him, point blank!" The horror on the boy's face made a few of the trappers chuckle.

"Well, really. It was the most treacherous act I have ever witnessed," he shouted. "You may think yourselves better than the Indians, but I think the act contemptible."

Bridger snickered at the boy. "Somebody get this boy a drink and keep him in camp till we return." He shot the Yankee a hard look. "While you're waiting, you get the camp guards to tell you about Indian tricks. They'll tell you Milt did right. If it'd been the Crow or the Shoshone he'd have handled it different. With Blackfoot there ain't no such thing as peace. They'd tell you that themselves. It was a trick, boy, pure and simple." He ducked his head in farewell and turned back to camp to collect his horse and gear.

"How far away you figure they are?" Bridger

asked the second rider who had fallen into step beside him.

"Can't be more'n five, six miles." He chuckled. "Most of them boys was still so full o' whiskey they couldn't stay long in the saddle. Milt let 'em off easy the first day. Said he could understand how they was feelin'."

"Most likely they're sobered up now," Bridger commented. "Ain't nothing like a village of Blackfoot to clear a man's head right fast."

Half an hour later over one hundred trappers were in the saddle, accompanied by Flathead, Nez Perce and Shoshone warriors. They covered the distance at a full gallop, the cries of half-sober white men mingling with the war cries of their red-skinned comrades.

Bridger rode at the lead with Fitz and Bill. The sounds of the battle reached them as they crested the ridge that led them out of Pierre's Hole.

"Listen to all that there caterwauling," Dupree yelled as the brigade leaders paused to determine their strategy.

Bridger gazed out grimly at the scene below. The Blackfoot had barricaded themselves in a grove of willows near a creek. "Looks to be a couple of hundred of them penned in good and tight. It's gonna be a long one," he commented as he spurred his horse forward down the slope into the next valley.

The sound of hundreds of riders thundering into the valley momentarily halted the exchange of gunfire in the two camps. The Gros Ventres could have pulled up stakes and made for the hills. But as he neared, Bridger saw the reason they did not. A willow-log wall had been erected in the thicket by the Indians. He swore under his breath. Milt must have been drunker than usual to have allowed the Indians to fortify themselves with such a vengeance before attacking.

"What the hell's the matter with you, Milt?" Bill scolded. "You lost your mind total, or you been nipping at the whiskey ration?" He jumped from his horse and faced his younger sibling with a wrathful expression.

Bristling from the tongue-lashing, Milt roared back, "Didn't see you galloping at them head-on, brother. You got any ideas, you go out there and try 'em yourself." He shot his partner, Fraeb, an ugly look, but the Dutchman merely grunted. "You try hauling a brigade of sops into order before a whole nation o' Blackfoot and see how far you get. Saved nearly every damned life. What'd you expect?"

"Ease up," Bridger said as he swung out of his saddle. The makeshift camp they had thrown together was not close enough to reach the Blackfoot by gunfire. "Reckon you could have got a mite closer," he mentioned after a moment. "Wasting shot and powder at this distance."

The old Dutchman nodded vigorously. "By damn, that's what I tell dem. Stupid ve are here and Injuns dere."

"You got casualties, Milt?"

"No!" Milt bit out.

Bridger's gaze swung to the Yankee, Wyeth. "You any good at tending wounds?"

"Yay-ah," the New Englander drawled.

"I'd be obliged if you'd do me the favor of helping out."

"Be right neighborly if you'd return the favor sometime."

Bridger noted the twinkle in the man's eye, but his expression did not soften. For the past ten days the Yankee had been questioning the trappers about the best beaver streams, but even soaked like sponges in alcohol, the men would not reveal the source of their livelihood. "I did already. Kept that young cousin of yours back at camp. Won't find a bullet hole or arrow in him anywhere." He turned away abruptly. "Fitz, you see a way outta this fix?"

"Looks like the only thing to do is to move up closer and commence to blasting them out of that thicket," Milt volunteered before Fitz could speak.

Bridger studied Fitz's furious expression. Fitz resented being cut off by Milt. After what he had been through, Fitz thought it his right to mastermind the bloody attack on the Blackfoot. Still, Milt was a good fighter, tough and dependable, and would not be for making a fool of himself a second time. "Okay, Milt. It's your fight."

Milt's grin, never far away, split his face. "I say we take a few of the seasoned boys and rush the grove. Move in tight and sit and pick 'em off a few at a time. We rattled 'em good, scalping their war chief. Gave 'em somethin' to think on."

Bridger cocked an ear to the renewed war chants rising out of the Indian barricade like a howling Blue Norther. "They don't sound too upset by their loss. They're putting on paint and working themselves up for a real to-do."

"We brought some Flatheads," Bill reminded him. "There's a few of them who'd take it right kindly if you'd include them in your party. They've been fighting Blackfoot with sticks and stone arrows so long they just about need to test their new rifles against McKenzie's issue."

"We'll give 'em their own side o' the thicket," Milt suggested. "We'll take the white volunteers in on one side, the Flatheads and other Injuns can have the other flank. Get them together, Bill, and you got it."

"A mite chancy," Fitz murmured at Bridger's shoulder when the men were assembled and the two parties divided up to rush the willow grove.

Bridger sat on his heels, his rifle balanced on his knees and his body shielded behind a clump of scrub. "Milt knows what he's doing. Anyhow, he and Frapp are in charge. It's their fight. We just come along to join the fun." He snorted in mirth.

Fitz whistled. "This piece of revenge should be mine."

Bridger cut his eyes to the side. "You don't look especially frisky to me, yet. Could've stayed back at Pierre's Hole. None would have faulted you. Damn, have you ever heard such screeching in all your born days? Ain't enough we got to listen to them Blackfoot; Milt's gone and stirred up the Flatheads."

Fitz shrugged and moved a little away. He knew the end of a conversation when he heard one.

Milt's shout to rush the log barricade roared over the yowling cries of both sides. Bridger jumped to his feet, the thirst for battle moving him and forty other trappers into the open. A hail of arrows from the enemy camp fell short of their marks, but the sight of the barbed steel arrows made Bridger's flesh crawl. He would rather have lead shot in him than one of those damned things.

A bullet whizzed past Bridger's right ear and he dived headfirst into a scrawny sagebrush patch. Milt's party ran on, roaring battle cries and holding back their shot to get a closer vantage point.

"Damn idiots!" Bridger grumbled under his breath. He lifted his rifle to pick off a Blackfoot warrior who had climbed the barricade to take aim at Bill. The rifle recoiled against Bridger's shoulder and the Blackfoot toppled from his perch. But the warrior fired his rifle as he fell. And Bill, too, went down howling with pain.

Automatically Bridger reached for his powder and lead in the sack that hung about his neck. His eyes riveted on the fallen Indian until he saw him move. "Winged him," he murmured. The Indian was struggling to position his rifle so that he could fire it, but his right arm was useless.

Bridger popped several lead balls into his mouth while tamping gunpowder down the barrel of his rifle. It seemed like an eternity to a man under fire, but he had his rifle reloaded in twenty seconds. "Goin' after Bill," he mumbled.

Tearing a large clump of sagebrush from the plant, he went down on his belly to crawl out into the grassy field. He edged forward on his elbows, his rifle grasped in one hand, the sagebrush clutched in the other. Ahead of him the battle raged in full force, arrows flying in all directions. One arrow swooped in on Bridger so closely it pinned the fringe of his buckskin sleeve to the ground. He sucked in a breath, tore his arm free, and moved on a little quicker. He knew the clump of brush afforded no real protection, but it did make a precise shot on his head more difficult. Crawling on his belly was not the best of strategies, as it left him exposed to random gunfire and flailing arrows. But he was able to move, and Bill, wounded as he was, would sooner or later be picked off.

"Get back, you whiskey-sotted idiot!" Bill yelled when he spied Bridger edging up on him. Before he could say anything else, the rangy mountain man was on him. Not caring to argue the point, Bridger raised up and delivered one swift uppercut that rendered Bill unconscious and easier to carry. Bridger lay in the grass a few moments, took his time in aiming, and picked off another warrior peering cautiously over the top of the barricade. He poured powder and spit a ball into his barrel, packing another shot. He smiled. He had made his point. His medicine was powerful. A warrior would think twice about attacking him. Maybe that would buy him enough time to get Bill back to camp.

Bridger hitched Bill onto his back. Balancing the heavy man with one knee on the ground, he waited for a barrage of arrows to strike a deadly pattern about them. Then he lurched to his feet and started racing back in the direction he had come.

"Suppose you expect my thanks," Bill grouched a few minutes later as he sat propped up by a cotton-wood trunk.

"Don't expect nothing," Bridger returned mildly as he dressed Bill's wound. "You're lucky. Flesh wound. It'll heal. Still, you're out of the fight."

Bill winced as he tightened the bandage. "You're calling me a fool."

"Didn't say that. I'll be going back to the front now. Milt and Fitz looked about ready to take cover, last I saw of them." He made a final knot in the cloth and picked up his rifle. "Milt's wasting powder and lead. Ain't nobody gonna blast them Blackfoot out from behind that wall they built. Mountains to the rear, river beside them, they're inside indefinitely. It won't take him much longer to figure out what's to be done."

"Must you always make a body beg you for your opinion?" Bill snarled, the pain in his arm adding to his sense of uselessness.

Bridger turned back, his eyes hidden behind the brim of his flat-crowned hat. "You asking my opinion? We can sit here four or five days peppering the hillside with shot. Or, we can give up and go back, hoping them Indians will clear out, which they probably won't."

"There's got to be another 'or.' "

Bridger struggled to keep the laughter out of his voice. "So there is. It's—"

"Hellfire and damnation!" Fitz came tearing through the underbrush. "You got to get back out there, Gabe. Milt's trying to do the only sane thing a body can and them Flatheads are fit to chew nails, saying it ain't fair they fight and lose everything."

Bridger turned a weary look on Bill. "Milt wants to burn them out. Flatheads are worried they'll destroy their hopes of collecting the Blackfoot's possessions."

"I ain't entirely void of ideas," Bill muttered. "Time was, Jim Bridger, when you needed a feller like me to wipe your nose and bait your traps."

"Learned my lessons real good, didn't I?" Bridger replied over his shoulder as he hurried away.

The exchange of fire had lessened but the din of traded insults more than made up for it as the noisy exchange between the camps continued. Bridger edged slowly toward the temporary barricade erected by the trappers near the Blackfoot foxhole. A few brave men had begun to pile loose brush against the willow-log wall in preparation for a fire.

"Over here!" Milt raised his rifle in salute to Bridger. "You got to talk some sense into these Injuns," he demanded. "Tell Running Buffalo this ain't no blood feud, just a matter of gettin' them Blackfoot outta our path. They can chase what's left of 'em from here to kingdom come once we flush 'em."

Bridger noticed that one of Running Buffalo's warriors held a peace pipe in his hand. They wanted to parley, a procedure that would take up the rest of the day. He brushed aside the symbol gently. "We agree that the Blackfoot should be punished, Running Buf-

falo. But this battle is ours. You understand? It is our
right to decide how they are to be treated. Just as we
abide by your laws when the battle is yours."

Running Buffalo spoke in an undertone to the
warrior beside him, cutting off the man's protest with a
slashing movement of his hand. Turning back to the
tall white man he said, "We will abide by your laws.
The battle is yours, the victory yours."

Bridger smiled inwardly. The sly old devil wanted
a share of the spoils. "Your people, so brave and great,
shall not be denied a just reward. When the Blackfoot
have been frightened off, their possessions are yours, in
thanks for joining in our defeat of an enemy."

"I suppose that takes care of—" Milt broke off at
the sudden cry rising abruptly from the main camp.
"Now what in blue blazes is that all about?"

"Here comes the Spaniard," one of the trappers
said. "Looks to be the devil himself is on his tail."

"Capitán Bridger, you must come!" Loretto burst
into the midst of the men. "The Blackfoot, they say
they are not afraid to die in the fire. They say they will
be avenged. Two hundred of their brothers are coming
up the pass from the north end of the valley."

"That means they'll find the rendezvous camp
first," one man fretted.

"Now, hold on," Bridger began, but he was immediately shouted down.

"The camp's unguarded with all us here!"

"Got a squaw and five kids back there," another
man exclaimed as he set out on a dead run for his
horse.

"Me, too! I got a woman and a boy I sent back
there to keep safe. We got to go help 'em out!"

Loretto wet his lips, his black eyes bright with the
fever of fear. "My wife, she is big with child. She can-

not run far. They will kill her for she is Blackfoot. We
must go back!"

That lamentation was all the reminder Fraeb
needed. The grizzled Dutchman had been dabbing at a
scalp wound on his skull, but he dropped the rag and
grabbed his rifle. "My voman, Gurtie! She's got de
pains. Dey no git my boy, by damn!" He issued a wolf-
like howl of rage and took off.

Bridger put out his arm to stop the Dutchman and
nearly had it taken off. Bridger yelled after him,
shouting curses and reminding him and those going
with him that they would be losing the village trapped
in the willow grove if they left. But they were beyond
thinking clearly and swarmed out over the valley floor
as soon as they were saddled.

"If that don't beat all!" Milt threw his hat on the
ground and kicked it. "Now what the hell am I supposed to do with three-fourths o' my men hied out for
rendezvous and two hundred plus Blackfoot at my
front?"

"Prudence, Milt, lad. We go back to the cottonwoods till they come back," Fitz suggested with a
merry twinkle in his eye. "The ties of love run deep, do
they not, Gabe?"

Bridger ignored the jibe. "Stands to reason we'd
have heard something from Pierre's Hole if they'd been
attacked. That soft-handed Wyeth boy would have
been the first one out of camp." He scratched his jaw.
"Still, them Gros Ventres might be telling the truth.
Better round up what men are left and keep an eye on
that willow fort till we get word."

Fitz fell into step beside Bridger. "You amaze me,
Gabe. Ain't you got a little twinge of misgiving for
your squaw back on the other side of the mountain?"

"Told you before I ain't got no woman. Costs a
man his sanity. Just look how ol' Frapp took outta

here like his britches was on fire. Women make a man do foolish things. Don't need that kind of trouble. Life's bitter hard enough."

"Sure, lad, sure. That's why you're gripping your Hawken like it's struggling to be free," Fitz quipped. "You done a foolish thing, gambling that she'll be waiting for you next summer. Could be her father could trade her out of his tribe altogether. There was talk of the Bannocks strengthening their ties with the Shoshone. Marriage helps cement treaties. Milt told me about seeing Ear-of-the-Fox in the Snake camp. Whole brigade saw how she doted on him last summer. Her father'd be doing himself a good turn, marrying her off to a warrior like him."

Bridger stopped in his tracks. "You finished?"

Fitz threw up his hands in mock terror. "Sure, Gabe. Anything you say."

Bridger took a swipe at him with the butt of his rifle, missing intentionally. "Your turn to turn out mess. And I'm mighty hungry."

The trappers came riding back into the cottonwoods well after dark, their horses lathered and snorting. "It was a trick!" one of them shouted to the waiting camp. "Weren't no Blackfoot to be seen anywhere."

Bridger rose to his feet, stifling the weakness invading his limbs. "Nobody at all?" he asked.

Loretto slid from his horse and hurried over. "No one, Capitán Bridger. The women and children, they wait for word of our victory." His face reddened. "We go loco."

Bridger sighed. "You did what you thought right. A man's got a family, he's got to look after it." He eased back down and poured more coffee into his cup. "Have a sip." He offered it to the Mexican. "We got them Blackfoot sewed up tight. They'll keep till morning."

But the morning proved a bitter disappointment to all. Bridger watched the dawn break with misgiving. The camps on both sides had grown quiet with nightfall. Yet the quiet that pervaded the valley seemed more complete and empty than hours earlier. The longer he sat with his rifle across his knees, the more he became convinced that something was wrong.

Finally he rose and started across the empty plain between the camps. He kept to the edges of the brush as much as possible, jumping from one bush to another as he checkered a path across the open land.

The muscles in his neck and shoulders grew rigid as he neared the willow grove. An arrow could at any moment put an end to his life and he would join the dozen men they had lost the day before. Noiselessly he edged himself forward until he reached the rough wall of the barricade. He pressed an eye to a gap between the logs and drew a sharp breath.

The willow thicket was empty. Half a dozen dead warriors lay in the clearing just beyond the barrier, and in the distance he saw a number of butchered horses. Those they did not take they had rendered useless for their enemies.

He turned back and sent up a cry of alarm before scrambling over the wall into the camp. Grimly he counted their losses and compared them with his own. Fifteen bodies lay scattered about in the trampled grass. There must have been more, he reasoned. By custom a tribe always carried off as many of its dead and wounded as it could. To leave the body of a comrade behind was to risk leaving him open to insults and mutilations that would follow him into the Spirit World. He paused by the body of the only white man to make it into their camp. A ball had hit him squarely between the eyes and the Blackfoot had done their work on the rest of him.

Bridger swallowed and turned away. A little farther on he found the dead bodies of two children. It saddened him to think that one of the balls lodged in the two little bodies might be his own. He heard the others coming up behind him, their cheers of victory or howls of frustration at being cheated out of their prey giving vent to their attitudes.

"I found one," a trapper yelled from the riverside of the thicket. "Got myself a sure-enough live Blackfoot."

Bridger turned and ran toward the bellowing man, hoping to reach him in time. But he was too late. The man was in the act of rising from his knees, a Blackfoot squaw's scalp dripping with blood in his left hand.

He turned to Bridger and smiled. "Got myself a real, nice trophy. She busted her leg trying to get away," he boasted, pointing to the figure at his feet. "Took care o' that for her."

Bridger looked down at the mutilated body with a single hatchet chop cloving the skull, and he gagged. His eyes were cold as glass when he looked into the face of the grinning man. "I know you?"

The man shook his head. "No, sir, you don't. But I know you. Signed up with one o' your brigades, Cap'n Bridger."

Bridger spat on the ground near the man's foot. "You come to see me when we get back to rendezvous. You'll get your contract back. Don't hire squaw murderers. Don't need that kind of filth in my outfit."

The man opened his mouth to reply, but Bridger's wordless snarl checked him and he sidestepped uneasily, the bloody scalp swinging guiltily behind him.

Bridger swung his big body around, anger and disgust knotting his stomach. They were supposed to be more human, less savage than the Indians they fought. Men like that snickering carrion-eater made him ashamed of his kind.

The image of Little Fawn stayed with him too closely for him to shrug off the mutilation he had just witnessed. He had wanted to kill that bastard who stood there grinning at him. He would have, too, if it would have brought the woman back to life.

"Hey! Where you goin'?" Milt called after him as Bridger pushed past him in a blind rage.

"Back to rendezvous," he called over his shoulder. He could not go back to the Shoshone camp after the way he had treated Little Fawn, but he could satisfy himself that she had come to no harm after leaving him. Perhaps, he thought, come the new year he would be willing to reconsider his feelings about marriage. Right now the season was ahead of him, the hills ripe with the promise of a bountiful harvest—and of course, there was Vanderburgh. That was a lot to think on for a man who took each day at a time.

Vanderburgh watched in seething frustration as the last of the Rocky Mountain brigades pulled out of Pierre's Hole. Once again Bridger had outfoxed him. He had been deprived of the pleasure of refusing the compromise which he felt certain Bridger was a party to. The refusal had cost him. Low on shot and powder, he could not hope to follow the Rocky Mountain forces into the field. They had even gone so far as to announce that they would begin the fall hunt on the Snake River, knowing he would be left behind.

Vanderburgh checked the letter he had just written to be delivered to Fort Union. In it he informed McKenzie that supplies had not reached him and that he was being forced to turn back toward the Green River in hopes of meeting Fontenelle and his pack train. He had also reminded his superior that it appeared as if the Gros Ventres had never heard of a peace treaty, citing the recent battle as evidence.

"Let him forward that to New York," he murmured angrily. Of course, McKenzie could not. "He expects me to march alongside the Opposition's brigades without any means of keeping my men fed and armed."

There was nothing else to do. He must find Fontenelle or lose another season.

"Get me Drips," he barked to Fletcher. "Tell the mess leaders to pack up and be ready to march at dawn."

"We goin' after Cap'n Bridger?" the steward inquired doubtfully.

"Does that not meet with your approval?" he barked.

"Oh, yes, sir," Fletcher answered quickly. "Only the men, they're a mite jumpy, what with the Blackfoot infesting the mountains."

"That's about the size of it," Drips seconded, appearing in the doorway of Vanderburgh's tepee. "This child's not for stickin' his neck out with no fire to protect it."

Vanderburgh recoiled out of habit, but somebody had tumbled Drips into the river only the day before and his aroma was considerably diluted. "I know quite well that we are low on fire power, as you so quaintly put it. That is why we're heading for Green River."

"Fontenelle's got Injun trouble, he's like to have turned back," Drips replied sourly.

Vanderburgh gave him a contemptuous look. "I think not."

Drips shrugged. "Can't never tell what a Frenchie might do. Aw, I ain't sayin' he lost his nerve. Most like he's fightin' and cussin' his way over the South Pass.

Been bad weather up north, what I hear from the trappers thereabouts. First they had a bad flood in the spring, then a terrible alkali dust storm. Probable the Frenchie's up to his fancy britches in mule dung and arrows." Drips smirked, revealing broken yellow teeth. "He's a scrappy 'un, give 'em that. He'll pull through."

"I have no intention of waiting to find out," his partner shot back.

Drips' expression turned blank. "If Fontenelle ain't dead you kin bet real safe he's got a pretty story to tell. O' course, I'll get my possibles together, seein' as how we're gettin' under way."

Chapter 15

Three Forks—Fall 1832

Bridger rode out ahead of his brigade, a dark silhouette against the mauve sky of dawn. The first week of September found him in the Yellowstone Mountains north of Colter's Hell. Vanderburgh and Drips had cut his path little more than a week back. He had thought himself beyond the Company's reach when he had pulled out of rendezvous a month back. He had taken it easy, stopping to trap the first of their private streams, though keeping a close watch for raiding Crows. He had sent Fitz out ahead to pay tribute to the friendly tribes. The packets of tobacco they held out for were plentiful for the first time in two years. But it was all in vain if they were giving away the location of their reserves with every change of stream. And he meant to tell Fitz so as soon as he appeared.

In the distance, Fitz advanced, recognizable now by his pure white hair. He came riding in slowly, picking a path down the steep slope of the canyon wall. They were deep in the country of the Continental Divide where the high, frigid streams yielded the finest pelts around.

Bridger raised a hand, cupping his mouth as he delivered a hawklike cry. Fitz waved in response to the birdcall.

"What's got you up and about so early in the day?" Fitz shouted a few minutes later.

"They found us," Bridger said flatly.

"Well now, I'll take that to mean the Company boys," Fitz replied in a thoughtful tone.

"Cut our trail a week back, right after you rode out. Lost them right quick. But them boys is been getting lost so often out here these last few years I reckon 'lost' is looking familiar to them."

Fitz pulled out his fur cap from his saddlebag. "You're thinking of a scheme, Gabe. I can feel it in my bones."

"Was pondering making a stand of it, like we done with the Blackfoot at rendezvous. Vanderburgh's boys versus ours. We could just blast away at each other. And when enough of us has gone under, the rest can feel free to ride on."

"You're talking blarney, lad," Fitz returned mildly, his brogue thickening to its persuasive best. " 'Tis what they're hoping for to slow us down. They've nothing to lose by pinning us to the underbrush till the snow's so deep we're trapped up in these mountains till May. It wouldn't do at all, I'm telling you, to go and lose the management of that fine and wondrous temper of yours."

Bridger shot him a sour look. "You get me mumbling mad when you're trying to get around me. What you got to offer instead?"

Fitz scratched his head through the thick fur of his cap. "Now, we made a pact back in '30. I'd head up the business, see to the books and such, and you'd be commanding in the field. Seems to me the problem's yours."

"I ain't swallowing that hogwash," Bridger answered. "But if I was to take you serious, I'd have to be obeyed, no questions asked." He peered at his friend from under the brim of his hat. "It'd mean a powerful lot of trouble. We'd lose some pelts till we shook them, finallike. There'll be the usual bellyaching to deal with and lots of hard riding that'll take us nowhere," he warned.

"Who are you trying to convince?" Fitz questioned. "Could it be you're growing too old for the game?"

Bridger shrugged, the taunt not getting a rise out of him. "You been seeing the signs, Fitz? There's disturbing news in some of them. Beaver ain't hardly to be found on the Salmon no more. The Bighorn River's the same. There were damned few signs of beaver coming up the Yellowstone either."

Fitz swayed slightly in his saddle from weariness. "Maybe it's a bad year. We're off one year, twice as good the next. Don't go looking for trouble. We got enough here before us."

They turned their horses in unison and began riding back toward the brigade. "Reckon Vanderburgh's any good at reading Indian sign?"

Fitz's eyes brightened. "You're thinking of playing Indian, Gabe?"

"Maybe."

"What do you mean we've lost them again?" Vanderburgh slammed his fist down on the pommel of his saddle. The constant days in the saddle had done their part to fracture his nerves. There had been no other way of catching up to the Rocky Mountain brigade after losing precious days tracking down Fontenelle and resupplying his men. "For the better part of a week I've been riding in circles while you scouts tell me we're getting somewhere. Can't remember the last time we cut the Opposition's trail."

The Company scout snarled. "You got no right badmouthing me, Mr. Vanderburgh. Them Rocky Mountain boys got more tricks up their sleeves than a Crow shaman. Me and Richard and Dudley done followed the broadest trail right smack up against that canyon a mile and a half further on. Met a small band of 'em Kicked-in-the-Bellies out there. Told me they ain't seen no white men 'cept us in days. Figured they must a doubled back on us during the night, like they done last week up on Madison Fork."

Vanderburgh flicked his riding crop against his leg. "Bridger couldn't have gotten past us, not even at night. Look about you. Tell me where they could be?"

The sound of Vanderburgh's harsh voice so close by grated on Bridger's nerves and he stifled a curse. At the edge of a shallow gully overgrown with brush, he and forty members of his brigade had taken cover. He edged up from his painful crouching position until his head was level with the floor of the plateau. A hundred yards away on the flat bottom land the entire Company brigade had come to a halt. The jingling of harnesses and snorting of their pack animals provided a certain amount of cover noise for his own crew, but Bridger held his expectations of eluding them in reserve. He had hurried his people north as far and as fast as he could, taking the women and children under his command. Fitz, Dupree, and Loretto were sent out with a few men each to set up dummy campsites and leave long, winding trails to nowhere.

But Vanderburgh was no longer a greenhorn who followed any new lead. He had simply detached a few of his men to run down the end of each trail. Still, the soldier in him would not allow him to lead his party too far afield for fear they would need to double back.

It was this cautiousness Bridger had counted on as he crisscrossed the territory.

A fretful cry snapped Bridger's head about in anger. His eyes immediately fell on the culprit. Frapp's wife had not been the only woman to give birth this season. Loretto's wife had delivered a fine-looking boy three days ago. She had delayed them half a day while she writhed in pain, sheltered by the burnt-orange canyon walls of the Great Divide. As Bridger raised a hand to signal for silence, the mother reached out and gently squeezed her baby's nose. Instantly he was silent, and Bridger gave the mother a grateful smile before turning back to his surveillance. Thank God she had been taught to be a decent mother, he thought. That old trick had saved many a migrating village their game when a child's sudden cry might have frightened it off. And while Vanderburgh might not know the difference between an owl's call and that of a redskin, not even he would mistake the wail of a child.

Bridger eased himself up to the rim of the gully again, stripping his hat from his head so that it would not give him away. His people needed rest, rest they would not get till the Company brigade moved on.

"I don't give a damn what you think!" Vanderburgh roared at the end of a long tirade. "Find them!"

Bridger watched them pull out. They were doubling back, unknowingly choosing the path he had meant to follow. He was low on water and in need of a few idle days to hunt game and replenish his stock. The mules were balking at the meager grazing they were forced to endure under the cover of night. And worst of all, he thought in frustration, he was hiding out like a yellow-tailed skunk, slipping in and out of brush like he had lost the taste for a real fight—like he was a coward!

He did not know he had gripped it till he heard it

snap and looked down at the broken trunk of a young sapling. That settled it. Enough of this playing hide-and-seek like a damned rabbit. He threw the limb from him in disgust. It was time Vanderburgh realized once and for all that he did not hold the only hand worth wagering on.

"I share your feelings, Gabe, but I'll say it again: To stand and fight is all Vanderburgh dreams of." Fitz took a long swill of whiskey from a battered cup. "Don't you see?"

"I see I'm sick to my stomach of crawling into a hole every time a rider appears on the next crest." Bridger tossed off his cupful and refilled. He had called a meeting of the entire brigade to put his plan to the test. "You tell me in one breath they're here to stay. In the next you're mouthing reasons why we should keep ahead of them till it's safe to trap our own streams. I say we fight."

"That do sound sweet to these ol' ears!" Dupree cried. "Been thinkin' we're turnin' tail a mite too often for my likin'. Give 'em shot for their effort, h'yar's what I say!"

A general agreement sounded through the grim-faced men.

"Got to fight back, ain't no other way."

"Show 'em this beaver's got teeth."

"Them doin's don't shine in this crowd. No way! Man's got to stand his ground."

"Gabe," Fitz whispered below the din. "You know you don't want a fight. If you and me go under, Vanderburgh's got it his way."

"Sometimes you think too neat, Fitz. What if Vanderburgh was to meet with an accident? Could happen to any of us. Loose boulder, snake spooking his horse, there's a number of ways of bushwhacking a man."

Fitz drew back as if he had seen a snake wriggle out of Bridger's eye. "You ain't that mad, Gabe. That ain't your way and you know it."

Bridger shrugged his burly shoulders. He was hunched over to keep off the sleet sliding out of the night sky. The moisture hissed and streamed as it dampened the stone-banked fire around which they sat. "You figure me for too good a soul, Fitz. That's the trouble with you book-learned folk, always trying to figure a man for more than he's worth." He wiped the rain from his face. "You figure that lowlife son of a bitch Vanderburgh's got a soul or some such. To me he's vermin, plain and simple. What's a man do when he runs across vermin? He steps on it or, if it's big enough, he blasts it away with his buffalo gun. Simple, like I said."

Fitz sucked in a long breath. "Didn't know it'd got to you so bad, Gabe. Maybe I was wrong from the beginning. Maybe this here company business wasn't to your liking after all."

Bridger's head swerved toward the Irishman. "Took that long to figure it out, did it?"

"Horseshit!" Fitz roared suddenly. He had been so busy worrying about the outcome of this council he had not heard the deadpan tone of Bridger. "You're stuffing me and I'm swallowing it whole, like some greenhorn who doesn't know how to wipe his own arse."

The acknowledgement drew loud, unsympathetic laughter his way. "Son of a bitch, Gabe. It ain't right, you suckering me in like that."

Bridger did not speak at once. His eyes were again opaque in that funny way Fitz knew meant he had something serious on his mind. "I don't aim to keep up what we're doing," Bridger said in a loud voice that included all the men. "I say if Vanderburgh wants to wager his life just to make us miserable, then it's time we upped the ante."

The men kept quiet, knowing that they were about to be asked to make a decision that might well hold their lives in the balance.

"It's my own opinion. Ain't saying any man ain't got a right to pack up and leave when he learns what we're about to do. I'm a mite disgusted with teaching them Company boys the lay of the land. Bill and Fitz offered them a split and you all know they threw it back in their faces. We ain't trapping enough beaver to make it worth our while to stay in the mountains. If we don't shake them soon, won't be no season left."

Bridger swallowed the last of his whiskey. "So, here it is. Vanderburgh says they need to learn the country before they'll deal. I say we show it to them, right up close. So close they'll be lucky if the view don't lift the hair right off their heads!"

"Goin' north to Blackfoot country!" Dupree hollered. "Knew it! Hoo-wee! That'll separate fat cow from poor bull, anyhow."

A cheer of agreement went up around the campfire.

"That's plumb crazy. It's suicide," Fitz objected.

"Seems to me it's letting nature take its course," Bridger retorted matter-of-factly. "If they want us bad enough, they'll have to come after us. If not, they lose us."

"It's risking our lives," Fitz insisted halfheartedly, for in his mind, the idea was beginning to sound intriguing.

"It's a test of courage, same as if I was to let you shoot this cup of whiskey off my head at a hundred paces. Vanderburgh will either hitch up his britches

and come after us or he'll hang back and lose. I ain't
going to crawl again for any man. Let him sweat it out
like we've been doing. And it ain't bushwhacking neither," Bridger added in an amused tone.

"But, it's surely close enough to have its charm,"
Fitz countered with a devilish grin. "Where do we begin?"

"We've been straddling the Great Divide all
month. Was hoping to steer the Company out over the
western slope, where the first snow would keep them
locked up till spring. Now I'm figuring we'll cut back
across the Divide, head east. We'll call in all the boys
and march in one tight line that couldn't be missed by
a shortsighted mole.

"It'll take Vanderburgh a few days to catch on to
the fact this ain't another decoy." Bridger smiled for
the first time. "Course, we don't want them to be too
easy on that account. He'll be learning to tell the difference between Indian sign and Bridger sign before too
long."

He looked at the smiling faces of his men. "No
sense in me warning you you're laying your life on the
line this hand. You fellers know the Blackfoot. We
could be making their season, offering up for their taking a couple of dozen prime scalps. We ain't going after beaver. So don't fool yourselves into thinking
otherwise. It's Company men we're out to skin, plain
and simple."

Dupree snorted and spit into the glowing embers.
"This soul ain't never backed down in a fight. Ain't
backin' down now."

"Been with you a long spell, Cap'n," another man
declared. "Seen things most mortals ain't dreamed of.
We covered a piece o' ground, we have. Been where
the mud bubbles up outta the ground like a Shoshone
stewpot. Smelled the bowels o' hell and dipped our

sticks in streams so cold the fishies a-wearin' long
johns. Ain't runnin' out on you now."

"It's our livin' them bastards is after. I'm for blast-
in' 'em all the way back to St. Louis!" still another exclaimed.

"H'yar's fire!" Dupree roared. "We should stand
and throw the lot! But," he added, dropping his voice,
" 'ye boys, what's bein' a touch squeamish, is hopin'
the Blackfoot'll do the butcherin' for 'ye. Hitch up ol'
Betsy and this child's for comin'."

Bridger and Fitz herded the last of the brigade
into a crudely fashioned camp in a protected corner of
the valley. They had sent men ahead to secure the spot
and strip the trees of bark for fodder. Since they had
left the Salmon River area the weather had turned
steadily worse. The first Blue Norther of the season
had ripped down the canyon slopes a few days earlier,
blinding them with sleet and grainy flakes of snow.

Bridger turned a measuring eye to the valley
ahead. They had come nearly thirty miles in the last
week, most of it over terrain so wild and rough he had
almost despaired of the Company brigade keeping up
with his own. This was not where he wanted to lose
them. The streams were brimming with beaver, and the
temptation to pause and hunt might overwhelm Vanderburgh's orders if the going got too difficult.

The sky was clearing up ahead. A red rim appeared on the horizon to the north. By morning they
would be seeing the last of the snow. The valley floor
below looked darker than the surrounding hills. Hopefully, the bitter cold had remained in the mountains
and the bunchgrass, necessary for grazing, had sur-
vived to keep enough buffalo this far north. That
would mean his people would be eating hump and ribs
before the week was out.

Early the next morning, Dupree and Loretto came riding back to camp waving a flag. "Cap'n Bridger, Injun sign down the valley a piece," Dupree announced. "Me and the Mexican seen 'em up close. Snake, Cap'n, that's a fact. Huntin' that herd of bufflar we was after."

Bridger and Fitz exchanged looks. "What are the Shoshone doing this far north?" Fitz asked in puzzlement.

"Most likely they're Bannocks," Bridger addressed the two scouts. "You recognize anyone?"

"No sir, this hoss weren't eager for a lifted scalp."

Bridger drew a deep breath. "That many?"

Loretto nodded. "*Sí*, Capitán. Dupree say a war party leads them. Plenty paint on their faces."

"Could be they met a party of Blackfoot and came off the winners," Fitz suggested. "At least they'll know if there be any of them nearby."

Bridger nodded absently, his mind absorbed in a new thought. He had been expecting trouble since he had awakened in a sweat, his knife half-drawn in expectation of some life-threatening specter. The fear and weakness in his gut had become an unavoidable but strangely accepted part of his nights. But this last one had come upon him like the low-riding clouds of a prairie storm when the earth holds its breath and shivers in helpless impotence. Just the thought of it made the hairs on his neck bristle.

He knew it was a warning. The Indians called it a visitation from the Manitou. Some men sought it out in wild and lonely places. Others felt it thrust on them from behind. If it was a warning of death, he was ready to meet it.

He swung his rifle to his shoulder and turned to Fitz. "Better pick up a couple of packs of tobacco. A keg o' whiskey might come in handy, too. But keep it

hid. I don't much like the idea of leaving a handful of
drunk Bannocks in Blackfoot territory."

"You go? Just two?" Loretto asked in frank
amazement.

"Don't want them thinking we're out to jump
them. Two's plenty." Bridger rubbed his heavy shoulder.
He was not nearly as weary as he would be before this
was all over, but he did not like the ache in his spine.
Bannocks were a touchy subject, a branch of the
Shoshone family who held a permanent distrust of
white faces. But they would parley. Not even the Bannocks would be foolhardy enough to make war on
them.

"Don't look especially happy to see us," Fitz murmured as he and Bridger rode at a slow pace into the
Bannock camp.

Two dozen tepees were stacked up tightly in a
narrow grove of juniper. The warriors acknowledged
their white flag with silence, each of them with a rifle
or bow openly displayed.

Bridger dropped from his saddle and moved
toward the leader. The stocky, battle-scarred chief was
adorned with the black face paint of mourning, which
Bridger surmised his people had adopted from their
neighbors, the Crows. He made the sign of peace and
the chief quickly answered in kind, though neither man
spoke.

Indian tricks, Bridger thought in resignation. It
would be a long parley, lasting maybe into the next
day. He signaled to Fitz to dismount, and the two of
them silently followed their hosts to the largest, most
colorfully decorated lodge, which belonged to the chief.

When the soapstone pipe had been passed around,
Bridger relaxed and let his eyes roam the wall of
stone-faced warriors standing behind the circle of

seated men. His gaze, passing over the line in indifference, suddenly became deadlocked.

The warning went off in his head like the scream of a wounded she-bear. But his eyes continued to travel the wall very casually as if he had chosen to count their number. He paused, eyes just short of his goal. Yes, he felt it again—an emanation of hatred so strong it had a smell, like a bitch in heat or a frightened skunk. The warrior wanted him dead. The recognition of the anger did not surprise him. He would have to be careful, that was all.

"You come to us. You are in need." The chief spoke, his painted cheek puckered by an old knife wound.

Bridger chose his words carefully. "We come in friendship. We are allies of the Shoshone. We would be allies of the Bannocks against our common enemy, the Blackfoot."

Dark implacable eyes studied Bridger intently. "I am called Beaver Tail, War Chief of the Bannocks," the chief continued. "We fight Blackfoot. We win many horses and take many scalps. We do not need white man's friendship."

Fitz's hand moved from his lap to his rifle lying on the floor before him, but two of the warriors checked his move by stepping on the barrel.

"Don't be a fool," Bridger mumbled under his breath as he reached casually for the pipe making its second pass by him. He inhaled, counted the number inside the tepee at twenty. Through a halo of blue smoke he said, "We do not seek the Bannocks' help. We are heading for Blackfoot territory to trap beaver."

That bit of information had the desired effect. The warriors fell at once into a hushed discussion, giving Bridger a chance to cut his eyes to the left and snatch a long look at the warrior who sought his scalp.

The features were the same. Two years had made the expected differences, but a man remained essentially the same unless marked by knife, gun, or tomahawk. None of those had touched the broad planes of cheek and brow smeared with war paint. The only changes were deep lines from nostril to jaw on either side of his wide, narrow mouth. But they did not disguise him. The single ornament, a red foxtail, still rode the lone plait in his thick, shiny hair. Ear-of-the-Fox.

Bridger glanced away. It had to be Washakie's adopted son, and yet . . . He shut his eyes briefly to recapture his impression of the young warrior. Out of the young warrior's eyes stared the rigid mien of a fox when it had spied its prey.

"What's wrong?" Fitz asked in an undertone. "Look like you've seen a ghost."

Beaver Tail turned to them before Bridger could reply. "We will tell you what we hear in the Blackfoot camps. They have pledged to the Great Spirit to rid this land of all their enemies, white and Indian. The Nez Perce have suffered at their hands. The Flathead ride in groups too big to attack in fear of their lives." A smile quirked the corners of his flat mouth. "Only the Bannocks dare to ride into their land, steal their horses, and ride away."

By exerting the full force of his will, Bridger hauled his attention to the speaker. "You are brave and skilled warriors. The Blackfoot themselves acknowledge this in their lamentations for their dead. But tell me, where do they get their power, the medicine that gives them the courage to declare war on all who live in and near the Shining Ones?"

The old warrior shook his head sadly. "They tell of a powerful treaty with the white one call McKenzie."

"I know, at Fort Union," Bridger stated quickly to hurry him along.

"That is so. The white man promises the Blackfoot control of their sacred streams if they trade only with him."

There was movement at his back. Bridger ran his big hand up his thigh to his hip, gently fingering his Green River. His voice betrayed nothing of the message of danger his senses screamed through his brain. "They believe that this white man called McKenzie can be trusted to carry out his side of the treaty?" One swift action was all he would get before they jumped him.

Fitz's cry of warning came just as a blow caught Bridger on the upper left shoulder. Bridger moved away, lunging forward from his cross-legged position, his weight on his left hand. His knife emerged in his right as the tomahawk came crashing down, wide of its mark.

The tepee erupted at once, warriors reaching out for the white men and the Indian who had attacked one of them. Bridger took several brutal blows before four men wrestled him to the floor. He took a deep breath and waited for the bite of steel that would crush his unprotected neck. It never came. Instead he felt his knife wrenched from his hand, and then he was released.

He sat up, his wary glance taking in Fitz, who was unarmed but free, and the warrior who had wanted his life. "Why?" he shouted painfully at the Shoshone who had once been his companion.

Ear-of-the-Fox came out of his trance slowly, the emergence like a rising from the depths of a deep, clear pool. The red film of rage lifted from his eyes and he knew what he had done. Or, rather, failed to do. He shook himself free of the restraining hands on his shoulders and bent to pick up his weapon. Beaver Tail spoke to him in a low angry growl that brought a hidden flush of anger to his features. He turned and walked out without a glance at his victim.

"I'll be damned!" Fitz turned to Bridger. "We know him."

"Shut up," Bridger hissed. He reached slowly for his knife and resheathed it under a score of watchful stares. He took his time in rearranging his buckskins, precious time that gave him a chance to still his own temper and convince himself that the warriors who had jumped him had not broken a rib.

Steady, Jim, he cautioned himself. You ain't got no reason to die in a Bannock camp tonight. Get yourself outta this mess. You can mull it over a fair distance from here.

"Ear-of-the-Fox brings shame upon the lodge of Beaver Tail," the old chief acknowledged. "The Shoshone comes to us as a friend. He remains with us a warrior. It is to him we owe our victory against the Blackfoot soldiers. His heart is strong and without fear. Whatever you have done to incur his wrath is between the two of you. I will warn you because he attacked one who should be safe in my lodge. Nothing you say or do will deter him from his revenge. You must look to your back, Peejatowahooten. Though your medicine be strong, his is no less."

"How do you know I am the one called Peejatowahooten?" Bridger asked.

Beaver Tail quirked his mouth. "Your Manitou sits at your shoulder. The Golden Grizzly saved your life."

Bridger shrugged aside the proclamation as typical Indian mystic talk, but the amusement in the chief's eyes left him uneasy. "We will leave you now," he said shortly. "I do not like being the target of crazy men."

"Ain't you even a little curious to know why he jumped you?" Fitz questioned, marveling at his friend's restraint. "Jesus, I thought you a goner." They had ridden in silence until the Bannock camp was a mile behind them.

Bridger turned, his face an unreliable shadow in the night. "It don't matter much. Beaver Tail spoke the truth when he said Ear-of-the-Fox wants my life. The 'why' don't make any difference."

Of course, that was not quite true, he thought to himself. He had turned the matter over and over in his mind this last mile. He and the Shoshone had never truly been friends. The warrior had saved his life and then said the debt was cleared by the gift of the horse. There had been no other intercourse between them. Bridger hitched his shoulder as an uncomfortable thought entered his mind. No traffic if he did not count Little Fawn.

He had never asked her pointblank whether she would marry the warrior. He had walked out of rendezvous telling himself that he expected it. In fact, he wanted her to tie herself to some man so she would not wait for him to come back. The notion did not sit so well with him these last weeks. The thought of that hard-faced young buck stretched out between her beautiful soft thighs gave him a twinge of jealousy so sharp he sucked in his breath. No, the boy had gone funny in the head. He would not do at all for Little Fawn. If Ear-of-the-Fox ever found out she had shared a white man's robes . . .

"Can't do nothing about that now," he grumbled angrily to himself. He was committed to bringing the Rocky Mountain brigades through another season. He would not have a free day until wintering. Besides, Ear-of-the-Fox had hitched himself to the Bannocks for a while. Bridger would be busy just staying alive till he got himself out of Blackfoot country.

"I'll look for Washakie's village come winterin'," he told himself. What he would do when he got there he had no idea.

The thought of looking upon Little Fawn's face just made him feel better. She would be mad enough to scratch his eyes out. He smiled. He didn't much care.

Ear-of-the-Fox had watched the two American trappers ride out of the Bannock camp from the shadow of a cottonwood. The overriding hatred had calmed to a dull throb in the middle of his chest. He had disgraced himself in Beaver Tail's lodge. He would not be welcomed there again for some time. His recent coups at the Blackfoot's expense would keep him from being banished from the village entirely, but that did not concern him now. He would be leaving as soon as he had convinced himself that the trappers were beyond circling back on him for revenge.

Anguish enveloped him like it had so many times before while waiting in agonizing patience for a visitation from the Manitou. Three times he had taken himself to the mountains where the wind sings. He had looked for the ledge Little Fawn had described in her vision, but found only a sliver of rock too small to support him. He had purified himself in the sweating lodge before setting out, and had fasted so long he would have died had not two companions come looking for him. Each time he had failed. The delirium of starvation had not brought him an image of his fate, but only the image of Peejatowahooten. No matter how precise and intricate his preparations, his Manitou failed to speak to him. Instead, sweating nightmares visited, each time displaying the face of the man who stood between him and all that he desired.

Even in self-mutilation, Ear-of-the-Fox could not shake the image that rose like a veil between him and the face of the Great Spirit. He had hung from the sun dance pole by two leather thongs attached to his chest, skewers of wood passing through slits in his flesh. Numbed by the pain of frenzied dancing, he had begged for the vision that still escaped him. The medicine man had wanted to deepen the gashes in his flesh when he had not worked himself free at the end of the day, like the other warriors. But he had not allowed that. All through the night he had cried, praying that the Great Spirit might send him a vision of his fate. Again he was denied. Then, at last, when he could no longer support his own weight, the bearded face of his nightmares had risen up to blot out the campfire. Peejatowahooten!

With a cry of despair dredged up from the core of his being, he had lashed out at the image with his hands. The fury of that assault tore him from the sun dance pole and covered him in a bath of his own blood.

Ear-of-the-Fox trembled, his face slick with hot tears. "My life is under the shadow of the one called Bridger. I shall never be free until he is dead," he murmured brokenly. The white man's medicine was strong. The trapper denied him the right of the protection and guidance of the Spirit World. "I failed tonight because I hesitated to strike," he whispered to himself. The great Peejatowahooten must think him a squaw to have failed so miserably. He would laugh and tell others of the folly of Ear-of-the-Fox.

A wail of pain burst forth from Ear-of-the-Fox. "My shame will know no bounds!"

Then he thought of Little Fawn. The darkness that often came to him these days receded as her image filled his mind. She would understand. Perhaps if he went to her she could interpret what the medicine men could not. She had been visited by the Manitou. She would help him. He would seek her out at once. She would be his protection against the white trapper's medicine. And then, when he was ready, he would kill the one called Bridger.

Chapter 16

Walking the measure of his camp, Vanderburgh felt the first sweet taste of victory. At last he had managed to put the Rocky Mountain brigade on the run. He had followed them over the most rugged terrain yet encountered in the wilderness at a pace hardly to be imagined. They were in flight, tumbling down the mountains and into the plains like the devil himself had singled them out for his attentions.

He rubbed his hands together in glee. He could not stop grinning. He alone had finally forced the Opposition from their fall hunting grounds. They were hoping to lead him on a merry chase and he wished them well at it. He would not be shaken this time. He would keep them at their decoying and making of false trails until winter closed in good and proper. And if the light blanket of snow already on the ground was any indication, winter would come early this year. In the first week of October the frosty breath of the Arctic had stripped the mountains behind them of foliage. The buffalo remained on the plains, thank God, but soon they, too, would look for the warmth of the land further south. Bridger and his brigade would then be forced to make their wintering without enough pelts to keep them warm.

"God, but it's a glorious day," Vanderburgh commented to a couple of his men as he walked past. The air was bitingly cold, but the sun shone with particular clarity on the golden prairie. And somewhere in that vast expanse, Bridger would be sitting about his own campfire, chilled to the bone and steeped in his own worries. What did it matter if the Company brigades were hungrier than he would like? They had to keep the Opposition on the alert, keep them moving and too frightened to stay too long in any one spot. He and his men had passed a couple of half-butchered buffalo carcasses only a few days ago. The Opposition had dared not remain long enough to finish the business.

Vanderburgh smiled again. Just wait till his latest express reached Fort Union. McKenzie would have to swallow many of his nastiest barbs, and with his own home brew, too. That old devil of a dealer had built his own still up at Fort Union. Said that with Meriwether Lewis watching their every move he could not bribe enough people to keep himself in supply. So he had removed the touchy subject from the hands of his enemies. Nobody would know if his bootleg whiskey found its path into the Blackfoot villages. The Indians were not about to tell. No one else would live who learned of the secret by a visit to one of their camps. The system was foolproof. As a soldier and an American, Vanderburgh thought it might not be the wisest of McKenzie's moves. However, after this rout of the Opposition from their streams, he doubted anything would bother him in the future. The Rocky Mountain Fur Company would fold come spring. It did not take much more than a shrewd guess to know that they were up to their necks in debt.

Vanderburgh barked a few orders to the mule tenders, then turned back toward his horse and packs. He could not resist trapping a few of the more abundant streams they were whizzing past in an effort to keep the Bridger brigade on the move. Drips had argued, as usual, about the unnecessary chances they would both be taking by splitting up now, now that they were in the heart of Blackfoot country. Vanderburgh had reminded him that McKenzie's dream of a treaty with that tribe was a reality and that soon they could expect to receive a copy of it by messenger.

"What the hell kind o' rider is McKenzie gonna be sendin' through Blackfoot land?" Drips had scoffed. "Reckon he'll send Injuns?"

Vanderburgh chuckled as he swung into the saddle. With McKenzie's delight in the eccentric, he would not put it past him. A frown momentarily ridged his brow. He really should not be trapping the Blackfoot territory. The treaty promised they would only trade. He shrugged and sighed. The streams would tempt a saint. If they had to give the Indians the pelts and buy them back, so what? It just made him feel better knowing Bridger was wearing the leather off the seat of his buckskins while he had the leisure to trap and follow.

So high was he riding in the saddle that the news, thundering back to him from one of his scouts that same afternoon, left him momentarily nonplused.

"We found 'em again!" The scout reined in beside the Company partisan, a cocky grin on his face. "Dogged, Mr. Vanderburgh, 'em Rocky Mountain boys musta figured they was rid o' us. They been headin' back toward Madison Fork just up ahead. Goin' back toward the hills to hunt beaver. Don't that beat all?"

"We'll just have to see if we can't make them a little more cautious the next time we're out of sight," Vanderburgh replied slowly. He was grateful he had found them, of course, but it rankled to think that Bridger did not yet consider him a worthy enough opponent to spend even an extra day or two in the field to make certain he had been shaken. And though he hated to admit it, luck had played its part in his scouts finding them. If not for the delay in rounding up his small parties of trappers, he might have beat the Opposition to Madison Fork and crossed it, missing them entirely.

By nightfall his edginess at the near miss turned to consternation. The Rocky Mountain brigade had ridden in at dusk, the same as if they were alone. He thought they might turn north and look for a covered area by which to sneak across the water. Instead, he watched Bridger send men out to set up traps right alongside the Company floatsticks.

"What's he got in mind now?" Vanderburgh growled as he marched back into his tent. Time alone would tell. Out of habit—and the nagging doubt that he was about to become the dupe of some as yet unknown hoax—he sent out a double guard. "Bridger is going to need every ounce of the medicine the Indians charge him with if he means to steal another march on Henry Vanderburgh," he vowed to Fletcher before turning in.

"Two days and nothing's happened," Vanderburgh muttered. At least he had the consolation of knowing he was delaying Bridger. He had not talked to the bourgeois, and for that he was sorry. He thought he would have handled himself well in an altercation. The Opposition men were edgy, spoiling for a fight. He had to wonder at the strength of his rival, who managed to keep those trigger-ready mountain goats in some semblance of order. Bridger and he both knew their men wanted nothing more than to start a no-holds-barred battle. There had been one or two disputes over the ownership of full traps. One of his men would bear the scar of the disputer's Green River to his grave. Yet the Opposition acted like a band of men with time on their hands.

The morning of the third day showed the early risers in Vanderburgh's brigade that the opposite bank, where sixty-odd rival trappers had spent several nights, was as empty as the unbroken plains to the north.

"Reckon they gone north?" the scout inquired of his boss.

Vanderburgh chewed his lower lip as he studied the vacant riverbank. "If you were Bridger, what would you do?"

The scout scratched his head. "Dogged if I wouldn't set out for the Divide 'afore this snow piles up, blocking the pass."

"Precisely." Vanderburgh turned from the man to dictate orders for his men to pull in their equipment. "Bridger will take the easier path up the Madison to the Jefferson Fork, cutting across to the Divide just west of it. In order to halve the distance and cut them off before they reach the goal of the mountains, we will lead our men due west to the Jefferson Fork."

The scout cleared his throat. "Mr. Vanderburgh, I don't— That is . . ." He cut his eyes to the side, a red flush creeping up his neck above his buckskin shirt. "I don't want you thinkin' me lackin' in grit, only there's been a powerful lot o' Injun sign hereabouts. We might do ourselves a favor, followin' that Rocky Mountain brigade. Anythin' to be flushed, they'd be doin' it."

"Feeling skittish, are you?" Vanderburgh eyed the

scout with a derisive glance. "Thought you claimed to be an experienced Indian-fighter. If you're turning yellow you can start back to Fort Union alone. The rest of us are going after our prey." He smirked. "Find me an Indian, a live one, and I'll consider our next move. In the meantime we march tight and straight across the watershed to Jefferson Fork. Is that clear?"

The scout nodded reluctantly. "Yes sir. Reckon it is."

"Yep, it's Blackfoot all right. I do know a few things," the scout announced belligerently. He stood with a dozen other men and his boss over the half-butchered carcass of a buffalo calf.

"You see them cuts, that's Injun butcherin', sure as I'm born. And them moccasin prints. Musta been a score of 'em ridin' outta here less than a day ago. The guts is still warm deep inside the bufflar. Best take care. Make camp while a few of us scout it out."

"Shut up!" Vanderburgh growled. "Any more of your mewling and I'll have an insurrection on my hands. God's blood, man. Can't you tell real Indian sign from Cap'n Bridger's grubbings in the dirt?"

The wind carried his laughter to the caravan halted some yards away. "It's another of Bridger's tricks," he called back to them. "He found out we were cutting across to head him off and he sent a few men to smear our path with bogus signs of Blackfoot butchery."

He turned away in disgust. His entire brigade had a case of Indian jitters. Many times in the past two days his scouts had to be forced to carry out sound military canvassing procedure after being frightened by signs on the trail. Each time they had returned with the news that they were mistaken, that there were no Indians ahead. The scouts had been useful in the beginning when he had not known one plain or ridge from the next. But now that he could read the timberline with ease, he found that he did not need their advice. In fact, they were infecting the entire brigade with their superstitious fears, and wearing down his nerves in the process. It was all those wild stories they had been swapping around the campfires.

"It's plain they've frightened themselves," he said to Fletcher as they walked back to the head of the mule train. "They just need to be prodded along."

But when he called for the brigade to mount up and fall into line, not one man moved. "What is this? Didn't you hear my command?" He shot a withering glance down the line, but still no one moved. "Well?" he demanded.

"It's like this, sir," one of the men drawled when it seemed no one was going to speak. "We're trappers, Mr. Vanderburgh. We fight Injuns when we have to. We trail a man havin' more'n his share o' luck once in a while. Only, we don't go lookin' for our death. Many's the way a feller kin go under out here. I'd just as soon not go the Blackfoot way."

A murmur of assent surged through the line of men.

Vanderburgh sat in stony silence. One did not give mutineers a hearing. In the military they would have been court-martialed and shot. His eyes went carefully over the throng once more, memorizing every face. A tight, empty smile stretched over his mouth. He could not court-martial them but there was something he could threaten to do. "If that is all, we will mount up and be on our way." He turned his horse and would have moved off if some instinct had not warned him that he would be setting off all alone.

Irritation turned to fury as he jerked his horse back to face them. "What is the matter with you? Are you telling me, after all this time, that you're finally afraid of one of Bridger's little schemes? Damnation! You've seen to what lengths the man will go to throw us off his tracks. We've wasted weeks circling back over cold trail looking to cut his path. One lousy dead buffalo is mild compared to his usual techniques."

"That's what's botherin' us," the trapper volunteered. "It ain't like Cap'n Bridger to try to put us off with one little cow. That's reason enough for it to be Blackfoot work."

"That's tellin' him!" a man shouted from the rear. "Ain't settin' one foot in front o' t'other till we know for certain them redguts ain't waitin' up a piece to claim our scalps!"

The murmur became a bellowing cheer of agreement as each man felt free to express his resentment at their treatment in recent weeks.

"Ain't like we come to fight Injuns," one complained. "This hoss is a trapper, pure and simple. 'Tain't Injun scalps I'm after, but beaver."

"Ain't leavin' this spot till 'em scouts's gone clear up beyond the next ridge and come back with the all clear," added the perpetual troublemaker, Jessup Cain.

"You expect me to sit still while you dictate to me under what terms you will work?" A tremor in his voice betrayed Vanderburgh's rage, but his face remained impassive. "May I remind you that most of you are under contract to the American Fur Company; that you are under *obligation,* signed in your own hand, to submit to the judgment of the Company Field Commander, and that *I* am *he?*"

"Don't make no difference was my mama tellin' me to move out," one man objected. "Ain't takin' one goddamn step till I hear tell the way is clear." Having said his piece, the speaker turned to his mule and began unhitching its packs.

"Looks like to me you're stuck," Cain snickered as he glanced up at the thunderously angry partisan.

Vanderburgh lashed out and struck the scout with his riding crop. "It is to you, Jessup Cain, I owe my debt of gratitude for stirring the others up!" Feeling his advantage over Bridger slipping out from under him with every wasted breath, Vanderburgh wheeled his horse and rode back toward the men setting up camp.

"Which of you big, brave souls will offer to ride with me as a scouting detail? That's right, you don't think I'm about to let you poor, misguided fools ride off to your deaths without me along to protect you, do you?"

"Don't go a-talkin' that way, Mr. Vanderburgh," the man nearest him advised. "Ain't no tellin' what you're liable to find. Take it real slow and easy. Don't force no matters you ain't got the right side of."

"I take it I'm receiving the benefit of your wise counsel because you're too yellow to ride with me," Vanderburgh spat.

The man colored up and turned away, cursing under his breath.

"Are there none of you brave enough to come, or are we to sit down and wait for the Blackfoot to come and find us huddled in a corner?"

The taunt forced a few men to the front of the line. One hour later, Vanderburgh found himself leading a tight little band of six volunteers. As he led them upstream, he kept up a steady stream of verbal abuse. He would not soon let them forget that they had countermanded his orders and that most of them were holed up in the river valley a few miles back like frightened sheep.

Shortly after noon, the scout riding out in front lifted his arm in signal and took out across the land.

Kicking his horse into a gallop, Vanderburgh called after the others to follow.

The sight that sent the scout streaking across the plain turned out to be a second butchered carcass, still oozing blood. Beside it a small fire blazed, melting the snow in an ever-widening circle in the grass.

"Look about you, Mr. Vanderburgh. Blackfoot tracks is everywhere. This ain't trappers' work," the scout said.

Vanderburgh slid from his horse and walked around the perimeter of the campsite. What if he had been wrong? What if they were on the trail of a Blackfoot hunting party and not falling prey to one of Bridger's tricks? He counted the prints carefully. How many of them could there be? Why, they had not even scared off the herd of buffalo grazing in the distance.

"Can't be more than half a dozen if it is Indians," he announced firmly. "Even a tenderfoot like myself can make sense of these signs. How many could there be when they did not completely divide up the kill? Perhaps they were scared off by the sounds of our arrival. You all know how Indians will not attack white men unless they outnumber them. These poor savages went off without their meal. That alone should tell you there can't be many of them." Vanderburgh's tone grew more confident with every word. It made sense. It had to be the only explanation. "Well? What do you think now of your suspicions?"

"Where'd they go? That's what I'd like to know," one of the volunteers wondered, his eyes straying from one horizon to the other. "Injuns is damn funny. They'll back off and then attack a body just so's they can have the advantage of surprise."

"What does it take to convince you?" Vanderburgh roared.

The flock of raised brows brought him quickly to

himself. "All right. We'll keep riding till we find the hunting party. We'll bring them back to camp, give them a few trinkets and whiskey, and let them go their way satisifed that we are Company men and that we are honoring the treaty." He would have to send a man ahead to warn the others to hide every pelt in camp, of course.

"Don't like it. Hanged if it makes sense," a man grumbled as they mounted up again.

Three miles upstream they spotted a grove of trees, the only cover of any kind within their view.

"If they've stayed around, they'll be in there," Vanderburgh said, pointing out the stand of trees. It was a small enclosure, and would hide ten men at the very most. "None of you is to make a single move until I authorize it. You may draw your weapons, but the man who fires a shot before my command can be certain I'll empty my lead into him."

He pulled his rifle from its holster and laid it across the saddle in front of him. He could expect a few arrows and shots when the Indians realized that they were discovered. Just in case, he nudged his mount a little ahead of the others. He would need a split second advantage to determine whether the hunters meant to make a stand of it, or parley first. Whatever happened, he had already lost a full day while Bridger got closer to reaching his goal of the mountains. He would have to push hard to catch him. "And I will," he vowed.

One hundred yards from the grove a narrow gully stretched across their path. Vanderburgh jumped in first, the exercise little more than a missed step for his animal. The others followed promptly, all eyes glued to the trees ahead.

Vanderburgh reached for his handkerchief, which he meant to use as a flag. He never drew it out. The day suddenly split open to the unearthly sound of a hundred savage cries.

They wheeled their mounts in unison, but it was too late. Pouring out of the tiny gully behind them, lances and rifles raised over their heads, came wave after wave of painted Blackfoot warriors.

Vanderburgh cried out for his men to hold their fire but it was lost as the first gun exploded in the hands of the trapper closest to the Indians.

The Blackfoot suddenly stopped, looks of surprise in their faces as they gazed down at their fallen comrade who had been carrying aloft an American flag. A guttural cry of rage rose from the rear of the war party. Dozens of rifles were lowered to take pointblank aim at the little party of six men. Sick fear enveloped Vanderburgh's body.

The scene changed, picking up speed until the only thing that mattered was the split second timing that made the difference between life and death. Vanderburgh's horse reared under him as once more the air vibrated with the blood cry of the most feared warriors in the West.

The man beside him gave a yelp of pain and toppled from his horse at Vanderburgh's feet. He had not yet drawn his rifle to his shoulder but he did so now, yelling automatically over his shoulder, "Don't give them an inch of ground! Stand and fight to the last man!"

He did not realize that he was surrounded. His horse went down and he discarded his spent rifle for the pistol in his waistband. He never got a chance to use it. Two strong warriors were upon him, each grabbing an arm. They lifted him from the ground as four rifle balls tore through him simultaneously.

Eagle Ribs looked down on his work with great

pleasure. War chief of the Blood Indians, he had not found his task as messenger of the white man, McKenzie, to his liking. But he had come south with his people in search of Vanderburgh with news of a peace treaty he did not like nor meant to honor beyond its use. Fort Union had supplied his warriors with the weapons necessary to wipe the mountains clear of both their tribal enemies and the trappers. And when the last of them were dead or frightened back beyond the north fork in the Great River, he would turn his rifles on McKenzie himself. This would be a lesson for the white man to beware. One false move and his people would leave him just as they were leaving this stupid white man.

Eagle Ribs signaled for his warriors to dump the body into the river. He smiled as he stroked his trophies—symbols of his victory over the white man's grasping ways. He would ride back to Fort Union now and say that he had not found the man he was sent to look for. And the white man, McKenzie, would smile and shrug, and break out a fresh keg of brandy, too afraid to question Eagle Ribs about the trophies swinging from his saddle.

Eagle Ribs kicked his pony, eager to return north, the stripped, bloody bones of Vanderburgh's forearms and fingers dangling at his knee.

Chapter 17

Bridger set the last stone in place over the bones of his vanquished enemy. His face was a mask of anger and grim determination. The bones were all that remained to be buried of what had once been the man named William Henry Vanderburgh. And there wasn't much left of the Canadian, either. The Blackfoot had done their job too well. Even the trappers were reluctant to cheer the loss of an enemy.

Bridger glanced up quickly at Fitz and the other trappers who were with him. Then his eyes fixed on the scout who had led them all to this terrible spot. The man averted his gaze. He had been lucky to escape—and he knew it.

Looking down again at the meager pile of stones, Bridger found himself strangely empty of any feelings of hatred. Vanderburgh's death was worse than any man deserved. When the exhausted and bedraggled scout had stumbled into Bridger's camp, he had recounted a grim story. But even so, Bridger had been unprepared for the sight that greeted him at this spot. The Canadian had been shot a dozen times and his scalp lifted. But it was Vanderburgh's condition that made even the toughest of the men turn away. Every bit of flesh had been stripped from the body. Most of the sinew and muscle had been dragged off by wolves and vultures. By the time Bridger and his men returned with the terrified scout, only the bones remained to be buried under a pile of stone.

Rising to his feet, Bridger unconsciously pulled his fur cap from his head. "Damnedest thing I ever saw," he commented to himself.

The murder left him uncomfortable. He had taken Vanderburgh into Blackfoot country hoping to scare him off or to keep him so busy dodging Blackfoot sign that he would lose the Rocky Mountain brigade. He had not meant for it to end like this.

" 'Twas a fair chance," Fitz whispered at his big friend's elbow. "He took it the same as the rest of us. Knew what he was doing. Had to." Fitz took off his cap, and a direct look at the others had them snatching their coverings from their heads. "We aren't rightly what you could call good Christians, but it would seem the man deserves a few good words said over him."

Bridger looked over the circle of men. When none of them volunteered he cleared his throat and said, "Dear Lord, this man, William Henry Vanderburgh, might not have been a particular friend of ours but we stand ready to say for his part that he was a tenacious soul. He saw his duty and tried his darnedest to see it through. Ain't much worse could happen to a man than what the Blackfoot done to him. Reckon hell will look quite comfortable to him now, if that's where he's at. Of course, if he made it to heaven, ain't a man here going to deny he earned it, dying the way he done. We do what we have to and Vanderburgh, well, he saw it different than most of us. Can't fault a man for doing his job. Amen."

Fitz clapped his hat back on his head and raised his hand high to lay it on Bridger's shoulder. "You done that real nice. Maybe you'll say a few words for me when the time comes."

Bridger made a sour face. "Let's get the hell out of here!"

That night, huddled in their robes with the smallest of campfires before them, the Bridger brigade reviewed its plans.

"It's nearly November," Fitz said. "By the time we reach the best streams, they'll be iced over. Three weeks at the most."

Bridger nodded. "Looks like we wasted our time, all right. Just what Vanderburgh wanted. Suppose he's laughin' his head off at this moment if he's looking over from the Spirit World."

The comment produced a round of chuckles, diluting the awesome silence that had remained with them the rest of the day. The best way to get over a bad experience was to turn it lighthearted, Bridger thought with an easing of his own tension. And seeing as how they were far from being out of danger themselves, he sought to buck up flagging spirits with a round of whiskey, a breach of most brigade routines.

"Of course, we got to get to wintering, meet up with Frapp and Milt and their boys. That means we got to first get out of Blackfoot territory."

"Do ye reckon 'em Injuns will come after this camp?" Dupree asked between swallows.

" 'Tain't likely," Fitz put in with a hearty tone. " 'Tis one thing you lads keep forgetting. Vanderburgh should o' ridden out with his whole brigade. A few men were sitting targets for even the tamest tribe. The horses alone would have tempted the Snakes or the Crows."

"That's the truth," another trapper added. "We

ain't settin' one foot 'afore t'other without ever' man followin' close behind."

"I've no quarrel with that," Bridger said. "Common sense and swift travel will keep us bunched together." He shot Loretto a keen glance. "It's the squaws and younguns that concern me. We been pushing hard for the better part of two months. We'll be pushed even harder to get to the west side of the Divide before the snow locks us on the Blackfoot side of the mountains. We must travel sometimes at night, especially if the sign becomes too fresh for comfort. Can you do it?"

Spurred by memories of the day, the agreement was unanimous. Only Loretto flushed to his forehead, his voice high and tight as he said, "My wife, she is Blackfoot. She travels the land of her people. I dare another squaw to do as well."

"Well now, boy, I reckon I might take you up on that, only I'm minus a woman at the moment. Maybe next season," a man called from the edge of the camp.

Loretto's flush deepened as he jumped to his feet and walked away.

Bridger looked about in question.

"The Spaniard's feelin' a mite peevish on account o' his woman," Blackjack Henry volunteered. "Some o' the boys is been makin' comments about a man sharin' his bedroll with the enemy."

"That's a truth that needs mouthin'," a man said. "Blackfoot squaw's bound to be trouble. Mark my words."

The meeting broke up quickly after that. The talk of Blackfoot had the effect of closing the whiskey barrels long before they were dry. No man wanted to be too drunk to make his shot count if needed.

Bridger did not roll up in his robes until after most of the camp had bedded down. He could not shake a feeling of danger and he never ignored his instincts. He sat hunched over, his knees drawn up and shut his eyes to sort out more clearly the feelings trembling in the purple haze of his subconscious. More and more his quiet moments were filled with images of Little Fawn. Memories of her bent over the stewpot or in the act of undressing came often enough to make him uncomfortable in a purely masculine way.

His mind wandered to Ear-of-the-Fox. Why had the warrior tried to kill him not so many weeks ago?

Bridger struck the question immediately from his mind. He felt a more pressing warning, and he knew by gut reaction that it was meant for him.

He pulled a cigar from his pack and lit it. It could be that Vanderburgh's death plagued him with guilt feelings. He faced it squarely in his mind. He felt a momentary twinge of sorrow for the man who had died a painful, torturous death. He felt neither victor nor traitor. He had been in the same area, at the same time. His odds had been the same as Vanderburgh's. An unlucky chance had separated them.

When his mind shifted to the Blackfoot, his feeling of alarm grew. He would not deny that he dreaded the fate he could meet at their hands. He told himself he would fight to the death if it came to that. For his brigade he felt responsibility and a camaraderie that would remain with him until they were safely over the Divide. After that . . .

Bridger took a long drag on his cigar. After that, he would go back to the Wind River Valley to look for the woman he would have as his wife.

He exhaled a breath in a deep sigh. He did not know quite when he had made up his mind. Perhaps Ear-of-the-Fox had something to do with it. He doubted it. While he had been shouting his vow never to return to Little Fawn, part of him had realized, with an uncommon amount of pride and fear, that she had just proclaimed her love for him. Now, hundreds of miles from her, he could listen to the echo of her words singing in his heart.

A grin spread over his face when he thought of how cocky she would be when he went to Washakie to ask for her hand. She would probably make him listen to every word of denial he had heaped on her, and more than likely parade the big Pelouse about the village in victory. He reckoned he could stand the teasing. When all was said and done, she would be rolled up with him in his robes, her soft, smooth body tangled with his, and her cries of victory traded for ones of passion. Yes, come wintering he thought he would let Fitz stew and fret over the brigade while he journeyed south.

"Maybe it's just bridegroom jitters," he taunted himself and, rolling over onto his back, stretched out his legs to sleep.

The weather turned nasty the next few days as arctic winter rushed down to meet the party of trappers trying desperately to reach the haven of the western slope. They made their way up the Madison Fork of the Missouri, surging winds howling down the horseshoe-shaped canyons of the rugged terrain. Sleet raked the unprotected faces of the riders and their mounts.

Bridger and Fitz had called in their scouts when the storm commenced. The scouts had fallen back to within a hundred yards of the main body and closed up the rear to within the same distance. There was nothing to be seen far enough in advance to do them any good.

The feeling of trouble persisted as the days wore on until Bridger's suspicions hardened into a conviction that they were in terrible danger. But he kept it to himself.

On the fourth night, after the camp was forted up against the miserable cold, Bridger stayed out of his robes. He moved through the camp on noiseless, moccasined feet, prowling back and forth like a caged beast just out of reach of its prey.

"What's eating you, Gabe? And don't be telling me it's the moon." Fitz and Bridger both turned up their faces to the sky where a ripe harvest moon hugged the eastern ridge of the Gallatin Range.

"Weather's clearing," Bridger murmured. "That'll help the going come morning."

"Any particular reason you're wanting the going to pick up?" Fitz persisted.

Bridger leaned his back against a boulder. They were on the eastern border of the Three Forks area where the Madison joined the Jefferson. "Come morning we'll begin to climb. We'll move quicker if we can see where we're heading. Flatheads will be a welcome change from Blackfoot sign."

Fitz slung his rifle over his shoulder and folded his arms. "So, it ain't just my Irish temperament making me dodge shadows. You got a wee touch of the nerves yourself."

Bridger's brows rose. "You feeling it? Thought I was jumpy cause of what happened to Vanderburgh."

"Did you now? And why should you be quailing before sights the likes of which we've witnessed many a time these last years?"

"This here is serious." Bridger hunched his shoulders against a painfully sharp blast of wind. "I got a reason for wanting to make it in safe this year. Don't know quite how to put it." He spared a quick glance at the Irishman and then slanted his eyes away. "Don't tell my feelings well, you know that. Ain't no other man I'd even say this to." He cleared his throat of its suddenly tight feeling and pulled himself upright to face the other man. "I'm thinking of marrying," he roared out in his deep bass voice.

Fitz's white brows flew up like the wings of a dove. "Faith! 'Tis that what's got you trembling like a bull downwind of a cow?" His grin went undetected in the dark, but Bridger heard it in his voice. "Tell me now, lad. Who is the fair colleen?"

Bridger's mouth turned down at the corners. "Little Fawn, of course."

"Of course." Fitz shot out his hand. "Congratulations, Gabe. Must say I'm delighted to hear it. When I'm gone you'll be needing a body to look after you proper. 'Tis a fair, fine lass you're having."

Bridger stared at him, ignoring the handshake. "What do you mean, when you're gone?"

Fitz lowered his hand. "Here! Let's sit a minute." He indicated the stump of a tree. "Don't go saying you never thought I'd leave the territory. I've been spending a great deal of time on the trail these last years. The adventure appeals to me. Time was, hunting beaver was more adventurous than it is now. Sure'n we've just beat out maybe the greatest threat we've ever had but there's a difference you'll not be telling me you don't understand."

Bridger rubbed his jaw with his knuckles. "No. I won't say I didn't figure you'd one day up and seek the city again. But, well . . . Hell! Thought you'd wait till we had these Company boys all beat to hell and back."

Fitz gave a heartfelt sigh. "Once we had no more concern for the folk back in civilization than a beaver had for the fashionable hats worn by the gentry in Europe. The threat to them was there all along but they hadn't seen its direct effect. Now the beaver are mortally scarce in places where a few years back you could hardly count their number. The beaver's got to know he's a hunted beast. 'Tis the same with you and me. We've known all along we were in a business that made the lucky rich. We've known the price of pelts was rising with each year and our presence here made it tempting for others to join us. Only now, we're seeing the results.

"McKenzie, Vanderburgh, Fontenelle—they're only the beginning. Talk back in St. Louis last spring was there'll be settlers heading out on the Platte River trail soon. Farmers, mind you. Faith! We'll soon be up to our necks in quilting bees and barn raisings."

Bridger was silent. He knew it all, had thought of it on his own, but the words spoken gave it a new pertinence. "Don't make me no difference. I'm out here for what time I got left. Nothing back East for me. But you, what will you do, Fitz?"

The Irishman shrugged. "Maybe see what's left of the territory to the west. The Santa Fe trail offers some unique opportunities. Most likely I'll not be drifting too far. But I'm thinking the time has come to settle down, like you're thinking of doing."

Bridger's head swung around. "I ain't said nothing about settling. Don't aim to, not as long as there's beaver anywhere about. Little Fawn's an Indian. She'll know what's expected of her on the seasonal hunts. She's born and bred a mountain child."

Fitz smiled. "Little Fawn's a woman. She'll be giving you sons before long. She'll need to have a home of her own to raise them in. You'll have to protect and feed a whole family. Marriage will settle you, Gabe. Be there no mistaking it."

Bridger had no answer for that. He had not gotten that far in his thinking. Marriage was a big enough hunk to swallow. He was not certain he would accept any curtailment of his wanderlust, even for Little

Fawn. But he wanted her. He could always trade her off if it did not work out, he told himself, even though he knew in his heart that it was a lie.

"Here now!" Fitz cried when Bridger burst into laughter all of a sudden. "What's the matter, lad?"

Bridger sobered slowly. "Just pondering the worth of hellfire in pintsize," he said between chuckles.

"Injuns! *Lêve!* Injuns!"

The cry went up at dawn, the wail of squaws and children floating sharply above the barks of orders. Howling trappers scrambled for their rifles as the brigade camp awoke to the signal of mortal danger.

Bridger rolled out of his blanket and to his feet in one smooth motion, his rifle clenched in his fist. He ran to the front of the camp and looked out across the open prairie where the scout pointed.

"Over yonder, Cap'n Bridger."

Bridger's eyes thinned to slits as their gray, knife-edged gaze cut through the blue mist hanging thickly about the valley. The forms were indistinct, mere shades of darkness against the pale drifting fog, but the signs were unmistakable to his experienced eye. He swung back toward the brigade, bawling orders for an immediate saddle-up.

"Can we outrun them?" Fitz cried, running full out beside the Rocky Mountain bourgeois.

"Your guess is as good as mine," Bridger shouted back over his shoulder. "We'll head for those mountains to the west. Hope to cache up in the rocks before them Indians catch on to our direction. They won't be happy about running into us either, I reckon."

They took cover quickly, women and children fleeing on foot toward the eastern foothills of the Divide. Mules and horses were herded on ahead of the armed trappers who formed a human barrier behind the retreating brigade. Two hours later they dug into the tumbled debris that formed a high, irregular fort of natural rock at the base of the mountains. The thin yellow sun had risen, dragging from the valley the winter veil of haze. The sight that greeted Bridger's eyes was not heartening.

"Damnation! It's a whole migrating village of Blackfoot!" Bridger sucked in his breath. He had counted on the fact that a full brigade, numbering better than sixty men, would put off any real attempt at aggression by the redmen. But they were outnumbered better than two to one. Blackfoot with a taste of a fresh battle still pumping in their veins would be eager for another victory.

As he and his men watched, the Indians quickly flushed their women and children to the wooded grove just abandoned by the trappers. The warriors rode to the fore, their rifles and lances displayed in full view.

"I count a hundred and fifty up front," Fitz whispered.

"Close enough," Bridger answered out of the corner of his mouth. His limbs had gone taut, but his men read nothing of that strain as he called out a deployment of his party. Two to one Indians preferred. But that did not mean they would not fight, he told himself, not when it was Blackfoot.

"It'd never have come to this if the day before had been fair," Fitz said quietly, his eyes glued to the enemy camp. "Lord knows how we kept from stepping on each other's toes in the fog."

Bridger did not reply. If the Indians chose to attack, he would make certain every man's shot counted. When the Indians emptied their rifles, they would turn to arrows. Knives and tomahawks, weapons used for close-quarter fighting, would be held till they broke through the trappers' defenses.

Tensions wove a pattern of silence about the grim-faced mountain men. The Blackfoot, too, were uncharacteristically silent. They rode back and forth before the grove where they had taken refuge. They seemed as uneasy as their foes.

"What's so almighty wrong?" Dupree called down from his position. "Injuns ain't quiet by nature."

"They're doin' some figurin' on whose scalp each of 'em wants," another trapper chimed in.

"Reckon that makes you safe, Jack, seein' as how you're buzzard-egg bald."

The banter died down quickly. A war chief, his face painted a brilliant red and yellow, kicked his mount into the open space between the two armed camps. The trappers' rifles were lifted to their shoulders immediately but Bridger's curt command kept a shot from being fired. Several other warriors followed the young chief, until half a dozen warriors stood in the open.

The first rider raised his arm in greeting, tassels of fur swinging from the sacred pipe he held aloft.

"What do they take us for? 'Tain't hardly likely we'd be falling for that old trick, not after what they done to Vanderburgh," Fitz voiced in derision. But to his astonishment, Bridger moved away from his side and started toward his horse tethered a little behind the rock where they had taken shelter.

"Are you a madman, truly?" Fitz yelled, running up to grab at the reins of the horse. "You don't have to go out there. Make a bit of sense. They'll jump you, sure as I'm a Mick. 'Tain't nobody expecting you to risk your life for the sake of a bit of a show."

Bridger paused, one foot in the stirrup. "You can count better'n me, Fitz. In the Indian way of thinking, we're nearly evenly matched. Two to one is as good as it's going to get on our side. If a few of the boys go under on the first charge, we got worse troubles than now. We got our backs against the mountains. They got the water and the cover. Maybe we can fake them out of attacking. It's worth a try."

Fitz's face hardened, his blue eyes frosting over. "Then I'll be the one to go. You're in charge. The brigade won't care if I take a gutful of shot."

"No." Bridger hauled his big frame into the saddle. "It's got to be me. My responsibility. I know Indians. Maybe they'll hear me out. You stay put."

Fitz fell back a step, his complexion blazing beneath a wealth of freckles. "So that's it! The great Jim Bridger is out to add a notch to his legend, and he'll not be having another to share in the glory."

Bridger pulled his hat down to shade his eyes, his expression unreadable. "Sorry you feel that way, Fitz," he said evenly.

"You're a madman!" Fitz yelled after him. "You don't have to do it!"

Fitz's cry carried out into the plain as Bridger urged his horse from behind the rocks. His rifle lay across his saddle, his finger resting on the trigger.

You don't have to do it. The sentence ran through his head. Yet something was drawing him out into the open, testing the very fiber of his being. Once before, when he was nineteen, he had listened to the voice of reason. A persuasive, sensible voice had lured him to an act which he had never been able to outrun nor forget in every breath, conscious or asleep. He would not buckle under again. Fitz did not understand that. Perhaps no one could.

His palms were sweating, the muscles in his chest so rigid he could hardly breathe. He felt the hundred arrows aimed at his flesh and the dozens more rifle barrels leveled at his gut. It took every ounce of will he had to keep himself upright in the saddle when instinct told him to crouch low and deliver his load of shot into the nearest Blackfoot. He moved out in the middle ground, a lone, unprotected figure in dirty buckskins, to meet his fate.

A dozen curious eyes swept over him as he approached the Blackfoot peace party. He slowly raised his arm in greeting, his rifle gripped tightly in that hand.

The first rider moved his mount a little closer until they stood side by side. "I am Wild River, Chief of the Dog Soldiers," the Blackfoot began in his own tongue. "You trespass in the land of my people. We will not allow that."

Bridger unlocked his clenched jaw. The Blackfoot had spoken first. That was a good sign. Perhaps they were as anxious as he to avoid a full-scale war. "I am called Bridger."

He turned carefully in the saddle to point to the rocks from which he had come. "Those are my people. We do not come to the land of the Blackfoot to trap. We were driven east over the Great Divide by our enemies, white enemies."

He paused, but the Indians gave no indication that the information was of any importance. "We go back to the land of the Flathead at this very moment. We wish no harm to your people nor your land. By the next sunrise we will have vanished into the land of the setting sun." He pointed a finger to the west.

He never learned what the Blackfoot war chief might have answered. A cry, a woman's shriek, pierced the silence, followed by a man's anguished yell. It was too much. Instinctively Bridger's finger tightened on the trigger.

The Blackfoot chief saw the move and threw himself across the white man's lap to grab for the weapon.

Shouts went up on both sides as the two men struggled for control.

Bridger jerked free and raised his Hawken. In the split second between the click of the hammer and the explosion of the shot he waited for death. So this, then, was what his hunter's instinct had warned him of. Strangely, his last thought was not fear, nor the sense that he had failed his people, but of a sweet sadness that Little Fawn would never know how true her prophecy had been. She had gotten into his blood and now she would never know it.

Two barb-tipped steel arrows arched out of the frigid blue sky and slammed into his back. His shot went wide as he was shoved hard against his horse's neck with the impact. His rifle was stripped from his suddenly numbed fingers. A skull-cracking blow from his own rifle sent him tumbling from the saddle and into a pool of blackness.

"Didn't I tell you that Blackfoot squaw was up to no good? Damn 'em all to hell, anyhow! Her and that bawling half-breed baby near about got us all killed. Five good men dead. Well? What do you think? He gonna make it or we stuck up out here without a booshway?" The trapper, his head bandaged where a Blackfoot ball had scraped his scalp, peered over the Irishman's shoulder.

"Don't like the looks of it. Arrows went in his right shoulder but his eyes are bloodshot. Must be bleeding inside his head from that clubbing."

Fitz bent over the unconscious form of his friend and felt for a pulse. He had not been able to sneak out into the middle for Bridger until after nightfall. The battle had raged all day once the first shots were exchanged. He had thought Bridger dead and went out just to keep the body from being mutilated and scalped. When he had reached him, the body was still warm, his breaths shallow but even.

Bridger's eyes opened at the touch of cold fingers on his flesh. It was so dark he thought at first he had been blinded. But gradually the light from a single campfire penetrated his exhausted senses. "Fitz? That you?"

Fitz expelled an oath under his breath. "You damn fool madman!" Tears of anger and fear sprang to his eyes, mercifully hidden by the darkness. "Told you you'd get yourself killed. Just look at you, arrows sticking out every which way. You look like a damned porcupine!"

"Made . . . a mistake," he quavered faintly.

"Like hell!" the trapper exclaimed. "It was that damn Blackfoot squaw. You no sooner rode out than she came pushing to the front of the line. Must o' spied a relative in that party of warriors what rode out to meet you. She let loose with a screech that'd take the hair off a grizzly and tore off into the open 'afore any of us could stop her. Loretto commenced to yelling, too. Next thing we know both camps was firing away."

Bridger tested his arms and legs. They would not move. He was face down on a buffalo robe. "Arrows still in?"

"You bet." Fitz chewed his lip a moment. "They got to come out, Gabe. Wish Milt or Doc Newell was here. They're better at this kind of thing."

Bridger tried to raise his head but nothing seemed to work anymore. "You . . . Fitz. You do it," he muttered.

"Of course I'm going to do it," he answered jauntily, but was glad the man could not see his face. "Only, maybe we better wait till morning."

Bridger managed a tiny movement of his head.

"Now. It cuts me up . . . something fierce, them arrows."

Fitz sat back on his heels and directed one man to grab Bridger's ankles and two more to hold his arms. "It's gonna hurt like hell. You need some whiskey?"

Bridger mouthed a denial. "One thing," he whispered so softly Fitz got down on his hands and knees to lean over him. "I don't make it . . . you tell Little Fawn . . . She won the Pelouse fair and square. You tell her. She'll know."

Fitz swore. "Of all the crazy notions to take you at this moment, Gabe, me lad, that's got to be the maddest. I'll be telling your colleen nothing, and that's a fact. You do your own courting."

"You're a bastard, Fitz," Bridger murmured.

"Don't I know it," the Irishman shot right back. "Now you hold still and pretty for old Fitz while he slips these hatpins out of your back."

Fitz tucked a thick wedge of rawhide between Bridger's teeth and rose quickly to his feet. "All right, lads, you hold him tight." He bent over and took a firm hold on the first arrow shaft, gritted his teeth, and yanked.

A gut-wrenching cry roared up when the three-inch arrowhead was yanked from Bridger's flesh.

"That's one of them," Fitz announced proudly as he held up the prize. "Ready for the next one?"

One of the trappers at Bridger's head looked up at the Irishman with a sour smile. "Reckon it don't much matter to the booshway. He's done fainted."

His first conscious feeling was that of movement. He lay a long time in the darkness of closed lids, testing by minute flexings of his muscles the response of his limbs. His last thought had been fear that, if he did not die, the arrows might leave him paralyzed. But his fingers grasped the buffalo robe over him, answering his brain's command. Toes that felt like lead shot twitched slightly, and he relaxed. He could face being alive now.

"Mr. Feetz! You come. Cap'n Bridger, he's movin'!"

Bridger opened his eyes at the sound of the woman's voice. The sharp, clear curve of sky told him at once that he was in high mountains. A painful but possible movement of his head had him glancing overhead into the grinning faces of a Flathead squaw and two black-eyed children leaning over the rump of the horse pulling the travois on which he lay.

"Gabe, lad! So you've come back to us." A moment elapsed between the sound of Fitz's voice and his appearance in Bridger's view.

"How long?" His voice grated against his throat, but the sound came forth.

"Well now, you'll be recovering just fine if you can worry about the date." Fitz's smile stretched his face to its limits. More seriously he said, "Thought we lost you three different times—between my butchering and the damage them murdering devils done to you. We gave you up I don't want to think how often. Was the brain fever that had us the most worked up. You were yelling fit to kill the lot of us when you wasn't so still we thought you was gone under."

"Meaner'n a grizzly, that be the truth," Dupree offered over Fitz's shoulder. "Took four of us to hold ye down."

"One thing, Gabe." Fitz lowered his voice. "I didn't get that second arrowhead out of you. Shaft broke off below the skin and I wasn't up to cutting you up any more. You'll have it forever."

"How long?" Bridger pushed past dry lips a second time.

"Oh, you want to know how long you've been

sick? A few weeks, long enough for us to make it over the Divide. We're practically to Snake River. Blackfoot cleared out before sunrise the very next day after your accident.

"Milt and Frapp was even in to camp to greet us a couple days back. Told them if you wasn't dead by now you'd be in the saddle by the time we pulled into their camp. They're making up their wintering in the valley."

Bridger hesitated in an effort to speak but Fitz went on quickly. "You ain't never gonna guess how bad a time old Milt had on the hunt to the south. Took to starving before it was over. Should have heard Joe Meek talking about the taste of fresh roasted crickets. Lord, they was drinking mule blood before they got to water and hooked some fish. Reckon they had a worse time of it all around."

If he expected an answer he did not get it. Bridger had fallen back into a heavy sleep that lasted intermittently for the next week.

Chapter 18

His strength was slow in returning, and by midway
through wintering, Bridger began to despair of ever re-
gaining his old feeling of power. He knew the others
watched him from under their brims, or with a quick
cut of their eyes when he was up and about again. He
heard the whispers about dead men walking, and how
his belief in the Indian Great Spirit had given him a
special protection against the Blackfoot arrows.

He grunted unconsciously as he lifted a hundred-
pound pack of pressed skins. The wound had healed
over, and by working his muscles, the tightness had
eased. But a deep ache checked his once easy movements. He cursed and dropped the load on the ground.

"Give it time, Gabe." Fitz came strolling up behind him. "You'd think you had something left to
prove."

Bridger turned on him and blushed. "Guess I'm
acting like a long-eared jackass," he grumbled.

"I never correct a man when he's right." Fitz
nearly reached out to help the man until his judgment
stopped him. "You plan on gearing up for the spring

hunt alone? There's a few of us figuring to do our share."

"I got to make it up to the boys," Bridger insisted. "Because of me they lost a whole season. I aim to be back in the field with the first thaw. Maybe get into position sooner. We'll make it up if we have to stay in the field clean through one season into the next."

"Ain't you forgetting something?"

Bridger cocked his head to one side.

"Little Fawn."

Bridger shook his shaggy head. "I was talking nonsense last fall. Musta been a wild hair kinking up my thinking. Just look at Milt. He's turned all doe-eyed and sloppy over that little Mountain Lamb he married. Can't do enough for her. A man would think he's the squaw and she's the master the way he's forever fetching and carrying for her."

"You never shut up about her," Fitz mentioned matter-of-factly.

"What say?" Bridger's look was suddenly wary.

"Little Fawn—you never said more'n five words that weren't about her while you were feverish."

Bridger made a disclaiming gesture with his hand. "Fever talk ain't nothin' a sane man would own up to."

"Maybe not," Fitz agreed mildly. "But it's certainly what's on a man's mind."

"Did I bawl it all over camp?" Bridger's usually firm voice sounded edgy, like a child caught at some mischief.

Fitz brightened considerably. "Faith, lad, you think I'd let you shame yourself while I'm about? No one heard you. I made certain of that. Nursed you myself through most of the bad days."

Suspicions unallayed, Bridger eyed him. "Who was riding bourgeois?"

" 'Tis a curious thing, that. The Mexican

Loretto's going to make a fine scout. He sat at the head those first days, along with Dupree. Guess he needed something to take his mind off the loss of his wife and babe, 'cause he volunteered."

"They dead?" Bridger had not asked too many questions about the battle after he was given a brief accounting.

"No. The Blackfoot took them with them. Guess the girl was more homesick than Loretto guessed. Nobody fired a shot when Loretto dashed across the lines to hand her the baby. Strange doin's that day. I'll not be saying, but there's some truth to the rumor."

"What rumor's that?"

The Irishman smiled. "Why, that Peejatowahooten's powerful medicine kept us from being smeared from here to the Snake River."

Bridger smirked. "That so, how come I'm near about busted up so bad I can hardly get by?"

"You're alive," Fitz returned quickly. "If you'd seen yourself when I brought you in, you'd believe in Manitou and spirit protection, too. Now, about the girl. Want to tell me why you're moping around here when you could be riding after Little Fawn?"

Bridger searched his friend's face with dark, smoky eyes, looking for any sign of amusement. There was none. "Plain and simple, I'm broke. Flat busted. Washakie's a proud man; he'll be expecting a fair amount of gifts for his oldest child. I ain't got nothin' and can't expect that to change until we make good on the spring hunt. It may be clear to the fall till I can afford what I want to give for her."

Fitz nodded. He understood, but the question had to be asked. "What if Washakie gets it into his head to marry her off to some warrior?"

Bridger's famous deadpan look made itself apparent. "I'll face that if I have to. Till then, what hap-

pens ain't no business of mine. If she's my woman,
she'll wait for me."

Little Fawn skirted the campsite of the American
trappers at the rendezvous. Her father's command that
she keep away from the white men's lodges rang
clearly in her ears. But the errand that brought her
here against his wishes was greater than her fear of
reprimand. The Rocky Mountain brigades had begun
arriving in the Green River Valley days before. She
knew because she had asked Raven's Song, one of the
bolder women of her tribe. Raven's Song made a daily
trek to the American camps looking for ways to earn
the baubles she paraded so proudly in the Shoshone
village.

Little Fawn had dressed in her oldest clothes and
pulled her hair back with a leather thong. On her
cheeks she had smeared a smelly concoction of mud
and herbs, hoping the paint would repel any man she
might encounter. Despite her father's order, she could
wait no longer. She had to know if Jim Bridger was in
the white trappers' camp before she set herself up to
oppose her father once again.

"I will marry no man but Bridger," she whispered
to herself. She had vowed it many times in her heart
since the last time she looked upon his face a full year
ago. She had countered her father's every attempt to
bind her in marriage to any of several young warriors
who had come to him in hopes of winning her for their
bride. She had sent back every gift from the suitors.
She even refused horses, which she knew her father
needed to improve his herd, and precious buffalo robes
and fine furs that she wanted for herself.

"My daughter, you must remember your promise
to me," Washakie had finally reminded her only the
week before. Her objections to a Bannock war chief

who wanted to take three of Washakie's daughters into his lodge had cost her village a needed alliance.

"I will not be one of a set of wives purchased for the purpose of swelling the prideful heart of Running Elk," she had retorted hotly. "Besides, Twin Arrows would drive me to weep before the moon ran its course in the sky. I will not share my husband with my sisters!"

Washakie had not voiced his sympathy. Instead he had said to her, "My daughter, will you look into your heart to recall that you promised to obey me in my choice of husband for you if you passed the fall unwed?"

Little Fawn had grown angry at the reminder of her humiliation in losing Bridger, but, realizing that it was not her father's fault, she had hidden her anger. "Father, surely you would not force upon me a man I despise."

Washakie had smiled. "You are so young you cannot know your heart. A woman's duty is to please her master. You asked me once to tell you how to gain a man's love. With time, and the willingness to please, you will have the happiness you seek."

"Then happiness is not to be for me," she had said woefully. "The warrior who marries me will not be pleased and will quickly turn to his other wives for the comfort he will not find in me."

"Would you make life so unpleasant for the man?"

Little Fawn had lowered her lashes as she spoke. "I would make life too terrible to be endured for Running Elk."

"He would beat you. It would be his right as your husband," Washakie had reminded her.

"I would leave him. That is my right as a Shoshone woman."

And so, for a time, she had won her father's begrudging concession to her refusal. This time the matter was different. She could not refuse this proposal without the backing of the man she desired.

Little Fawn shook herself slightly. Ear-of-the-Fox had returned last week after more than two years. When first she had seen him riding into her village with a herd of six stolen horses, her heart had gone out to him in her pride at his accomplishment. Not many warriors, even with twice his years, could boast of so fine a conquest. Word of his other great deeds of bravery and cunning had filtered back to her ears through the many months of his absence, but nothing could compare with the joy of seeing him ride into the Shoshone village. His bare chest had been intricately adorned with the paint marks of an honored warrior with many coups and several scalps of their enemies to his credit. It was rumored that the scalp decorating his war lance was the hair of a Blackfoot Dog Soldier.

She had run across the open yard of the camp along with all the others who came out to greet him, her smile the broadest of them all. It had not lasted. He had looked over the people circling his mount until he saw her. The look in his eyes had caused her to stumble back in surprise. The flat, black stare was the look of a stranger. No—it was a contemptuous look that had as its intent a wish of death. She knew in that moment that word of her life as Bridger's lodge-keeper had reached him.

Angry and resentful of the piercing glance, she had squared her shoulders and walked away. He could think what he wished. She did not need his regard. She was a woman now, fully capable of accepting the results of her actions. If he regarded her as a whore, it did not matter. She had given herself to the only man she ever hoped to lie beside. So mighty a warrior as Ear-of-the-Fox could buy himself half a dozen wives. He did not need her adulation.

But she had misinterpreted that look. She later learned that Ear-of-the-Fox wanted her as his bride.

"My father cannot force me into this alliance," she had assured herself, but she was less confident than usual. Ear-of-the-Fox was now a famous man, a legendary figure up and down the canyons of the territory. He was an honored guest and a son, by adoption, of her father. Even her mother, Blue Feather, was in favor of the match. When Little Fawn did not gather the abundant gifts Ear-of-the-Fox left before her lodge door that morning, her mother did at her father's instruction. Washakie's patience had run out. He would not ask her this time, she realized in growing panic. And without shaming her village and her father, she could find no way of refusing, other than to seek out Bridger.

Little Fawn hunched her shoulders lower as two men passed her. She, who had known a pride uncommon in a Shoshone woman, was preparing to go with Bridger as his woman, without the words of the marriage ceremony binding them to one another. Her father would disown her. Her mother would never be allowed to speak her name again. They would think her ungrateful and disobedient. But none of them had seen the look Ear-of-the-Fox kept guarded until his eyes fell on her. None of them had witnessed the hatred and promise of revenge that lurked in that gaze. No one knew what she knew—that a madman lay hidden behind the eyes of the man she had once loved as a brother and a friend.

A large hand reached out to grab her by the arm,

forcing a frightened gasp from her as she was jerked around and into the arms of a stranger.

"Glory be! Looky what I done caught sniffin' 'round our tepee, Fitz?" the tall white man yelled, enveloping the tiny girl in a bearlike hug. "And just my size. I do like 'em small."

Fitz looked up over his shoulder with a rakish grin. He was well into his second keg of whiskey. "Want me to try her on for size for you, lad? There's a trick to mounting a wee thing." He rose unsteadily to his feet and lurched over to the man who held a violently struggling girl in his grasp.

"Go gently, lad. You'll mar the merchandise." Fitz leaned forward to peer into the girl's face. Little Fawn struck out at him with a fist and he ducked back. "Ah, the fair colleen thinks we should be paying up front for our pleasure." He swung about, feet tangling, and nearly fell flat. Righting himself with consciously measured movements, he yelled to the men around the campfire, "Any of you lads willing to take a small IOU on a pair of bead necklaces till morning?"

Immediately half a dozen glass-bead necklaces flew up from the men and landed at his feet. "Much obliged," he slurred jauntily and bent quickly to pick up a few. He turned back to the trapper holding on to Little Fawn and smiled. "Would seem the lass objects to you, lad. Let a real ladies' man show you how it's done."

"Hold on!" the trapper cried, letting go of the girl and pushing her behind him as Fitz held out the necklaces to her. "This here squaw is mine. Go find you own— Hey! Where're you goin'?"

Little Fawn did not hesitate when the man loosened his grasp. She ran as fast as her slender legs would carry her out of the trappers' camp. She had been foolish to go there at night, she told herself as she heard the cries of the two men close behind her. She should have waited and come during the day when she might have been able to spot Bridger at a distance. Now she had piqued the lust of two men who were too drunk and too filled with the urgency of their desire to listen to her.

Running through the underbrush near their camp, she suffered unflinchingly the sting of thorns that raked her arms and legs. It was the pace of her breathing that finally slowed her at the water's edge. She put both hands to her mouth to smother her harsh breathing and squatted low in the reeds of the bank.

After a few minute's silence in which the loud voices of her pursuers retreated in the distance, she rose and stepped slowly into the open.

"Got you!"

The triumphant cry rang out as a heavy hand once more fell on her arm. She swung around with fists curled to deliver a furious assault. But she checked her blow as she faced in the moonlight the lopsided grin of the smaller man.

Fitz held out his beads in one hand and put the fingers of his other hand to his lips. "Ssh! Don't want the lad to hear us," he whispered. "Brad's a sore loser. We'll just stay out here a while till he finds himself another woman."

Little Fawn drew back slightly but did not flee. Here, with one man, she might learn what she needed to know.

Fitz reached out and gently took her hand to place the beads in her palm. "Just so you know, darlin'. I'm not a welsher." He sniffed the air lightly and wrinkled his nose. "What's that smell?"

Little Fawn turned her palm down, her wide eyes never leaving the white man's face as the beads slid to the ground. "Bridger," she implored when he turned a puzzled stare on her.

Fitz cocked his head to the side. "You looking for Gabe?" When she did not answer he realized she must not speak English. His perception was a bit fogged by the Taos Lightning and it took him three tries to find the right Indian language. "So, you're Shoshone. Well, you can't . . ." He reached out and wiped some mud from her face with his sleeve. "Little Fawn?"

She nodded cautiously. "I come seeking the one you call Jim Bridger," she said softly. "He is here?"

Fitz had begun wiping his hand on his buckskins. "Faith! What is that concoction? Buffalo dung?" He bent and picked up the beads. Bridger had been right about the girl after all, he thought with a smile. She was waiting for him, just like he said she would. "You want Bridger. Sorry, lass, he is not here."

A slow thudding began in Little Fawn's chest. "He is not here? He is dead?"

"Nah!" Fitz shook his head vigorously and immediately regretted it as the night spun wildly with red and yellow stars. "Though the Blackfoot sure enough tried. Last November Gabe took two arrows and got a cracked skull in a battle. 'Twas touch and go for almost a month. Patched up fine, though. A tougher man never drew breath." He wagged his silver head in admiration. "We're friends, he and I. I'm Thomas Fitzpatrick, at your service, ma'am."

Little Fawn studied the man in silence, his words unclear. "Where is Bridger?" she asked finally.

"Down by the Platte River. He and the lads are spending their time in the field this year. He doesn't plan to come in to rendezvous."

"Not come?"

The plaintive anguish in the girl's voice tugged at the romantic heart of the Irishman and he touched her cheek gently with a finger. "It does hurt to love that man, doesn't it? He's pricklier than a Mexican cactus and harder to track than an Arikara."

He started to add that Bridger cared very much for her, that in fact he had heard it from the man directly. But he decided it was Bridger's place to tell her that. "Can't tell you when he'll be back this way. Maybe— Hey! Where're you going?" he called after her as she suddenly turned and fled.

He watched her go with a sad expression. Hell! What did Bridger expect him to do? He had not so much as mentioned the girl since wintering. No, the only time Bridger had asked him to tell her anything was when he thought he was dying.

"Now, what was that?" Fitz muttered to himself. "Oh yes. Hey! Little Fawn!" he yelled, setting off in the direction which she had taken. "Listen, darlin'! Gabe said you're to keep the Pelouse. Won him fair and square!"

But she had disappeared. "It'll keep," he said under his breath. In fact, it would probably keep till he had a chance to talk to that fellow, Wyeth, who had shown up again. He had a bug to put in that Yankee's ear. Something that could keep the American Fur Company out of the Rockies forever. Then, when Washakie came in to trade, he would find Little Fawn and give her Gabe's message. "It'll keep."

"My child, what is wrong?" Blue Feather knelt beside her oldest daughter who was sprawled across her robe in one corner of their lodge. "Come, talk with me," she urged, gently shaking the trembling shoulder of the girl whose face was buried in the coarse blanket.

Little Fawn sat up slowly, her face flooded with tears. "Mother, I am so afraid," she whispered huskily and, throwing her arms about the woman's shoulders, began to sob uncontrollably.

"What is it, Little Fawn?" her mother asked when most of her daughter's tears were spent. "It is not like my warrior-hearted daughter to weep. What has disturbed you so?"

"It is Ear-of-the-Fox. I cannot marry him," Little Fawn answered.

Blue Feather's face, once as beautiful as the daughter's she looked upon, turned disapproving. "It is your father's wish. It would shame him and our village if you refuse a warrior as great as Ear-of-the-Fox. Your father will be very displeased."

Little Fawn struck the tears from her eyes. "I will never marry him. I will leave our village, never to return."

Blue Feather shook her head. "Do you think that will free you from your father's command? Where will you go? No Shoshone village will welcome a disobedient daughter of Chief Washakie. Nor will they welcome a girl so foolish that she spurns the powerful warrior Ear-of-the-Fox." Her dark eyes suddenly grew wide. "You would go to the white medicine chief, Peejatowahooten?"

Little Fawn sighed. "No, Mother. Peejatowahooten does not want me. He does not come to the rendezvous this year. He has forgotten me."

"My daughter, I am sorry for these things. My heart aches for you. You must be strong. The Great Spirit has blessed you with the offer of marriage from one you have known and loved all your life. Marriage will not be difficult with one you respect and know."

Little Fawn raised her eyes to her mother's face. "Ear-of-the-Fox does not love me. I fear that I will be dead—or wish that I were so—before our marriage is many moons old."

Blue Feather gasped. "What manner of foolish talk! Ear-of-the-Fox has been waiting for you to reach the proper age for many years. He has claimed no other wife before you. You will be the center, the heart of his lodge."

"I will be the sacrifice he makes to soothe his pride," she answered with a little return of spirit. "You must listen to me, Mother, and I will tell you why I fear Ear-of-the-Fox."

Blue Feather rose and tended her stewpot when Little Fawn finished the story of her visit from the Manitou. She had been in ignorance of her daughter's vision and of her talks with Ear-of-the-Fox about it. When she had expressed concern over Little Fawn's visit last summer to the lodge of Peejatowahooten, Washakie had calmed her misgivings with a promise that no harm would come to her child.

It had not. Little Fawn had returned without a swelling belly, and with a beautiful, strong horse. She had thought the matter satisfactorily closed. She had two other daughters with suitors and hoped to see them both happily settled by fall. She needed to think of a plan that would save her eldest daughter from the wrath of her father and the violence of a jealous warrior. She had seen the looks Ear-of-the-Fox gave Little Fawn and thought them fired with the heat of a young man's lust for his first woman. Enlightened by Little Fawn's story, she now saw great danger in his glances.

An hour later, Blue Feather had found a solution. "My younger sister, White Blossom, is big with her first child," Blue Feather said as she stirred the stew with a willow stick. "Word comes to me of the happy event with one of the warriors who accompanies Running Buffalo. She is the only wife of Red Fox. The fall will be difficult for her, so far from her family and without the helping hands of a second wife. My heart is heavy for this reason. They live in the land to the south and west, where the earth is bitter and the water filled with salt. I would go to her myself, but Washakie will not hear of it."

She turned to face her daughter and a blush colored her cheeks. "I, too, will grow big-bellied soon. The Great Spirit is most generous in his choice of my husband." She turned quickly away, her stick slowly spinning the stew. "I think now I will send someone in my place. It must be a strong, healthy woman who can keep a lodge and help White Blossom deliver herself of the child. Then, too, it will be good training for a girl who is soon to marry. I will send my choice with Running Baffalo at dawn. Washakie cannot object to a bride going to learn how she must conduct herself when she is to bring a child upon the earth."

Little Fawn leaped to her feet and threw her arms about her mother's waist. "Oh, Mother! I love you so. Thank you, thank you! I do not deserve your protection, but I shall not make you regret it."

Blue Feather lifted her daughter's chin and held the sparkling eyes with ones of concern. "It is not a solution, my daughter. It is only a way of saving time. I will speak with your father while you are gone, but he is my master as well as yours and I must obey him."

"I understand, Mother, and I thank you for your help. If this marriage is my fate, which in my heart I cannot yet believe, then I will return to you in the wintering season and accept what the Great Spirit demands of me."

Chapter 19

The hooves of the big horse moved easily through the winding, snow-packed trail of the Wind River Mountains, as easily as did the thoughts of its rider. Bridger tilted his face to the thin light of the winter sun and smiled. He would always remember the year of '33 as the hardest and most satisfying of his life. A small band of rough-mannered trappers had won their right to remain independent from the greed and influence of the biggest business empire the United States had ever seen. News riding in on the latest express from Bill Sublette in St. Louis proclaimed that the American Trust had bought a whole parcel of trouble in operating a whiskey still in Indian Territory. The U.S. Congress was demanding an investigation that could break the great Astor business empire.

Bridger chuckled, wondering if McKenzie would ever know that it was the gossip, spread by one little white-haired Irishman at last summer's Green River rendezvous, that had brought about that state of affairs. " 'Twas certain we could not be bringing in the complaint ourselves, not with there being the pitched battle between us and the Astor folk to start with," Fitz had said when pressed on the matter by a rowdy crowd around the campfire. "But, there was Wyeth, the poor ordinary soul, who felt it his duty as a citizen to report that breach of the law. 'An all-out flagrant attempt to bamboozle the United States Government,' is how he phrased it, I believe."

"We won!" Bridger shouted to the empty sky. They might have to share the land eventually with settlers and other independents, but the territory would not become the private preserves of a monopoly.

He, too, had at last won his own personal battle of the past ten years. The dream had visited no more after the Blackfoot battle. He did not question it, just accepted it as a gift from the Great Spirit. Then, just last month, he had learned that old Hugh Glass had fought and lost his last battle that very same fall. Blackfoot took him under. Such doin's made a man think.

Now all that stood between him and happiness was one scrappy bit of womanhood called Little Fawn. Fitz had told him about their meeting at Green River, how she had asked for him by name and then looked stricken when she thought him dead. She cared, by damn! He could feel her image setting up the fret in his blood. She would be waiting for him to come and claim her.

Descending the mountain to the valley below, he became lost in memory. He recalled her pliant lips moving beneath his rough kiss, her fierce embrace when he entered her, the lunge and roll of her hips to his thrust. Oh yes, he remembered her well.

The canyon opened suddenly from a narrow rise and Bridger found himself facing a rider—an Indian by his dress. He slowed his mount and gripped tightly the ropes of the three horses he led. He would be damned before he let any man steal his wedding presents.

The rider neared, slowed, and raised a hand in greeting. Bridger nudged his horse forward with his knees, his rifle clenched in his right hand. He picked a path down the frozen slope to meet the man, pulling up short at the last moment.

Ear-of-the-Fox!

The Shoshone warrior did not react visibly, but his horse whinnied and tossed its mane at the sight of the big bearded man on a stallion. Ear-of-the-Fox eyed Bridger impassively. Their last meeting of more than a year ago might never have taken place. He sat his mount with pride, his wide, sculptured features given new harshness by the stripes of vermilion and ocher carefully applied to his cheeks and chin. In the villages of his people it was whispered that he was the bravest of all warriors. Any brave could ride without fear with his medicine bag tied securely by his side. But Ear-of-the-Fox rode like the chinook winds into the midst of the enemy with neither protection nor fear. It was whispered that he had no need of the Manitou because he had made a bargain with the white man's God. But no one dared to ask. His courage and many coups were enough evidence of his powerful medicine, whatever its source.

Bridger hitched his reins over his left arm and lowered his rifle across his saddle. He was used to the Indian way of prolonging a meeting and felt no real danger in facing Ear-of-the-Fox. The enemy was before him. But was the Shoshone alone? In spite of himself, Bridger cast a quick, sharp glance over his left shoulder. The action brought several short barks of laughter from the Shoshone.

"You have nothing to fear from me, Peejatowa-hooten." His teeth showed in bright contrast to his skin. It was good the white man doubted his own medicine, he thought. "Why do you come to the wintering grounds of my people?"

Bridger saw the flicker of interest the Indian cast over his horseflesh and his trigger finger tightened slightly. "I come to counsel with Washakie," he responded in his deep, slow drawl. "I am thinking of setting myself up with a squaw."

Ear-of-the-Fox's features relaxed into a smirk and he lowered his war lance across the back of his mount. "It is a good thing to have a wife. I, too, am to marry. You will come to join in the celebration?"

Bridger ducked his head. "Perhaps."

"You do not ask who I am to marry," Ear-of-the-Fox taunted.

The hackles on his neck stiffened, but Bridger let nothing show. Only one bride would be of interest to him and they both knew it.

"I am to marry Washakie's eldest girl-child in ten days," Ear-of-the-Fox said. "We are promised to one another more than six moons. It is the will of Washakie that the marriage take place. I come to the mountains to welcome my wife back from her journey to the Salt Deserts. You will ride with me?"

The mocking tone was not lost on Bridger. For the first time in a long while he contemplated gunning down a defenseless man.

"See you in camp," he spat out. With a vicious digging in of his knees, Bridger sent his horse barreling forward past the Shoshone. He had not yet considered the full advantages of having the man dead.

Little Fawn to marry Ear-of-the-Fox. The thought brought forth no overt sense of anger nor impending loss after the initial flaring of his temper. As he rode into the village, nestled beneath a thick canopy of sweet cottonwoods, he supposed it was because he had considered the possibility a dozen times in the last twelve months. He had gotten cocksure of her feelings for a time after Fitz returned from rendezvous with news of her. Still, one could never be certain with a woman. Could be she had taken it into her head to marry when he did not show up for rendezvous.

"Hell!"

If she were any kind of real woman who cared about her man she would have tried to understand what he had been through in the past year—the wounds he had suffered and the struggle of making it up to a group of men who had followed him into hell for the sake of a dream and friendship.

Bridger checked his horse and swung down from the saddle. As he advanced across the frozen earth, words of greeting formed automatically on his lips for the man he had hoped he would soon be calling father-in-law.

The formalities of the greeting complete, Bridger entered the lodge of Chief Washakie to partake of Blue Feather's stew. Doubt penetrated his thoughts. Did Washakie consent to his daughter's marriage publicly? Would Ear-of-the-Fox have been audacious enough to lie about Washakie's approval of the proposal?

The meal was cleared and the pale-green soapstone peace pipe ritually filled and lit before Washakie spoke of his guest's unexpected visit.

"Our people are pleased and honored by the arrival of Peejatowahooten. Already the wintering season promises to be one of reward for us. The buffalo number greater than ever before in our valley. There will be no starving times." Washakie observed Bridger's new buckskins in a way that made the big man squirm. The new suit of clothes, the three horses on a lead, the unusual timing of his visit; Washakie understood without the embarrassing need to question why the white man had come among them. He did not address the matter directly.

"Our people prosper more with each year. We owe a debt of gratitude to the generous trade with the white man and the bounty of the Great Spirit. Among us there is one who can boast of many victories, where once we suffered sorely at the hands of our enemies the Blackfoot. We owe these great victories to—" Washakie's words were cut off when the lodge flap was thrown back by Blue Feather who cried, "She has returned, Washakie! The Great Spirit has returned to us our Little Fawn."

Both men rose and moved to the entry. Bridger lagged behind, lolling in the doorway while Washakie went forward to wait for his child. She came with a party of perhaps twenty Bannock warriors. The sight made Bridger uneasy. Twenty young bucks and a single squaw; what kind of protection was that? Then the words of greeting between Washakie and the war party leader drifted over to him.

"With my life I protect all that belongs to the mighty warrior, Washakie. Not so much as the loss of a strand of hair has she suffered." The Bannock warrior made a sweeping gesture toward the girl, and Bridger felt his gut tighten dangerously.

She sat proudly in the saddle, her slender legs encased in soft, doeskin leggings and an unscraped buffalo robe pulled tightly about her shoulders. Her hair streamed like the dipping wings of a raven over her shoulders. Bridger spied the silver hawkbells bracelet about her wrist.

In near fear he slowly raised his eyes to her face and his gut gave a second quick twist. Her face was painted in a delicate design. Vermilion reddened her cheeks, and on her forehead and chin, tiny blue dots had been applied. But it was her expression that rendered his tongue useless and riled his blood. Terror, pure and unrestrained, marked her soft features.

Bridger's shoulders came away from the lodgepole he leaned against, his big fists curling into weapons. The action brought her eyes his way and her tiny gasp made him pause. He saw her eyes cut quickly to her side and knew without question that the fear stamped on her face had its cause in the man by her side, Ear-of-the-Fox.

Was that all? he wondered in a curious easing of his anger. If she were afraid of Ear-of-the-Fox alone, then he could wait to settle that score. Bridger came forward with the light step of an Indian, his face set in a slight smile. The son of a bitch he would deal with later.

He waited for Washakie to lift his daughter from the saddle before moving forward to speak to her. His heart beat heavily in his chest. If she gave him the slightest encouragement, he would take on the whole damn camp, here and now.

Little Fawn stood with her eyes to the ground while she commanded her trembling body not to provoke her intended husband. She knew that his eyes bored into her; they weighed her down with anxiety and foreboding. But stronger still was her need to look full, just once, into the face of the man she loved and thought never to see again. The meeting of their gazes—one brown and wide as the summer prairie, and the other gray and clear as a snowcapped stream— met. It was over in an instant. But the knowledge that passed between them answered all questions on both sides.

"You remember my daughter, Little Fawn," Washakie injected into the brief silence surrounding the meeting. He saw the exchange of looks, and regretted the fates that had brought these three people together. The decision was his to make and he made it quickly.

"You will also remember my adopted son, Ear-of-the-Fox. You come among us on a most joyous occasion. The marriage of Little Fawn to Ear-of-the-Fox is to take place ten days from today. You are welcome to join us as a friend and ally of the Shoshone, Peejatowahooten."

Bridger did not ever remember how he acknowledged the announcement. Later, in the darkness of his lodge, he realized he had no ally in Washakie. Washakie wanted this marriage for his child, and he expected his friend and companion in war to accept his decision without question. Bridger thought it best that he leave immediately. But he would wait until the moment Little Fawn entered Ear-of-the-Fox's lodge.

With a partially stifled groan, he turned from his back to his side. He could not watch her walk away with Ear-of-the-Fox. He became obsessed with the image of Little Fawn standing before the hot, black gaze of the mad warrior loosening her clothes. He tortured himself with thoughts of her writhing under the man's brutal, relentless thrusts that punished her for having offered herself elsewhere.

A few ragged breaths later, Bridger bounded to his feet. "Won't give her up that easy," he vowed softly. "She belongs to me; saw it in her eyes today. Gotta find a way."

But Washakie was careful of his daughter in ways he had never been before. By the end of the third day, Bridger was pacing the village like a caged animal. Villagers scurried out of his path in fear of the black scowl riding his brow. He saw Little Fawn only when he was invited to Washakie's tepee, and then she came near him only to refill his wooden bowl or to offer him a drink. Her eyes spoke a thousand words but not one

of them was given tongue. His hands were effectively
tied by the polite hospitality of his host. He could no
more break through the flimsy social barrier than he
could hope to lick a village of Blackfoot single-hand-
edly.

If only the Shoshone were less civilized, he
thought in one moment of gut-busting anger. More like
the Comanche, who believed in a man's right to fight
for the woman of his choice, even if she belonged to
another. Right now he felt like breaking heads and rip-
ping out guts. But he knew Washakie would turn him
out of the village if he started a brawl. And he would
shame Little Fawn by making her an object of ridicule.

Inevitably this kind of thinking began to turn his
feelings against the girl herself.

"It's her fault," he declared while listening to
Ear-of-the-Fox pipe a wretched piece of music on his
willow flute outside Washakie's lodge.

"Damned lovesick warrior," he murmured more
loudly. "The pair of us pining and writhing in our own
sweat over a mere squaw. Hell! But she's thinkin'
hers is the only breechcloth I got under in the territory."

The mouthing off gave him brief respite. Remembering that Ear-of-the-Fox was never able to entice
Little Fawn to share his robes also eased his mind.

By morning he had resolved to leave the
Shoshone village. He could do nothing—outside of
committing murder. He dressed in his old rawhides and
rolled his new skins into a tight package to shove in his
rucksack. Perhaps Washakie would be interested in a
little horse trading before he left. If not, he would follow the trail south, maybe visit the Utes till the spring
thaw allowed him to travel north to his brigade.

These thoughts so fully occupied his mind that he
almost missed the pledge hanging outside his lodge. In

agitation he had thrown the flap wide, looking back only out of mere whimsy. The sight brought him up short. He dropped his saddle and packs with an explosive, "Damnation!"

Hanging from the flap to his lodge were a pair of beautifully beaded moccasins. The work of Little Fawn, he knew it at once. She had scowled at him for his shoddy footwear only the night before. Obviously she had not been satisfied with his indecision and had sought to take things into her own hands.

He observed the excellent workmanship. They were his size, too. And lined with fur for the winter months. If he took them down and put them on, he would be proclaiming to the village that he accepted her proposal of marriage.

"Damn sly bitch," he grumbled and turned to pick up his things. He headed directly toward the corral where his horses were kept, but his steps slowed as he neared. If he did not accept the proposal, everyone in the village would know she had made the offer by the time the sun had climbed to the top of the eastern ridge. It would mean trouble for her whether he left or stayed.

"Damned interfering woman! Why couldn't she have left it to me to find a way?" She must have realized that he had thought of nothing and was ready to give up. He was amazed at the courage she had in exposing herself to the inevitable anger of her father and Ear-of-the-Fox. He could not accept the challenge, but he could stay around in case she needed help.

Consequences of the act became known in a matter of hours. Bridger was not asked to Washakie's lodge that night nor was he sent a meal. As he lay in the darkness, his empty belly grumbling with the lack of warm food, he heard the dissonant flute of Ear-of-the-Fox. He listened carefully for sounds of movement in the lodge next to his. Finally he heard it, the whisper of a woman's feet over the threshold of Washakie's lodge.

Bridger sprang to his feet, darting across the floor of his lodge with the swift and silent tread of a cougar. Pride and caution kept him from flinging wide the flap of his tepee. Instead, he went down on his belly and, with no more sound than a leaf caught up by the wind, lifted the edge of the hides forming his dew cloth. He inched forward until his head was between it and the outer cover of the tepee, and then lifted the outer skins.

He could hear their voices, one low and sweet, the other heavy and angry. They were arguing. But why had she gone to the warrior if not to share his robes? Naugh, she wouldn't, he thought suddenly. The girl would not be so foolish as to confront Ear-of-the-Fox with her love for another man. But, as he listened, the voices grew louder and more strained. He could make out very few words, but the erratic pattern of their voices told him what he needed to know. She was denying her desire to marry the young warrior, refusing, in fact, to do so.

The crack of a blow came unexpectedly. Bridger tried desperately to remain still while he heard the woman he loved cry out as another blow fell on her. He bit clean through the inside of his lip in castrated rage, unable to go to her defense. A man had a right to punish his woman's insubordination. "Where the hell is that son of a bitch, Washakie?" he growled.

A commanding voice cut across the night. Washakie's tone was that of an enraged parent. Ear-of-the-Fox's explanation was cut off by a single cutting word and the night dissolved into silence.

For Bridger, however, the matter had yet to be settled.

He looked straight ahead as he made his way through the village to tend his horses. He heard the whispers of squaws, who had risen early to light the big fires over which they would make pemmican and boil fat. They giggled and pointed. A few rushed back to their tepees to distribute the news that Peejatowahooten had taken down the moccasins from his lodge flap and was wearing them through the camp. His Green River was tucked in his leggings. He could do no more. The insult had been offered. He would not deliver the first blow. That was for squaw beaters and other yellow-bellied cowards.

Ear-of-the-Fox went down on his knees in the snow of the valley floor and lifted his arms toward the frigid sky. "Great Spirit that rules the lives of our people, send to your servant, Ear-of-the-Fox, a sign of your favor! I come seeking you on mountain tops and in the agony of the Sun Dance! Yet you hold your face from me! Give me the vision that I seek!"

Tears ran freely down his face. Never before had he felt the burning anguish of the humiliation he suffered this day. His woman refused him his rights and gave, instead, for the whole village to see, herself in offering to the man who shadowed his life without mercy.

"My medicine is strong, Great Spirit. Those of my people who have seen me in battle praise and fear my cunning and bravery. Many coups I win to lay at the feet of my intended and she spurns me as she would the advances of an old man with a useless stick between his legs. Help me! Show me my future!"

Ear-of-the-Fox fell face down in the snow, the icy sting a comfort against his blazing cheeks. Gradually, without an awareness of the coming, he knew that he was not alone. Lifting his face from the ground, he looked up into the face of a grizzly bear. The beast reared up on its hind legs, its huge paws lifted in the sign of peace. Immediately Ear-of-the-Fox grabbed his lance and, gathering his full weight behind it, struck the beast in its belly. A horrifying roar assailed his ears. Then there was silence. Ear-of-the-Fox was again alone. His lance lay beside him, its tip bloodless.

Bridger kept clear of the village for most of the day. The sounds of the returning hunters reached his ears from where he stayed in the corral. If Ear-of-the-Fox did not come foward soon, he told himself, he would be forced to seek him out. The waiting was telling on his nerves and the cold had aggravated the three-inch arrowhead in his back. The metal seemed to draw the cold into itself, stiffening his shoulder and arm. By nightfall he was afraid that he would be too tense to fight a real battle.

The shadows grew long behind the corral, their purple depths portending a heavy snowfall by the break of a new day. Such a storm would sweep across the plain and bury them for several days, perhaps a week.

"Leastways, there can be no marriage," he announced to his companion, the Pelouse he had given Little Fawn two summers before. He stroked the horse's broad flank absently. He had not spoken to anyone this day. He knew that he was a leper among the villagers, that none of them would speak to him until this thing was resolved.

He waited another hour until the deep purple sunset had faded. The trees were shadows against the horizon and the lodges gleamed like lanterns lit by their warm fires. Deciding that he had been penned in long enough, he straddled the log barricade. The time had

come to settle matters with Ear-of-the-Fox. The swift
act left him vulnerable. He was unprepared for the
screaming fury that rushed suddenly out of the night. It
was Ear-of-the-Fox, a death cry on his lips and a powerful horse beneath him.

A tomahawk dug into the side of Bridger's right
shoulder, just below his neck. Dazed by the blow, he
spun around and grabbed his knife in one lightning
motion. In that instant, he looked straight into the face
of his attacker.

Ear-of-the-Fox had stripped himself of everything
but his breechcloth. His skin shone in the fading light
with the sacred unguents he had used in hopes of making himself invisible. His teeth were bared in a horrible
grimace. In his right hand was the blood-tinged tomahawk he had used to open Bridger's shoulder.

"You will die, white man!" he gasped out. "You
stand between me and the Spirit World!"

"Not for long, you bastard!" Bridger growled
back. He put a hand to his neck to wipe away the
blood tickling him, but his eyes never left the young
warrior. It was not a fatal wound. But its sting made
him conscious of the fact that it was serious enough to
cost him the fight if he did not strike soon.

"You will no longer ride the form of the whore,
Little Fawn," the Shoshone began to taunt as they
carefully circled one another. "When I am done with
you, you will mount no squaws. Peejatowahooten will
be a squaw himself and Ear-of-the-Fox will ride about
with the white man's stick hanging from his lance."

Bridger lunged forward. The warrior's laughter
told him his jab had gone wide. He recovered quickly,
the jarring of his wound making little impression on
the concentration in his eyes.

"I will marry Little Fawn when I have scalped
and cut you. I will make her clean your scalp and

stretch it for me," the warrior threatened. "I will take her to my lodge and she will learn what it is to ride a real man." His voice was deadly. "And when I am done with her, she will never seek out another man again."

Bridger looked up into the blood-tinged eyes of the mad warrior and knew he must kill him. It seemed inconceivable that this was the man who had once saved his life.

The fight commenced in silence. The grunts of the two men were the only sounds pervading the mountain valley. They stared into each other's eyes, searching for signs of weakness. There were none. They were equals in deadly combat, but only for a moment. Ear-of-the-Fox blinked. Bridger lunged, his knife slipping past the guard of his enemy. Ear-of-the-Fox cried out, stung by the contact of the knife with his stomach. Bridger felt a tomahawk bite into his left forearm and the arm fell to his side, useless. Blood smeared his clothes. They were both breathing heavily. Without the light of day to confirm it, Bridger thought he had hurt the Indian badly. His own shoulder felt like hot coals had been shoveled into it, and his old wound flared up with each move.

In desperation Bridger stepped into a long narrow shadow and halted, perfectly still. It was a slim chance. If Ear-of-the-Fox made a lunge, just a fraction miscalculated in its haste, he would have the one opportunity he needed.

Ear-of-the-Fox marked Bridger's rigid stand in midmotion and raised his tomahawk. The white man would die now. The weapon swung back to come down in a fatal blow. But when Ear-of-the-Fox glanced up over Bridger's shoulder, the stroke arched away.

He did not cry out when a hot blade sliced through him. The slow, falling away from consciousness meant nothing to him. He continued to stare wild-eyed at the image that was there in the shadow of Peejatowahooten. A final breath racked his body and blood bubbled over his lips with the dying words "The Golden Grizzly."

Bridger stood swaying over the dead body of the young warrior for a long moment. He had not heard the whispered word, but he had seen the incredulous look of fear come over the Shoshone's face just before he purposely threw himself on his blade.

"Damn shame," he panted huskily. He turned and started toward his lodge, unaware that most of the village had witnessed the fight.

Bridger lay with his chest against Little Fawn's back. The day had been a long one. The celebration had lasted until daybreak. He opened his eyes and surveyed his lodge. The beautiful war shirt that Little Fawn had spent two years making for him was in a heap by the doorflap. The equally beautiful elkskin dress that she had made for her wedding day lay in a smaller heap beside it. Only the exquisitely painted buffalo robe remained about them. He had asked her to explain the images of the Golden Grizzly. She had merely shaken her head and begun to undress. Her breasts were fuller and proudly upthrust this year, and he had teasingly asked her if she would continue to advance in beauty with each year.

"What are you thinking, my husband?"

Bridger rose up on one elbow and looked down into the face of his wife. "Well, truth to tell, I was planning the spring hunt. I left a parcel of boys stuck up north without a bourgeois. Of course, Fitz says he ain't quite ready to call it quits, but I reckon it's my responsibility. You reckon you'll be willing to ride up north with me?"

"Just try to stop me," she shot back.

"Easy, honey. You got to remember that you could be breeding come spring. It's a lonely, hard time for a woman who follows her man into the wilderness. You ain't gonna have no mother and no sisters to help with the chores."

Little Fawn snuggled against him. "Neither will I be forced to share my stallion," she murmured.

"You little devil," he growled in her ear. "I'm going to make you pay up, you keep teasing me."

Little Fawn turned onto her back, a soft provocative smile on her red mouth. "You make me one of the brigade, yes?" She murmured softly, burrowing into Bridger's back, and went to sleep.

Second in the Spectacular Series
THE AMERICAN INDIANS

BLACKFOOT AMBUSH

by Catherine Weber

It's 1868 and the Blackfoot reservation is seething with danger and discontent. An Indian agent has been murdered and the Blackfoot are accused. The only man who can solve the mystery of this crime is the new agent — an outlaw and killer by the name of Cole Sykes. He doesn't stand a chance until the beautiful Patricia Ashley makes him face the shattering truth. Through a maze of deceit and intrigue, the tender woman leads the vicious gunfighter to new realizations about himself — and about the Blackfoot people he is meant to serve. And the voluptuous Patricia promises a future for the man who once faced a life in prison.